To "

MW00388926

With love,

[signature]
9/'08

Self and Secrecy in Early Islam

Studies in Comparative Religion
Frederick M. Denny, Series Editor

Self and Secrecy
in Early Islam

Ruqayya Yasmine Khan

The University of South Carolina Press

Published by the University of South Carolina Press
Columbia, South Carolina 29208

www.sc.edu/uscpress

Manufactured in the United States of America

17 16 15 14 13 12 11 10 09 08   10 9 8 7 6 5 4 3 2 1

Library of Congress Cataloging-in-Publication Data

Khan, Ruqayya Yasmine.
  Self and secrecy in early Islam / Ruqayya Yasmine Khan.
      p. cm.— (Studies in comparative religion)
   Includes bibliographical references and index.
   ISBN 978-1-57003-754-2 (cloth : alk. paper)
     1. Islamic literature, Arabic—History and criticism.   2. Koran—Criticism,
interpretation, etc.   3. Secrecy in literature.   4. Self in literature.   I. Title.
   PJ7519.I84K48   2008
   892.7'09353—dc22   2008024031

This book was printed on Glatfelter Natures, a recycled paper with 30 percent postconsumer waste
content.

*To piarra Mikail . . . and to my long-departed nani Kulsoom Begum
for sitting me on her knee and teaching me the Arabic*

Contents

Series Editor's Preface

This original and intriguing study brings together important but quite diverse kinds of Arabic texts from the early centuries of Islam in a synoptic exercise in literary, religious, ethical, psychological, and cultural analysis and interpretation. The author focuses on the deep and abiding dimensions of secrecy and the human self as expressed in Islam's holy scripture the Qur'an, as well as in early ethical discourses and love poetry. The results of this comparative investigation include a nuanced understanding of fundamental dimensions of early Arabo-Muslim civilization's interrelated religio-ethical, social, cultural, political, and psychosexual realities.

Self and Secrecy in Early Islam draws on a rich variety of Arabic texts from early Muslim history and a wide knowledge of modern research, method, and theory in Qur'anic, literary, and psychoanalytic studies. Ruqayya Yasmine Khan has realized her challenging goal of overcoming a traditional compartmentalization of the study of secrecy and the human self in Islam into the separate fields of Sufi, Shi'ite, Qur'anic, and literary studies with scholars in each of those discourses usually not having seriously examined findings in the others. The result is eye-opening for our knowledge and understanding of not only early Arabo-Muslim life but also global psychological, ethical, cultural and spiritual ideals and realities of Muslim communities, movements, and individuals in our post-9/11 world.

Frederick M. Denny

Acknowledgments

This book has been in the making for a long time, and there are many whom I would like to acknowledge gratefully. The first is Th. Emil Homerin, who during the summer of 2004 read through a substantial part of the manuscript and offered detailed, insightful comments on it as well as steadfastly supported the book during a crucial phase. I would also like to acknowledge my dear friend Emily Haddad for her rigorous and intellectually stimulating feedback on the manuscript in its early stages.

In part, the genesis of this book lies in my dissertation, which could not have been completed at the University of Pennsylvania without the brilliant tutelage of Everett Rowson. Thank you so much, Everett, for making magical and pleasurable the reading of medieval Arabic texts and for always being there! A heartfelt thanks to my other teachers at the University of Pennsylvania, among them Roger Allen and William Hanaway. Without the Omid Safi's wise counsel, this book would not exist. I remain indebted to him for nudging me toward the University of South Carolina Press and toward Fred Denny, whose responsiveness and enthusiasm have been wonderful. The astute comments and constructive criticism of anonymous reviewers and readers helped me to strengthen the book. To them, I owe a big measure of gratitude. I thank Jim Denton, my editor with the University of South Carolina Press, for his diligence and efficiency.

Other colleagues whom I want to acknowledge gratefully for taking the time to read through and comment on parts of the manuscript are Shawkat Toorawa, Joe Lowry, Joan Burton, Sarah Pinnock, Fred Donner, Jamal Elias, Mark Wallace, and Jeffrey Kripal. An Andrew Mellon Postdoctoral Fellowship made possible an early intellectual home for the research and writing of the book at Swarthmore College's Department of Religion, and I thank all my former colleagues there, who were a marvelous source of support and encouragement. I am especially grateful to Mark Wallace for his intellectual fellowship, academic "street smarts," and engaging warmth throughout the ups and downs of the writing of this book. The Department of Religious Studies and the Center for Middle East Studies at UCSB graciously invited me to present material related to the book, and I thank my former colleagues there, including Dwight Reynolds, Juan Campo, Wade Clark Roof, and Garay Menicucci. Not to be forgotten are Pamela Eisenbaum and Mark George, who, during a 2004 Crosscurrents Colloquium at the Union Theological Seminary, read portions of my research regarding the Qur'an and shared insightful comments with me based on their biblical studies' work.

As for Trinity University, my first expression of heartfelt gratitude goes to Rashna Patel, a Trinity graduate and like a daughter to me, for her excellent editorial work on the manuscript in its various phases. I admire her for the cheerfulness and patience she has shown throughout this long process. I also am grateful for the summer research funds provided through the Trinity University Faculty Fellowship in Religion and the Office of Academic Affairs, and I thank Diane Smith for being so gracious about support during the last stages of the project. My thanks also go to my very fine colleagues in the Department of Religion, the former and present secretaries, Margaret Miksch and Irma Escalante respectively, and the library staff, including Chris Nolan. To my "gal" colleagues, including Alida Metcalf and Joan Burton, much gratitude is due for guiding me through the ups and downs of the publication process.

The presence of my dear friend Sumathi Ramaswamy has suffused the years of research and writing this book like a fine perfume. My profound debt to Salman Akhtar is apparent throughout the book. Thank you also to Diane Martinez for being there. The love, affection, and joyful company of my helpmate and husband, John, have incalculably smoothed the pathway in the last few years as I approached the landing of this project. My daughter, Marie Christine, in her gentle way, has stood by me as well during the journey. To my son, Mikail, whose childhood was at times overshadowed by his mother's intellectual quest, I dedicate this book. I can never make up for that time. With that comes a painful sense of loss somewhat tempered by my being witness to and enthusiastically supporting his own budding quest.

※※※※※※※※※※※※※※※※※※※※※※※※※※※※※※※※※※※※※※※

Introduction

A student penned this arresting observation in response to an exam essay question I once gave, demanding that the "central, organizing questions in each of the three [Abrahamic] religions" be identified: "Islam's question is how to best express the Islamic faith outwardly as a community. The . . . [Muslim] people take part in rituals that set them apart visually and mentally from the other Abrahamic Religions. . . . Two required rituals of Islam . . . [that] are highly recognizable by [and visible to] people of other faiths [are the] Hajj and salat."[1] I felt that the student had touched on something critical to the construction of Muslim collective and individual identities by drawing attention to dualities such as outward versus inward, visual versus nonvisual, as well as expression versus suppression. Her insight resonates with much of what I argue in this book: a marker of early Arabo-Islamic discourse, its textual productions and material cultures, is secrecy and its opposite, revelation. The phenomena of ciphering, deciphering, coding, decoding, signs, and semiotics are central to its discourses and material cultures.

Perhaps due to the logocentric qualities of Islamic civilization, it is the semiotic rather than the figurative that is paramount in it. Frederick Denny, a scholar of Islamic studies, has pointed out that "in relation to Christianity, the Qur'an may be usefully compared with Christ, in that it is believed to be God's Word that has miraculously come down into the world in history and humankind. If in Christianity the 'Word became flesh,' in Islam it became a book."[2] In Christianity, the Word became image and icon, whereas in Islam, the Word became a codex. Likewise, Stefan Wild states: "The importance of the Qur'an for Muslims and Islam is tantamount to the importance of the person of Jesus Christ for Christian and Christianity. It has been rightly observed that the Christian concept of incarnation corresponds to what one

My transliteration of Arabic in this book follows the system used for the language by the *International Journal of Middle East Studies* (*IJMES*), which is based on a modified *Encyclopedia of Islam* transliteration system.

might call 'illibration' in Islam. In Christianity, the divine *logos* becomes man. In Islam, God's word becomes text, a text to be recited in Arabic and to be read as an Arabic book."[3] Neither icons nor images but rather linguistic signs and ciphers prevail in Arabo-Islamic productions.[4] Derived from the Arabic word (*ṣifr, ṣafr*) that means "vacant, empty," the word *cipher* is especially meaningful here because its semantics embrace meanings related to secrecy and revelation (for example, deciphering and ciphering).[5]

The Concept of the Secret

This book is about the topic of secrecy and revelation in a selection of early Arabo-Islamic discourses including the Qur'an. The book maintains that individual *identity* is characterized by this marker of secrecy and revelation. I argue that the concept of the secret is integral to how self and subjectivity, as well as interpersonal relations, are imagined and constituted in early Arabo-Islamic discourses. I employ the term *concept of the secret* to convey the idea that what is important is not so much the content or substance of the secret but rather the form it takes and that this form is an integral aspect of the psychological state of possessing and/or divulging a secret. In these discourses more importance is assigned to the *psychological state of keeping and revealing secrets* than to the *nature of the content* of the secret—in other words, the human inclination toward secrecy and its opposite, revelation, is deemed more crucial than the issue of *what* the secret is. However, the content of the secret is not entirely irrelevant; for instance, in the Qur'an, the content of the secret does matter, but its importance recedes before the aforementioned psychological state. Hence, I use this term or phrase to refer to a conceptual model of human secrecy and its functions as set forth by the Qur'an and diverse classical Arabo-Islamic discourses.[6]

Whereas I analyze the *concept* of the secret in the primarily religious and ethical texts, when I turn to Arabic love literature, I address the existence of the *trope* of the secret. The term *trope of the secret* is used to describe the *literary* use of the idea or concept of the secret, and this usage is found in, but not limited to, discourses of an explicitly literary nature (for example, Arabic love poetry and romance narratives). These construct the secret as a literary theme, device, motif, or rhetorical element. To an extent, the trope of the secret is impossible without the concept of the secret, for the former reflects the elaborations and/or paradoxes of the latter within the context of literary language and genres. Nonetheless, in Arabic love literature too, secrecy and revelation are integral to how self and subjectivity are imagined and represented. This yields a certain unity in constructions of the self across the very different early Arabo-Islamic discourses and genres analyzed in this book.

I approach the subject of secrecy with two general aims: first, to examine the idea of the secret and its religious and literary significance in classical Arabo-Islamic texts; and second, to illustrate its utility in representing pre-modern notions of self and subjectivity in these textual discourses. This book argues that the keeping and revealing of secrets inform the creation and retention of identity and subjectivity in early Arabo-Islamic discourses.

Secrecy and Psychoanalysis

In modern Western culture, we do not think of human secrets and secrecy as a domain for the examination and exploration of human self and identity. We may intuitively understand that every human being has secrets, but the systematic exploration of secrecy as a vehicle with which to better understand human selfhood and personality is limited to one area.[7] That area is psychoanalysis. Gerald Margolis, a contemporary psychoanalyst, has observed, "Secret keeping is a psychological process of considerable importance if only for its ubiquity. But, while everyone keeps secrets, little has been written about it. It is a topic of special significance to psychoanalysts . . . [because] analysis deals with the personal secrets that people hide from one another and from themselves."[8]

To be sure, psychoanalysis is a modern, primarily Euro-American herme-neutic and practice; yet there are some interesting parallels between its object of study and the fascination with human tendencies toward concealment and revelation in my early Arabic texts. Fortunately my treatment of the topic of secrecy and revelation in early Arabo-Islamic discourses—while informed by approaches of psychoanalysis, religion, and sociology—does not need to rely on them because the Arabic sources themselves explicitly iden-tify secrecy as a prism through which to better understand human identity and subjectivity.[9] In other words, the concern with psychology and character as well as with psychology and personality already existed in early Arabic discourses and genres.

Secrecy and Islamic Studies

The field of Islamic studies reflects the major trends in history of religions scholarship on secrecy; it analyzes secrecy by situating it within mysticism and/or traditions of the esoteric.[10] However, *Self and Secrecy in Early Islam* departs from this by assessing secrecy's significance in terms of links with self and identity. The two primary trends in Islamic studies scholarship on secrecy are secrecy's links with Sufism or Islamic mysticism and secrecy's links with Shi'ism.[11] Annemarie Schimmel and William Chittick, among others, have written about secrecy in Islamic mysticism.[12] As for Shi'ism, Etan Kohlberg, Farhad Daftary, Devin Stewart, and others have written on the subject.[13] Jean-Claude Vadet has fleetingly addressed it with regard to

Arabic love poetry.[14] By and large, the field of Islamic studies evinces an approach to secrecy that examines it in the context of traditions and transmission of mystical knowledge, preservation, and protection of esoteric knowledge, gnosis.[15] This book examines literary, scriptural, and ethical traditions with a view to understanding how dynamic tensions between secrecy and revelation help us to understand constructions of self, identity, and self-and-other relations.

A problem associated with the scholarship on secrecy in Islamic studies is that it is compartmentalized. The scholars and critics writing about secrecy in Islamic mysticism are not informed by the work of those who have examined it in Shi'ism, and conversely, those who have written about its meanings for Shi'ism are not in conversation with those who have done work on it in the context of Sufism. If one takes into consideration fields contiguous to Islamic studies such as Middle Eastern or Near Eastern studies, the compartmentalization is even greater. Those who have analyzed secrecy in Middle Eastern literatures, especially in Arabic literature, are not in conversation with those who have treated it in Islamic studies, and vice versa. This is rather unfortunate because I think especially a topic such as secrecy is amenable to, indeed invites, the bridging between different kinds of genres and discourses.

Because my work on secrecy straddles Arabic literary studies and Islamic studies, I am able to avoid this kind of compartmentalizing. My methodology is distinguished on two grounds. First, in my examination of secrecy I cross disparate genres and discourses; in other words, I combine literary writings with texts that are mainly religious. Hence I examine the idea of the secret in several early Arabic discourses and genres: ethics, pseudocourtly love literature, the *paedeia,* and scripture. Second, I have grouped together these disparate discourses because I view them as being held together by the prominent way in which the concept of the secret bears upon the representation of self and subjectivity in them.[16]

There exists reciprocity between early Arabic literature and the Qur'an that makes the comparative approach more compelling. Just as the Qur'an has had a distinct impact on the development of the early Arabic literary heritage—including its belles lettres and love literature—so does that literature (especially its poetic heritage) explicate the Qur'an: early commentators and exegetes turned to pre-Islamic, Arabic poetry to explicate and interpret the Qur'an. Not surprisingly then, the classical exegeses of the Qur'an are replete with literary exempla from the poetic heritage.

Sources

The concept of the secret is most powerfully conveyed in the Qur'an's portrayal of the God-human relation, eschatology, and worship practices, and it is these three areas that are examined in chapters 1 and 2. The focus is not on divine secrets but rather on human secrecy and concealment, though at times there are points of contact between the two. My analysis hinges on a careful selection of the vocabulary, syntactical terms, verbal refrains, and metaphors that describe and characterize the concept of the secret throughout the sacred text. I do not undertake a lexicographical treatment of the whole Qur'anic vocabulary; rather, I analyze the most important words and phrases that play a recurrent and decisive role in characterizing the concept of the secret.

My approach to the Qur'an is informed by theories and paradigms from literary criticism, history of religions, and psychology. Issa Boullata's point regarding "concentrat[ing] on the literary structures of the Qur'an in order to elucidate how they produce religious meaning" is also important to my approach.[17] Moreover, I rely on intertextual approaches to the Qur'an "encapsulated in the dictum: *al-Qur'an yufassiru ba'duhu ba'dan* (different parts of the Qur'an explain one another)."[18] I work largely within a synchronic framework. As Mustansir Mir has pointed out:

> In a certain sense, the Qur'an is marked by a unity of content and style that admits of taking a synchronic approach. . . . First, historically as well as theologically, the Qur'anic revelation was mediated through a single individual, Muhammad. Second, it is generally agreed that the compilation of the Qur'anic text was finished, or nearly finished, in a short period of time—within Muhammad's lifetime, according to some authorities. On these two counts, the Qur'an comes to possess a unity that would justify taking the Qur'an in its finished form as the starting point of a literary investigation.[19]

I recognize that the Qur'an emerged and was canonized within a changing historical context. In other words, I approach the Qur'an with the stance of the empathetic but nontheological scholar of religion.

Several Qur'anic commentaries, including al-Tabari's *Jami' al-Bayan* and al-Zamakhshari's *al-Kashshaf,* have been consulted selectively. I follow the strategy outlined by Angelika Neuwirth in her remark that "their exegesis is referred to and discussed in cases where particular passages present hermeneutical difficulties or have provoked controversial interpretation. Independent interpretations, however, have been attempted, based on consideration of structural continuity in Qur'anic speech."[20]

Early Islamic ethical and didactical writings include works devoted to various character types and specific character traits. The writings that treat "secrets and secrecy" as a topic belong to this category—a category that dealt with an array of themes such as the different human emotions and affects (forgiveness, envy, anger) and human conduct (the virtues of keeping promises and oaths). The locus classicus on human secrets and secrecy is a ninth-century treatise entitled *Kitab Kitman al-Sirr wa hifz al-lisan,* or *Book of Concealing the Secret and Holding the Tongue* (henceforth referred to as simply *Kitman*).[21] This treatise was written by the eminent early Mu'tazilī theologian, ethicist, and essayist (*adīb*) named al-Jahiz (c. 776–868).[22]

Kitman is the principal text with which chapter 3 deals, and it bridges the religious and literary conceptions of secrecy.[23] It is a sixty-page treatise that provides an in-depth understanding of the concept of the secret. *Kitman* is a relatively well-knit work,[24] examining the topic of the secrets of the individual self rather than the subject of secrets of a group or collective practices of secrecy.[25] Although the topic of secrecy was not novel during al-Jahiz's time, what sets his treatment apart is his probing, investigative approach. He did not merely transmit existing ideas and traditions regarding the concept of the secret; the imprint of his own individual genius is present throughout the treatise. Charles Pellat's observations on al-Jahiz's works are relevant here: "What is more, al-Jahiz always sets his own personal and utterly distinctive stamp on his source-material, however neutral. In the field of the Arabic humanities, it could well be said that while al-Jahiz's predecessors collected and sifted the raw materials, al-Jahiz himself was the artist who brought an original touch to the whole edifice. He raised the study of manners to the level of psychological enquiry and brought an analytical approach to a scholarly and professional *adab.*"[26] The treatise is both descriptive and prescriptive: al-Jahiz not only describes and analyzes secrecy; he also offers counsel and guidelines on how to practice discretion.

Classical Arabic encyclopedic works, or the *paedeia,* consider secrecy as one of among many topics, and therefore "secrecy chapters" are found in many well-known encyclopedias.[27] These Arabic polythematic encyclopedias provide insight into what was deemed worthy of knowing by members of certain elite social strata connected with the court.[28] Textual excerpts from classical belletristic encyclopedic works (ranging from the ninth to the fourteenth centuries) are examined in chapter 3. These include Ibn Qutayba's ninth-century *'Uyun al-Akhbar* (*Choice Reports*), al-Bayhaqi's tenth-century *al-Mahasin wal-Masawi* (*Goodness and Equality*), the Andalusian Ibn 'Abd Rabbih's tenth-century *al-'Iqd al-Farid* (*The Unique Necklace*), and al-Nuwayri's fourteenth-century *Nihayat al-Arab fi Funun al-Adab* (*The Ultimate Ambition in the Branches of Erudition*). Because these encyclopedias were composed and compiled mainly for the court scribes and secretaries, the chapters on secrecy in them fall within the volumes devoted to subjects concerned with their arts and duties.

My examination of early Arabic love literature in the second half of the book draws primarily on two genres: pseudohistorical love story or romance narrative (*qiṣṣa* or *hikāya*) and expository treatises or tracts on "love theory" (*kitāb, risāla*). However, references will be made to the love prelude (*nasīb*) of the pre-Islamic ode and the love poems of subsequent periods of Islamic history—the *ghazals* of the Umayyad and 'Abbasid periods.

In particular I focus on the romance narratives or 'Udhri love stories. The Arabic word *'udhrī* means "chaste, virginal," and the narratives are so named because they are considered to be, according to both popular and scholarly views, "chaste" love stories in which sexual union is absent and marriage is thwarted. Indeed, the love tales are known for their portrayals of ostensibly chaste love affairs in which a poet-lover loses his beloved precisely because of his impugning her chastity. Hence, these stories are characterized by depictions of "love gone awry," with themes of (male) indiscretion playing a big role. Although the versions I rely on are mainly from the tenth century, the oral provenance of many of these pseudohistorical romances perhaps dates back to late seventh and early eighth centuries C.E. (the early Umayyad period). The literary antecedents for these romances, and the poetry contained in them, lie in genres of even earlier ages—that is, possibly in the Greek romance and certainly in the love prelude of the classical pre-Islamic ode. These love stories played a role in the development of chronologically later genres, such as mystical Sufi literature, medieval Persian and Urdu love poetry, and, according to some scholars, medieval European romance.[29] Because the narrative aspects of these 'Udhri romances are most richly developed in a tenth-century multivolume work entitled *Book of Songs* (*Kitab al-Aghani*), produced by a Baghdadi courtier named Abu al-Faraj al-Isfahani, I rely on the later renditions of the stories.[30]

The central characters in all these romances are poets who are also legendary lovers. Poets were also lovers because the links between poetic language and courtship in early Arabic culture were well established. Among the romances that belong to the 'Udhri corpus examined in chapters 4 and 5 are *Jamil Buthayna, Majnun Layla,* and *Qays Lubna.*[31] From among these romances, my chief focus is on precisely the romance of *Majnun Layla* for several reasons: it is the most well known 'Udhri romance with a rich legacy in Arabic literature but also in the Persian, Turkish, and Urdu literary traditions; and it is the love story that best exemplifies the hazards of "love revealed."[32]

The expository treatises or tracts on "love theory" describe, analyze, and explicate the phenomenon of love. They also contain individual chapters devoted to the ideas of concealing and revealing love. Among the major love treatises referred to in this book are the eleventh-century *Tawq al-Hamama* (*The Ring of the Dove*), by the Andalusian theologian and jurist Ibn Hazm (d. 1064), and the ninth-century *Kitab al-Zahra* (*Book of the Flower*), by the jurist and essayist Muhammad ibn Dawud al-Isfahani (d. 910).

Qur'anic Constructions of the Embodied Self

The Qur'an sets forth a particular "ideology of truth and deception."[33] According to this ideology, appearances or outer signifiers in general may be designed to deceive, but for those who can discern and discriminate, these outer signifiers disclose truth. The deceitful stratagems or deceptions characterizing the outer signifiers do not succeed and are not part of God's plan— God is certainly not deceived, and those close to God are not deceived nor do they deceive. What is hidden is inevitably revealed as part of God's plan and design.

This Qur'anic ideology of truth and deception is inscribed in its conceptions of the self. The Qur'an identifies secrecy as a marker of the self (*nafs*). When this secrecy of the self is linked with worshipping God, it signifies an invisible human structure of interiority. Often this secrecy of the self is linked with deception; indeed, the Qur'an implies that the self has a proclivity toward hiding and concealment due to deception. Even while it suggests this, however, the Qur'an privileges an ethical and moral self characterized by transparency. What the Qur'an attempts to forge is a human self and subjectivity, a definitive trait of which is its complete transparency vis-à-vis God. This transparency involves the recognition that the self is always known (including watched, observed, heard) by God and, most importantly, held accountable by God—thereby underscoring the profundity of the theme of human responsibility that characterizes the scripture.

Consistent with its ideology of truth and deception, the Qur'an suggests that secrecy of the self is always accompanied by revelation. Secrecy and revelation are inextricably linked. The self's inner recesses are ineluctably conveyed through outer signifiers that disclose truth. This is so because, according to the Qur'an, the self is embodied. It is through the embodied quality of the human self that the body is implicated in the secret's disclosure; that is, the outer body reveals the secret in spite of the self's (sometimes deceptive) intentions to conceal. In other words, the self's interior moral life and conscience are conveyed through exterior, physical signifiers. Hence, Qur'anic eschatology sets forth notions of self and body (as well as soul and body) that are intertwined and connected.

These particular notions of self and subjectivity, as presented in the Qur'an, provide a contrast to the model of the "public self" premised on honor/shame standards that prevailed in pre-Islamic Arabia. For this reason and others, I raise the question of whether the Qur'anic construction of a "religiously transparent self" helped to mediate a profound transition between pre-Islamic and early Islamic Arabian cultures from this "public self" to a "transparent self" personally accountable to God for secret and public thoughts and deeds. Islam embraced certain continuities of this "public self," but it significantly raised the stakes by also holding the human self accountable for its secret, hidden deeds and thoughts in addition to the known, visible ones. Again, an important aspect of this "religiously transparent self" was its embodied quality—the self's outer physical signs and signifiers attested to inner truths.

If, as I maintain, the Qur'an suggests that the self is embodied and the outer signifiers of this embodied self reveal inner truths (the body is implicated in the secret self's disclosure), then we have profound insight into how and why Qur'anic notions of self and body (as well as soul and body) necessarily would be intertwined and connected. It should be mentioned that the Arabic word for self (*nafs*) in the textual selections under consideration in this book draws on the Qur'anic conception. The Qur'an employs this same word *nafs* (plural *anfus*), and it bears the meaning of "the entirety of the human self or person."[34] Its meaning embraces both "self" and "soul." Th. Emil Homerin argues that in the Qur'an, "*nafs* and its plurals do not appear to designate a spiritual substance or soul, but rather aspects of human character, including selfishness, concupiscence, personal responsibility, and individual conscience."[35] The term *nafs* is central to discussions of Islamic ethics, psychology, and mysticism. The "Hebraic-biblical tradition . . . is [also] strongly holistic in its understanding of the human self."[36] Notions of body as understood in the Qur'an draw on the Hebraic model: the body is not separate from or exclusive of self and subjectivity; *soma* is not separate from psyche.[37] Fazlur Rahman comments on this: "The term *nafs*, which later in Islamic philosophy and Sufism came to mean soul as a *substance* separate from the body, in the Qur'an means mostly 'himself' or 'herself' and, in the plural, 'themselves,' while in some contexts it means the 'person' or the 'inner person,' that is, the living reality of man, but not separate from or exclusive of the body. In fact, it is body with a certain life-and-intelligence center that constitutes the inner identity or persnality of man."[38] My analysis of secrecy elucidates the Qur'anic meaning of *nafs* as "the entirety of the human self or person"—not separate from or exclusive of the body.

Inextricability of Secrecy and Revelation: A Marker of the Self

This Qur'anic construction of the embodied self has strong implications for understanding representations of self and subjectivity in early Islamic ethics and Arabic love literature. These ethical and literary Arabo-Islamic discourses display an acute awareness of and interest in the embodied self that reveals. Moreover, the Qur'an bequeathed to these discourses a powerful belief in how human intentionality and consciousness can be subverted through the body. The Qur'anic construction of the embodied self also has strong implications for understanding representations of self in Sufism or Islamic mysticism. This book does not deal with Islamic mysticism or Sufism, but Sufism too privileges the interior self as being determinative of the external self's expression and conduct. Hence, the psycho-spiritual development of the inner or interior self (*al-bāṭin*) is rendered critical.[39] This process of refinement of the self is often conveyed through symbolic language involving metaphors of secrecy and transparency: "removing the veils of the self"[40] or "polishing the mirror (the mental, spiritual, and mystical states) of the self." Not surprisingly, the Sufis drew on the Qur'anic constructions of the self in the articulation of their metaphysical doctrines and psychological theories.[41]

Indeed, there is a certain unity in constructions and representations of the self across the very different early Arabo-Islamic discourses (scripture, ethical writings, and love literature) examined in this book. This unity consists of the following three significant elements: that the dialectic of keeping and revealing of secrets is crucial to the very way that the self is imagined and constructed; that the self is always embodied and both conceals and reveals secrets; and that the embodied self is characterized by outer physical signs and signifiers that attest to inner truths.

No doubt the conventions of the genre or discourse dealt with here, the kinds of audience(s) intended, and the historical contexts all influence and color how secrecy and the secret are conceptualized as well as how secrecy explicates the representations of self and subjectivity in the texts under consideration. In other words, at a certain level, each discourse yields its own configurations of self and subjectivity. For instance, in early Arabic love poetry, the meanings and functions of secrecy are tropological; the meanings of secrecy and privacy also interrogate prevailing psychosocial realities pertaining to marriage, sexuality, and gender relations; and hence we obtain glimpses into especially male-gendered constructions of the "rhetorical self." However, the Qur'an makes claims about the absolute; it persuades, warns, admonishes, and is a prescriptive text offering guidance on how to live. Therefore, it is characterized by the "religiously transparent self" because the meanings and function of secrecy are designed to uphold individual accountability and responsibility in the context of the God-human relation. Islamic ethical and didactic texts, on the other hand, promote the notion of the "self as cipher" because the themes of secrecy in them concern earthly contexts involving discretion in interpersonal relations and modes of self-presentation. Hence, secrecy sometimes works in the service of individual accountability, sometimes it works in the service of ethical conduct and discretion, and at other times it works in the service of rhetorical embellishment. However, throughout these early Arabo-Islamic discourses, the emphasis is on how secrecy and revelation function as markers of the self.

In these Arabo-Islamic discourses, including the Qur'an, a strong dynamic of "inner versus outer," "interior versus exterior," and "inside versus outside" characterizes the workings of the human self and subjectivity, as well as interpersonal relations. Also, an impetus toward continually fortifying and policing the boundaries between this inner-outer binary informs this dynamic. Furthermore, what is on the surface, external, outer, or visible as well as the realm of the public often carries negative connotations associated with deception, falsehood, corruption, or danger. And yet, these external signifiers inevitably disclose the truth; they ineluctably reveal the hidden. By focusing on the concept of the secret, I interrogate some of these fundamental notions of self, identity, belonging, and not belonging found in the Qur'an and other early Arabo-Islamic discourses.

※※※※※※※※※※※※※※※※※※※※※※※※※※※※※※※※※※※※

I.

Self and Secrecy in the Qur'an

And my Lord is the seer of [all] that the breasts conceal (*wa-rabbī bi-mā tukhfī al-ṣudūr baṣīr*).

'Udhri romance of *Majnun Layla*

The themes of God knowing all secrets of the self and God holding the self accountable for all concealments that cover up impious and/or harmful deeds also are found in the scriptures of the other two Abrahamic religions, namely Judaism and Christianity. Indeed, conceptions of faith and ethics involved in all three scriptures—the Hebrew Bible, the New Testament, and the Qur'an—are based on divine omniscience and human accountability. In the Hebrew Bible, Deuteronomy 29:29 reads: "The secret things belong unto the Lord our God: but those which are revealed belong to us and to our children for ever"; Psalms 44:20–21 reads: "If we had forgotten the name of our God, or spread out our hands to a strange god, would not God discover this? For he knows the secrets of the heart"; and Proverbs 5:21–22 proclaims: "For human ways are under the eyes of the Lord, and he examines all their paths. The iniquities of the wicked ensnare them, and they are caught in the toils of their sin." In the New Testament, Matthew 10:26–27 states: "So have no fear of them; for nothing is covered up that will not become uncovered, and nothing secret that will not become known. What I say to you in the dark, tell in the light; and what you hear whispered, proclaim from the housetops." Luke 12:2 reads: "There is nothing covered, that shall not be revealed; neither hid, that shall not be known," while Luke 12:7 declares: "But even the hairs of your head are all counted." All these references to "knowing," "heart's secrets," "revealed," "eyes of the Lord," "covered and uncovered," and "ac[count]ing" resonate richly with Qur'anic themes and symbolism concerning secrecy and revelation.

However, as we shall see, secrecy and revelation as markers of the self are more prominent in the Qur'an. The Qur'an is characterized by a particular "ideology of truth and deception" that renders the hidden as being inevitably revealed according to God's plan and design.[1] Consistent with this ideology, the scripture sets forth the conception of an embodied self whose inner moral life is ineluctably conveyed through external, physical signifiers. An examination of the concept of the secret in Qur'anic eschatology reveals a clear example of this embodied self, and examination of a Qur'anic refrain elucidates further the links between self and secrecy in the context of the God-human relation.

Qur'anic Eschatology: "Skins That Speak"

Two principal themes inform Qur'anic eschatological passages. The first emphasizes the secret and hidden nature of eschatological events; these are God's secrets.[2] The second theme concerns the secrets of all creation, especially human secrets, and it emphasizes how during the eschatological drama all such secrets will be revealed. Up until the Day of Judgment, secrecy reigns, but once it dawns, the Day of Judgment is the Day of Revelation par excellence. Fazlur Rahman has pointed out that, according to the Qur'an, on the Day of Last Judgment, "all the interior of man will become transparent."[3] As 86:8–9 proclaims:

> Surely, [God] is able to return him [to life]
> On the day that secrets will be tested.

Among the most startling of Qur'anic eschatological passages are those describing scenes in which human bodies "rebel against and tell the secrets of their selves." The longest and most vivid is found in Qur'anic chapter 41 (Sūrat Ḥā-Mīm), which depicts how the exterior bodies of unbelievers— including their skins— will speak out against them as they approach their chastisement:

> 41:19 Upon the day that God's enemies shall be gathered together and herded to the fire . . .
> 41:20 Until when they come to it, their hearing and their eyes and their skins will bear witness against them concerning what they have been doing.
> 41:21 And they will say to their skins: why did you bear witness against us? They [the skins] will say: God has given us speech, as he gave speech to everything; He created you for the first time, and unto him you shall be returned
> 41:22 You did not seek to hide yourselves, [so] that your hearing, your eyes and your skins should not bear witness against you; rather you thought that God would not know many of the things that you used to do . . .

41:23 And that thought you thought concerning your lord, has
destroyed you, and therefore you find yourselves . . . among the losers.

What is striking here is the imagery of the "skins that speak and bear witness." Classical Qur'anic lexicons, such as Raghib al-Isfahani's *Mu'jam
mufradat alfaz al-Qur'an,* suggest that the word *skins,* or *julūd,* can function
as a metaphor for "bodies."[4] In this sense, it resembles other corporeal metaphors that proliferate in the Qur'an—metaphors that signify, for example,
belief, faith, unbelief, righteousness, sin, or impiety.[5] Commentators offer
various opinions on these verses. The twelfth-century commentator al-
Zamakhshari argues that God grants powers of speech to the organs of the
unbelievers just as he did to the bush that spoke to Moses on Mount Sinai.[6]
Other authorities, including the tenth-century commentator al-Tabari, declare that the term *skins* may refer to the limbs,[7] and indeed, in the other
two passages respectively from Qur'anic chapters 24 and 36 (Sūrat al-Nūr
and Sūrat Yā Sīn),[8] there is mention of "the hands that speak, the feet that
bear witness against the unbelievers as to their actions." Yet other exegetes,
among them al-Qurtubi of the thirteenth century, state that the term *skins*
functions as an allusion to the genital openings or orifices (*al-furūj*), specifically the female external genitalia.[9] This latter signification certainly suggests
that the testimony of the skins concerns "sins" of a sexual nature.[10]

This eschatological passage in chapter 41 illustrates how corporeal signifiers attest to the self's inner world, attest to individual conscience and
morality in a distinctly eschatological context; God's "enemies," destined for
hell-fire, discover on approaching this inferno that the most exterior and
largest organ of their bodies rebels against them and betrays their innermost
secrets. That it is the skin, a thoroughly visible and exterior sensory organ,
is pivotal in this Qur'anic passage because what is underscored is the manifold ways in which the whole outer body renders transparent what the secret-
holder desires to conceal inwardly. Although the other sensory organs are
mentioned (the ears and eyes respectively), it is the striking testimony of the
"skins" that "bear witness" that most disturbs the disbelievers: "And they
will say to their skins: why did you bear witness [*shahidtum 'alaynā*] against
us?"

Human accountability and divine judgment are at the core of the eschatological phenomenon of "bearing witness." The phenomenon of "bearing
witness" is identified as one among many events during the ordering of
events on Judgment Day (other events include, for example, "the returning
to life," "the gathering," and "the balances of justice"). Sight, knowledge,
and testimonial speech are intricately interwoven in the semantic spectrum
of the verbal root for the word *to witness* (*yashhad*) as found in the early
lexicons: "to give information of what one has witnessed, or seen with the

eye; to give testimony, evidence, or to declare such a thing as knowing it." Mustansir Mir points out that the literal meaning of a derivation of this word, *shahāda,* is "presence."[11] Pointing out the links between "presence" and "testimony" in the word's etymology, Mir enumerates the different modes of "bearing of testimony" found in the Qur'an:

1. Bearing witness to any event
2. Bearing witness to an agreement or transaction
3. Bearing witness to the truth of something
4. Representing or speaking for a group or people—a spokesman bears witness to the correctness of the stance or position of his people
5. Keeping watch over something
6. Martyrdom—a martyr, by giving his life, bears witness to the truth of what he stands for.[12]

The modes of "bearing witness to the truth of something" and "keeping watch over something" from this list are especially relevant to 41:22, which captures the corporeal dimension to the "body as testimonial against the self."[13] The corporeal body with its sensory organs is clearly aligned with the divine—it watches over, indeed, records on behalf of God, and then testifies to the truth of the self on Judgment Day. Bodily signs and signifiers provide a testimonial of the inner conscience and moral life.[14] In effect, 41:22 almost jests at the notion of the unbeliever's futile attempts to hide from God— attempts as futile as the unbeliever's incapacity to hide from his/her body what he/she sought to hide from God.[15] Issues of God's omniscience, human secrecy, and accountability pervasively inform this eschatological passage in chapter 41. This is underscored by a hadith specifically concerning 41:22 cited by al-Tabari in his commentary[16] and also found in the collection *Sahih Muslim:*

> Ibn Masʿud reported that there gathered near the House three persons among whom two were Quraishi and one was a Thaqafi. . . . One of them said: Do you think Allah hears as we speak? The other one said: He does hear when we speak loudly and He does not hear when we speak in undertones, and still the other one said: If he listens when we speak loudly, he also listens when we speak in undertones. It was on this occasion that this verse was revealed: "You did not conceal yourselves lest your ears, your eyes and your skins would stand witness against you." (xli:22)[17]

A certain degree of volition is associated with the body, a volition which subverts the will and intentionality of the "self" in these Qur'anic eschatological passages. Bodily symptoms, signs, expressions, and gestures are portrayed as beyond the self's control, and again the intention to retain the secret (as worded in the phrase from 41:22, "rather you thought that God would not know many of the things that you used to do") is undermined and reversed by the body as truthful testimonial.

If, as illustrated by chapter 41, revelation consists of public testimony (what is uttered or spoken publicly), another important dimension of the revelations that will occur on the Day of Judgment is that which is physically and materially turned "inside-out." Chapter 100 (Sūrat al-ʿĀdiyāt), verses 9–11 read: "Does he not know that when that which is in the graves is scattered abroad and that which is in the breasts is brought out, surely on that Day, their Lord shall be aware of them!" Physical surfaces—such as the earth, graves, and bodies—are turned inside-out to reveal the invisible and latent.[18] Both these dimensions—that of the testimonial and the "inside-out" motif—are found in chapter 99 (Sūrat al-Zilzāl), which reads:

> When the earth is shaken with a mighty convulsion,
> and the earth throws forth her burdens,
> and the human says, "What is the matter with her?"
> upon that day she [the earth] shall narrate her news accounts [*akhbārahā*],
> for that her Lord has inspired her.
> On that day, people will come forward in separate groups,
> to be shown their deeds and works,
> and whosoever has done an atom's weight of good shall see it,
> and whosoever has done an atom's weight of evil shall see it.

Here the modes of "bearing witness to the truth of something" and "keeping watch over something" are relevant to the description of the earth herself "telling or attesting to the secrets of human beings." The use of the words *news account(s)* (*khabar* or *akhbār*) is intriguing in this context; they basically mean something disclosed and rendered public, and often the medium of disclosure is oral and spoken. Chapter 99's final verses indicate that the earth's testimony and news will concern the public stocktaking and accounting of the past deeds and thoughts of each and every human being:

> On that day, people will come forward in separate groups,
> to be shown their deeds and works,
> and whosoever has done an atom's weight of good shall see it,
> and whosoever has done an atom's weight of evil shall see it.

As for the second dimension (that is, revelation defined as that which is physically and materially turned inside-out), it is evident in the phrase "and the earth throws forth her burdens." This phrase captures the inside-out eschatological dimension of the secret. This inside-out eschatological dimension of the secret is echoed again and again in many proverbs and pithy sayings from early Arabo-Islamic ethical and didactic writings. One example is a two-liner pithy saying, found in al-Jahiz's ninth-century *Kitman* (*Book of Concealing the Secret*), in which the one on the receiving end of someone else's secret showcases his excellent ability to keep that secret. It draws on Qur'anic eschatological imagery: "It was said to a man: how are you at keeping a secret? He said: I make my heart a tomb in which I bury it until the Day of Resurrection."[19] This dictum underscores the Qur'anic notion of how the self's inner life and conscience are conveyed by bodily signs and signifiers. Recall that chapter 100, verses 9–11 explicitly set up syntactic and symbolic equivalences between bodily cavities and graves—both of which hold hidden content until the Last Day, when they bring out what is inwardly concealed. This pithy saying is actually a variant of the following:

> It was said to a Bedouin: How [good] are you at keeping a secret
> [*kitmānuka lil-sirr*]?
> He said: My heart is but a grave for it.[20]

That the self is marked by an inextricability of secrecy and revelation is certainly conveyed by these sayings. Evidently, the ability to keep a secret was a recognized and sought-after character trait, so much so that there existed a quick, succinct interrogative for sizing up another person about this.[21] The response is equally pithy and relies on the metaphor of the heart as a sealed grave, a sealed mute grave—the main point being: if you tell me a secret, my heart will conceal it like a grave's concealing and sealing of a corpse. Other exempla from the Qur'an as well as Islamic ethics and Arabic love literature (and Islamic mysticism) show that the heart, as the center or locus of the self, is viewed as the container of all secrets of the self.

Selfhood: Secrecy and Transparency

In biblical studies scholarship, the themes of hiddenness and secrecy have often concerned God—for instance, the motif of "God hiding his face" as explored by Samuel Balentine in his book *The Hidden God*.[22] However, the Qur'an, though characterized by the symbolism pertaining to God's absence or presence, also foregrounds the themes and symbols regarding "the human presence."[23] The Qur'an is concerned with the degrees to which human beings are present or absent, open or hidden before God, and it is within the context of such symbolism that it attempts to forge what I term a *transparency of the self*. This transparency of the self is effectively conveyed through a Qur'anic refrain concerned with human secrecy and revelation[24] that is distributed fairly evenly throughout the text and occurs at least sixty to seventy times in it.[25] Qur'anic symbolism of human secrecy and concealment is by no means exhausted by this refrain: such symbolism is found in many instances outside of the refrain.[26] Indeed, the refrain is but one, distinctive element in an overall theme found in the Qur'an: what human beings conceal is inevitably revealed as part of God's plan—God knows all that is concealed and revealed. Examples of the refrain are provided below (rather than citing the entire verse in question, I often cite the portion containing the refrain):[27]

2:33 God said: "Did I not tell you that I know the unseen of the heavens and earth, and I know what you show and what you conceal?"

2:77 Know they not that God knows what they keep secret and what they reveal.

2:284 To God belongs all that is in the heavens and on earth. Whether you show what is in yourselves or conceal it, God calls you to account for it.

3:29 Say: Whether you hide what is in your breasts or disclose it, God knows it. God knows what is in the heavens and what is on the earth. And God has power over all things.

3:167 They were that day nearer to unbelief than to faith, saying with their mouths what was not in their hearts. But God has full knowledge of what they conceal.

4:148–49 And God is all-hearing and all-knowing. Whether you show a good deed or hide it.

5:99 The Messenger's duty is but to proclaim, but God knows all that you show and that you conceal.

6:3 And he is God in the heavens and the earth. He knows your secret and your disclosure. And he knows what you earn.

9:78 Know they not that God knows their secret and their secret conferences and God is all-knowing of the unseen realms?

11:5 Now surely they fold up their breasts that they may hide . . . from him. Behold [even] when they cover themselves with their garments, he knows what they keep secret and what they reveal. Surely he knows full well what is in their breasts.

14:38 O our Lord, indeed you know what we conceal and what we reveal, for nothing whatever is hidden from God, whether on earth or in heaven.

20:7 And if you speak aloud [it is no matter] for he knows what is secret and what is yet more hidden.

21:110 Indeed he knows what is open, uttered in speech and he knows what you conceal.

27:65 Say: none in the heavens or on earth, except God, knows what is hidden, nor can they perceive when they shall be raised up.

27:74 Indeed, your Lord knows all that their breasts hide as well as all that they reveal.

28:69 And your Lord knows what their breasts conceal and what they reveal.

29:52 Say: Enough is God for a witness between me and you: he
knows what is in the heavens and on earth.

35:38 Indeed, God is all-knowing of the unseen of the heavens and
the earth; indeed, he is all-knowing of that which is in the breasts.

40:19 He knows the treachery of the eyes and what the breasts hide.

64:4 He knows what is in the heavens and on the earth; and he
knows what you keep secret and what you reveal, and God knows full
well that which is hidden in the breasts.

67:13 And whether you keep secret your saying or say it openly and
aloud, he knows full well that which is hidden in the breasts.

86:8–9 Surely, God is able to bring him back [to life].

[On] the day that [all] secrets will be tested.

87:7 Except as God wills, for he knows what is open and what is
hidden.

100:9–10 Does he not know that when that which is in the graves
is scattered abroad . . . and that which is in the breasts is brought forth
surely on that day, their Lord shall be aware of them!

The refrain is bound to a seventh-century context involving the Meccans
and the Madinans, however clearly the Qur'an intends this refrain to also
bear a general and universal import. To assume that this refrain can refer
only to what the commentaries allege—that is, the secretive conduct of the
Meccans and /or the Madinan Jews—is an approach that is reductive; it is
also significant that sometimes it is found in contexts that have nothing to
do with either of the aforementioned parties. Some modern critics have
commented on the universality of secrecy. Critics have remarked on secrecy's
ubiquity [28] and how it characterizes and permeates, in varying degrees, every
human relation. [29]

The refrain is characterized by the repetition of certain key words and/or
phrases at intervals throughout the text of the Qur'an. At times "the meaning
of the refrain may vary or develop from one recurrence to the next . . . or its
wording may vary somewhat with each variation." [30] This Qur'anic refrain
repeatedly employs verbs of concealment and revelation and frequently syn-
tactically pairs them. It repeatedly employs the word *ṣudūr* (breasts, chests),
which conceal and reveal, and in this context it recurrently describes God as
the "knower" par excellence of what is in these human breasts. In the refrain,
rhetorically, the opposition of what is concealed and what is revealed by
human breasts is rendered analogous to the opposition between what is in
the heavens and what is on earth. God is as knowledgeable of the minutiae
of hidden human recesses as he is of the workings of the vast created natural
domain.

Human secrecy and revelation can have positive or negative connotations
in the Qur'an, depending on the human intentions or motives for which

they are employed. Not surprisingly secrecy acquires a negative cast when it is linked with deception. Sissela Bok observes that "to confuse secrecy and deception is easy, since all deception does involve keeping something secret—namely, that about which one wishes to deceive others. But while all deception requires secrecy, all secrecy is not meant to deceive."[31] If one treats the refrain as being contextually specific, then, one discerns a pronounced subtext of deception that begs the questions of who is deceiving whom, how, and why.

Secrecy and Alterity

Classical Qur'anic commentaries, including the canonical tenth-century one by al-Tabari, indicate that sometimes the Qur'anic refrain refers to the pagan unbelievers (the Meccans) and at other times it concerns acts of concealment on the part of those whom the Qur'an identifies as the Madinan Jews (*al-munāfiqūn* or "the hypocrites").[32] The second example of this refrain, 2:77, is preceded by verses that provide a narrative context that alludes to the involvement of the Jews of Madina. The verses (2:75–76) read: "Can you aspire [to the hope] that they will believe in you, [after] a party of them heard the word of God and then distorted it knowingly and this subsequent to their having understood it? And when they meet those who have faith they say 'we believe' but when they meet each other in private, they say 'shall you tell them what God has opened/revealed to you that they may engage you in argument about it before your lord?' Do you not understand?" Initially, the verse accuses the Madinan Jews of deliberately misleading people on the matter of the signification of "God's words" (*kalām allah*). This verse concerns the allegation that the Jews had "tamper[ed] with the actual wording of the Torah" (*taḥrīf* and/or *tabdīl*).[33] Scholars are in disagreement over whether this actually is a charge leveled against the Jews by the Qur'an. John Burton, a classical Islamic law specialist, maintains that "[Concerning the] . . . allegation that the Jews had even dared to tamper with the actual wording of the Tora—the *taḥrīf/tabdīl* charge, the Kura'an texts afford not a trace. What the Kur'ān does charge the Jews, especially the Jewish scholars, with is deliberate concealment of their knowledge that the Prophet spoken of in the divine promise contained in their scriptures was indeed this prophet who has now appeared i their midst, in the person of Muhammad."[34]

The Madinan Jews are accused of falsifying or misinterpreting sacred verses (presumably in their own sacred books, including the Torah). As for the second half of the verse, it portrays the Madinan Jews' alleged hypocrisy, namely, saying one thing in public but in private saying and doing something entirely different.[35] Classical Qur'anic commentaries suggest that the Madinan Jews, specifically their rabbis, were hiding portions of their scriptures from various parties (for example, 2:159, 6:91).[36] Grouping all of these allegations under the umbrella term *distortion of scripture*, Mustansir Mir, a Qur'anic-studies scholar, observes: "The People of the Book . . . are accused of distorting the scriptures . . . particularly those portions of the scriptures which prophesy the advent of the Prophet Muhammad. . . . The distortion may take the form of *layy,* which is calculated mispronunciation of words (3:78), or *tahrīf,* which includes tampering with the text and misinterpreting it (4:46; 5:41). *Ikhfā* (concealment; 5:15) is more comprehensive and covers not only the two types of *tahrīf,* but also concealment of certain texts from becoming known."[37] The reference to the latter phrase, "concealment of certain texts from becoming known," refers to the Qur'anic assumption that the Jews, in the words of Burton, "were deliberately concealing that part of their revelation that spoke of . . . [him as God's prophet] . . . 'who will come in the latter days.' "[38] According to some scholars, there is evidence for holding the view that there existed "messianism among certain Meccan Arab circles at the time Muhammad appeared."[39] Mahmoud Ayoub, another noted Qur'anic-studies scholar, talks about "the wide expectation among the Arabs of the coming of a prophet who would unite them and give them an Arabic scripure like the Torah of the Jews and Gospel of the Christians. This prophetic anticipation may have been inspired by Jewish messianic ideas, as the Qur'an reports that the Jews of Medina used to taunt their [Muslim] neighbors with the threat of a new prophet under whose leadership they would defeat them (Qur'an 2:89)."[40]

Certainly deception is an element characterizing all the practices that the Qur'an allegedly associates with the Madinan Jews: hypocrisy, withholding of knowledge, and deliberate misinterpretation of sacred verses.[41] Indeed, 3:167 from the refrain maintains that such deception has tied them with "unbelief" [*kufr*]: "They were that day nearer to unbelief [*kufr*] than to faith, saying with their mouths what was not in their hearts. But God has full knowledge of what they conceal." The external conduct and the spoken words of the Madinan Jews belie inner truths, and the Qur'an suggests that these truths have been and will continue to be inevitably revealed as part of God's plan and design.

Yet another form of deception that the Qur'an ascribes to the Madinan Jews is conspiring against Muhammad. Qur'anic chapter 58 (Sūrat al-Mujād-ila) contains a passage that effectively conveys, in the words of the well-known Islamic studies scholar Fazlur Rahman, "the Qur'an's recurrent criticisms of the small but frequent conspiratorial meetings of the opponents of Islam (whether Meccan pagans or Madinan hypocrites)."[42] After the oft-quoted proclamation of God's omniscience (for example, that God knows all that is in the heavens and what is in the earth), 58:7 announces that God is, in effect, an eavesdropper in each and every secret human consultation or conference, no matter where this gathering may be, when it may be, and how many are in the gathering. God does not just know; he sees, watches, and hears: "Do you not see that God knows all that is the heavens and what is in the earth? There is not a secret consultation between three but he is their fourth, nor between five but he is their sixth—nor between fewer nor more but he is amid them wheresoever they may be. Then on the Judgment Day, he will inform them of what they did; for God has full knowledge of everything."[43] Rahman points out that, "while the immediate meaning is that no matter how secretly they talk, God knows what they say, the more general idea obviously is that God is present wherever two or more persons are present."[44] The notion of God as an eavesdropper and watch guard (*raqīb*) certainly is not limited to this verse in the Qur'an.[45]

A key word employed in the passage is *najwā,* meaning "secret conferences or consultations." The semantics of *najwā* concerns collective practices of secrecy, or more precisely, it concerns interpersonal secrets that are deliberately confided, shared, and traded between two or more parties.[46] There are two qualities of the semantics of *najwā* that are very important. First, an aural dimension is present in its meanings, that is, the element of converse, talk, or whisperings.[47] Second, as Mustansir Mir suggests, the meanings of *najwā* are not necessarily linked with deception and wrongdoing. Indeed, there are several hadith that indicate the term has a sacred dimension. In one such saying, the Prophet declares: "Whenever anyone of you stands for the Salat (prayer), he is speaking in private to his Lord [*yunājī*]."[48] In another, *najwā* as a form of secret discourse between the believer and God acquires eschatological dimensions:

> Narrated by Safwan bin Muhriz: A man asked Ibn 'Umar, "What did you hear Allah's Apostle saying regarding An-Najwā (secret talk between Allah and His believing worshipper on the Day of Judgment)?" He said, "The Prophet said, 'One of you will come close to his Lord till He will shelter him in His screen and say: Did you commit such and such sin? He will say, "Yes." So Allah will make him confess (all his sins) and He will say, "I screened them (your sins) for you in the world, and today I forgive them for you.'" "[49]

Evidently, then, the term *najwā* also embraces the meanings of "private and / or secret converse" that is of a sacred, religious nature—in this hadith such converse is "between God and his believer on Judgment Day," but it can be used to refer to other contexts. A related term is *munājāt,* which, in the plural, also carries the meaning of "confidential, intimate discourse between the believer and God."[50] However, Mir points out that "while *najwā* may have a positive or neutral connotation (19:52 on Mount Sinai, God spoke with Moses 'in confidence' . . .), the word is often used in the Qur'an with the negative meaning of 'conspiracy.'"[51]

One effect of such Qur'anic verses imputing hypocritical and/or conspiratorial behavior to certain Jewish groups is to imply somehow that all Jews constitute a deceiving Other. The refrain (insofar as it is interpreted as being context-specific) and the passage from chapter 58 are important to what I label a dynamic of "othering" or alterity in the Qur'an. The fact is that the Qur'an is characterized by an intense spiritual drama of insiders versus outsiders. There is an air of "us versus them" that tensely pervades certain parts of the text. Moreover, in some passages—if not explicitly, then implicitly and as supported by years of commentaries—there is content that yields a worldview of antagonism against the Other (the infidel, the pagan, the Christian, the Jew).[52] Scholars have drawn attention to this dynamic of alterity that characterizes the Qur'an. David Marshall, in his book *God, Muhammad and the Unbelievers,* observes: "there is always opposition, a blameworthy 'Other' on whom the Qur'an comments, and whom it most characteristically calls a *kāfir.*"[53] Secrecy, insofar as it fosters exclusion, can be part of a trope and rhetoric of "othering" in the Qur'an. The German sociologist Georg Simmel has demonstrated that "excluding another" is central to secrecy.[54] "From Simmel's point of view, concealment is triadic: there are always (at least) two who share a secret, which they keep from a third (another person, society, etc.)."[55] The Madinan Jews, for instance, are alleged to be concealing, conspiring, and (with)holding secrets from and thereby excluding (Muslim) others. In turn, these (Muslim) others, by imputing secrecy and deception to the Madinan Jews, redeploy the trope of "othering" vis-à-vis the Madinan Jews.

In keeping with its emphasis on a "transparency of self," the Qur'an strongly condemns any form of hypocrisy (for example, saying one thing in public and saying and doing something entirely different in private). No doubt this condemnation of hypocrisy acquires a polemical subtext in the scripture, for it is mainly the Madinan Jews who are alleged to withhold or hide that which should not be hidden, that is, to conceal the truth from people. If we treat the refrain as having a universal import, then we discern how descriptively the Qur'anic refrain presents one conception of self and subjectivity, while prescriptively, it attempts to privilege and inculcate another. These two conceptions of self bear examination.

Secrecy of Self

The principal trait that the refrain associates with the (human) self is its proclivity toward hiding and concealment. The refrain identifies secrecy as a marker of the self. One powerful way that the refrain does this is through the semantics of "God knows what is hidden in the breasts" (*'alīm bi-dhāt al-ṣudūr*). Of the examples from the refrain, nine are characterized by the imagery of the breast, or *ṣadr* (the Arabic plural for which is *ṣudūr*), though the eye is also mentioned.[56] The refrain employs the word *ṣadr* as a metaphor for the inner, latent self. Sometimes it interchangeably employs the words *ṣadr* (breast) and *qalb* (heart)—as well as their plurals—as metaphors for hidden human recesses.[57] As 33:51 reads: "And God knows all that is in your hearts [*qulūbikum*] and God is all-knowing and most forbearing." Moreover, 2:284 from the refrain employs the very word for "self," *nafs* (plural *anfus*), instead of *ṣadr* or *qalb*.[58] Elsewhere in the Qur'an, 11:31 reads:

> I tell you not that with me are the treasures of God,
> nor do I know what is hidden,
> nor claim to be an angel. Nor yet do I say,
> of those whom your eyes despise that God will not grant them
> (all) that is good: God knows best what is in their souls/selves
> [*anfusihim*].

Islamic mysticism (*taṣawwuf*) richly developed the idea that the locus of the self, or *nafs,* was the *qalb* (heart) and that embedded within the *qalb*[59] was the *sirr* (secret). This is conveyed by the following passage, which quotes L. Massignon, a noted French scholar of Islam, on the subject: "the seat of thought and awareness of self lay not in the brain but in the heart, a bodily organ . . . a morsel of flesh . . . situated in the hollow of the breast whose beats both gave life and indicated the presence of life. There in the heart lies the 'secret and hidden (*sirr*) home of the conscience, whose secrets (*nadjwā*) will be revealed on Judgment Day.'"[60]

Evidently, the word *ṣadr* does not mean simply the physical chest or breast but rather also embraces meanings concerned with the latent, psychological aspects of the self. Early Arabic lexicons indicate that the word *ṣadr* also means "mind." Moreover, under the lexical entries for *ṣadr,* we find phrases such as "contraction or constriction of the breast or mind" versus "dilation of the breast or mind." "Dilation of the breast" signifies "joy, relief, freedom," whereas its contraction is suggestive of the opposite, "tension and anxieties." Positive affects are linked with the breast's dilation (suggestive of confession or disclosure), and negative affects are linked with the breast's contraction (suggestive of suppression).

Another way that the refrain identifies secrecy and revelation as markers of the self paradoxically is through its portrayal of human speech or what is uttered. Three examples from the selection of the refrain clearly concern revelations in the form of speech or something uttered (they employ derivations of the aforementioned verb *jahara,* "to proclaim, publish, be loud" [20:7, 21:110, and 67:13]). Human speech simultaneously reveals and conceals. However, God's omniscience extends to both human silence/concealment and speech/revelation.

Sirr: The Dialectic of Secrecy and Revelation

The Qur'anic refrain also makes prominent the inextricability of secrecy and revelation. In other words, the refrain makes prominent a psychological state of possessing and/or divulging a secret irrespective of its content. The mention of concealing nearly always accompanies that of revealing in the refrain.[61] The refrain pairs verbs of concealment and revelation: *asarra,* "to conceal, suppress, keep secret" (etymologically related to the word *sirr*); and *'alana,* "to publish, announce, make manifest, speak publicly," are among the most oft-used words conveying the semantics of human secrecy and revelation in the Qur'an.[62] With regard to *sirr,* seven examples from the refrain employ derivations of this Arabic word.

The most commonly employed Arabic word for "secret," *sirr* has contrary meanings: "something concealed, or suppressed" as well as "a thing that is made manifest or disclosed."[63] This contrariness in semantics is suggestive of a kind of dialectic of the secret: a secret is not a secret until it is disclosed to someone, so secrecy invites revelation, and this disclosure, in turn, necessitates concealment.[64] Certainly the telling or revelation of a secret to one person implies the concealment of it from a third party or another. The encapsulation of these contrary meanings in the word *sirr* suggests a kind of form or logic of the secret: a secret is not a secret until it is revealed to someone, so secrecy invites revelation, and this revelation, in turn, entails concealment.

Modern scholars have drawn attention to this inextricability in their conceptual models of secrecy. For example, Simmel introduced the concept of the "sociological form" of the secret.[65] He argued that the secret is a form that is neutral with regard to what he termed the "value functions of its contents."[66] In other words, Simmel held that what is important is not so much the content or substance of the secret but that "the secret is form which constantly receives and releases its contents: what originally was manifest becomes secret, and what once was hidden later sheds its concealment."[67] Elliot Wolfson, a historian of religion, described it thus: "A secret presupposes the concurrent promulgation and suppression on the part of the one who knows the secret. If I have a secret but do not divulge it to anyone, there is no sense in which the secret is meaningfully a secret. Analogously, if I impart the secret indiscriminately, there is no secrecy of which to speak. Possession of the secret on my part necessitates that I transmit it to some and not to others."[68] This inextricability of secrecy and revelation is integrally linked with Qur'anic notions of self and subjectivity.[69] Such a psychological state is also symbolized through the imagery of the concealing/revealing breast. In the context of the unique and specific God-human relation, this kind of subjectivity is problematic because there cannot be any secrets kept from God.[70]

Transparency of Self

According to the Qur'anic refrain, the nature of the God-human relationship is partly defined through its absolute inequality, with the role of knowledge and secrecy in this inequality being imperative: God always fully knows one, but one never knows the hidden God. It is precisely the cognitive verb—"to know," or *ya'lam*—that is most often used in the Qur'anic symbolism of secrecy and revelation (including the refrain): God "knows" the secrets of all human beings. One of the divine names of God is deemed to be *al-'alīm*, the all-knowing, and there is an overwhelming preponderance of this particular verb (and its derivations) in describing the deity in the Qur'an.[71] Among God's other divine names are *al-khabīr* (the all-aware),[72] *al-baṣīr* (the all-seeing), and *al-shahīd* (the all-attesting).[73] From the vantage of the deity, God, nothing of the human self's motives, actions, utterances, thoughts, and feelings can be hidden. The Qur'an assigns far more emphasis to God as the knower of what is hidden or concealed even though it often speaks of God as being the hidden one (*al-bāṭin*). As 57:12 reads: "He is the first and the last and the manifest [*al-ẓāhir*] and the latent [*al-bāṭin*] and he has full knowledge of all things [*huwa bi-kull shay' 'alīm*]."

The recognition that one is always watched, observed, heard, and known by God implies a transparency of self. What is crucial is that this transparency of self involves accountability—one is held accountable by God, especially for harmful and evil thoughts and deeds never known by others. The recognition that, in this relation of transparency vis-à-vis God, one is always held accountable by God is seen in the following verses from the refrain:

> 2:284 To God belongs all that is in the heavens and on earth.
> Whether you show what is in yourselves or conceal it, God calls
> you to account for it . . .
> 6:3 And he is God in the heavens and the earth. He knows your
> secret and your disclosure. And he knows what you earn.

Hence prescriptively the Qur'an privileges a self that is transparent, that is self-aware, one in which the disparity between the inner and outer aspects is at a minimum. What one earns is a cumulative result of the process of being held morally accountable in the eyes of God. Fazlur Rahman conveys this—that it is not just cognition (that is, that one is known by God), but that there is divine judgment involved: "God's presence is not merely cognitive, for His condition entails other consequences—most importantly, judgment upon cumulative human activity. This is the meaning of the frequent Qur'anic reminders that God is ever wakeful, watching, witnessing, and, so far as societies are concerned, 'He is sitting in a watch tower' (89:14) and 'no atom in the heavens or the earth ever escapes His notice' (10:61; 34:3)."[74] Indeed, the fear of the reality of this final accounting and judgment is integral to Qur'anic conceptions of faith and belief—as we have seen in the section concerned with Qur'anic eschatology.[75]

Resistance to the Transparency of Self

It may be asked what room there was for divine mercy and compassion rather than divine judgment regarding an individual's secret mental lapses or errors. A window is provided into this line of inquiry through a cluster of hadith associated with 2:284 from the refrain.[76] These hadith suggest that the Qur'anic call for a "transparency of the self" encountered a degree of resistance. They strikingly portray how the new converts, including the very companions of the Prophet, grasped the profound religious and theological import of 2:284 so much that they beseeched him with help in dealing with the verse and expressed their fear that "it is beyond our power to live up to it."[77] This Qur'anic verse was perceived as mandating something well beyond what the nascent religion already had asked of them (for example, to observe and comply with new religious practices and rituals). Indeed, there are several hadith references indicating 2:284 becoming an abrogated or "cancelled" verse.[78] According to the canonical hadith collections, the verse that abrogated or "replaced" it is 2:286: "God does not burden a self [*nafs*] except in accordance with its capacity. It gets what [good] it earns and it is charged with what [bad] it racks up. Our Lord! Do not punish us if we forget or err. Our Lord! Lay not on us a burden like you did lay on those before us. Our Lord! Do not impose upon us what we do not have the strength for and pardon us and grant us forgiveness and have mercy on us. You are our patron/protector." What is rendered prominent here is the human need for God's mercy and compassion rather than for divine judgment. To a degree, the omnipresence of God is resisted, and the resistance to 2:284 appears to be based not only on its novelty for the early Arab Muslims but also on the perception that it ran counter to what they humanly could comply with and follow. Without diminishing the importance of individual accounability and responsibility, emphasis is placed on divine forgiveness and mercy for human mental and/or emotional lapses and errors. If, as was argued by one Muslim scholar, "abrogation was generally directed to making things easier, and the earlier ordinance [that is, the abrogated verse] was retained as a reminder of God's mercy," then the abrogation of the verse in question (2:284) and its retention in the Qur'an became more explicable.[79] God mercifully responds by making his call for a "transparency of the self" commensurate with each individual's capacity (2:286: "God does not burden a self except in accordance with its capacity").

The Islamic Reinvention of the Self

It is possible that the Qur'anic transparency of the self mediated and facilitated a profound transition between pre-Islamic and early Islamic Arabian cultures from a "public self" bound to honor/shame standards to a "religiously transparent self" personally accountable to the God as mandated by Islam and the other Abrahamic, monotheistic religions. To delve into this, it must be asked how this Qur'anic transparency of self comported with standards of honor/shame that prevailed in much of pre-Islamic and early Islamic Arabia at this time (according to which it was what was done in public that mattered). For example, a saying attributed to Ibn Abbas (relayed by the tenth-century exegete al-Tabari) declares that "the pre-Islamic Arabs used to forbid such adultery (*zinā'*) as appeared but to allow what was hidden saying 'Concerning that which appears—it is a disgrace but as for what was hidden, that does not matter.' "[80] Clearly, a public/private dichotomy prevailed regarding what was permissible and impermissible among the pre-Islamic Arabs. The following hadith attributed to the second caliph 'Umar ibn al-Khattab (who came into power less than five years after the death of Muhammad and ruled the nascent Islamic community for a decade from 634 to 644 C.E.) demonstrates that this public/private dichotomy continued to prevail during the early Islamic era: "People were (sometimes) judged by the revealing of a Divine Inspiration during the lifetime of Allah's Apostle but now there is no longer any more (new revelation). Now we judge you by the deeds you practice publicly, so we will trust and favor the one who does good deeds in front of us, and we will not call him to account about what he is really doing in secret, for Allah will judge him for that; but we will not trust or believe the one who presents to us with an evil deed even if he claims that his intentions were good."[81] Though the calip 'Umar is shown reminding his Muslim subjects that they will be called to account for all they do in secret, and they will be judged by God for this, he clearly states that the new Islamic state will measure and judge individuals by what is publicly known and witnessed of their deeds, behavior, and conduct.

Nonetheless, as Pamela Eisenbaum observes, "it is striking that the cultures out of which Judaism, Christianity and Islam come are considered honor/shame cultures in which virtue was measured publicly. But if this is the case, how does one explain the theme of being accountable for acts done in secret?"[82] Actually, one can imagine a neat complementariness between this Qur'anic transparency of self and standards of honor/shame that prevailed in much of early Islamic Arabia at this time. Not necessarily contradicting the communal emphasis on virtue being assessed publicly, the religion upheld an ethical, moral self or a transparency of the self according to which not only the seen but also the unseen are judged and held accountable by God. Certainly, in the Qur'an, there is often the assumption that secrecy or privacy of the self lends itself to deception and/or wrongdoing. Perhaps, as a consequence of this, there is no notion in early Islam, according to Michael Cook, "that certain kinds of behaviour are inherently private,

and as such immune to public scrutiny."[83] In *Forbidding Wrong in Islam,*
while making the argument that in Islam there were no inherently private
behaviors immune to the public gaze, Cook also brings up the idea of
"immunity of hidden wrongs" whereby if a wrong is private (or secret) in
the sense that nobody knows about it, it is beyond the scope of the individual
Muslim's duty of commanding right and forbidding wrong (*al-amr bi'l-
ma'rūf wa'l-nahy 'an al-munkar*).[84] He points out that such a wrongdoing,
according to a prophetic tradition, harms only the wrongdoer.[85] Cook
adduces a saying of Ibn Taymiyya: "Manifest wrongs must be acted against,
in contrast to hidden ones, the punishment of which afflicts only the perpe-
trator."[86] If the secrecy of the self is indeed susceptible to deception and/or
wrongdoing, then the religious theme of being held accountable for acts
done in secret functons to combat this and to inculcate virtue, personal
responsibility, and ethical conduct.

Cook's analysis of early textual evidence concerning the Islamic duty of
commanding right and forbidding wrong sheds some light on the presence
of secrecy and concealment as a marker of self and subjectivity. He suggests
that Islamic law punished individuals for secret crimes that were found out,
such as adultery or drinking. Cook points out that there was a kind of clash
between the individual duty to stop wrongdoing and the injunction against
violating privacy.[87] For instance, spying in order to uncover hidden wrongs
was discouraged and deemed excessive.[88] One could stumble upon indirect
evidence, but one had no right to go looking for such signs.[89] Yet, often
punishment was meted out for secret crimes that were found out (in spite of
the admonitions not to spy).

There is another response to the aforementioned question of how the
standards of honor/shame in early Islamic Arabia comported with the
Qur'anic transparency of self: for the religiously transparent self whose conduct may be under public scrutiny, there potentially could be a deep clash
between an honor/shame culture that measures individual virtue commu-
nally and a religious system that privileges an individual's inner moral vigilance. In the aforementioned hadith attributed to the caliph 'Umar , he is
shown declaring that "we will not trust or believe the one who presents to
us with an evil deed even if he claims that his intentions were good."[90] In
such a situation, were the community to "misread" or "misjudge" the outward deed of the inner self whose intentions were good and who ultimately
is innocent, then one can imagine a profound tension between the practice
of virtue being measured publicly and the scriptural theme of the individual
being accountable for acts done in secret.

Precisely such a situation unfolds in the infamous Hadith al-Ifk ("The
account / saying of the lie") associated with the Prophet's favorite wife,
'A'isha. As Denise Spellberg asserts in *Politics, Gender and the Islamic Past,*

this account "contained the seeds of conceptual conflict regarding issues of honor and shame, belief and unbelief, and truth and falsehood."[91] In a nut-shell, the incident involved 'A'isha accidentally being left alone (unchaper-oned) with a young man unrelated to her. No doubt, it was on the basis of publicly defined notions of honor and shame that 'A'isha and also her hus-band, the Prophet, were judged during the controversy generated by this incident: "The attack upon 'A'isha's chastity was in fact aimed through her at her husband, the founder of the Islamic community. In this sense, Muhammad's male honor was merely maintained by 'A'isha as a woman. Women are not active in promoting or attaining honor, but demonstrate only passive proof of its maintenance in the public vigilance of male control and protection."[92]

Spellberg analyzes in detail the elements of the controversy, but several aspects are pertinent here. First, 'A'isha inwardly recognized that God knew her innocence. Yet, according to the honor/shame standards of the Arabian culture in which she lived, what held sway were public appearances and accusations: "Caught in the most serious crisis of her married life, 'A'isha understood that her testimony in the face of communal slander and doubt was worthless. At this critical juncture in her life, only divine intervention could exonerate her because the true danger of the accusation, now common knowledge in the community, would never be completely undone."[93] Poi-gnantly, 'A'isha is shown agonizing over whether God deemed her important enough to send down to Muhammad affirmation of her innocence, as only God knows the unseen: "By Allah, I believed I was too unimportant for God to send down a [Qur'anic] recitation which could be read in the mosque and in prayer. I hoped that the Prophet would see something in his sleep through which Allah would exonerate me from the lie, because Allah knew my innocence."[94] 'A'isha, through her privileged status as the wife of Muhammad, is fortunate enough to be among the people to whom the caliph 'Umar makes reference in the quotation cited earlier: "People were (sometimes) judged by the revealing of a Divine Inspiration during the life-time of Allah's Apostle." Ultimately, it is divine proof (indirectly conveyed by Muhammad) that saves her—God alone is the source of her vindication.[95] Yet, for those less fortunate than 'A'isha, their being wrongfully judged by the community would constitute an even longer and more trying test of religious faith than the one she appears to have suffered.

Actually, for the religious self, there really was no self outside of or apart from a transparency of the self. Consider the following quotation from a well-known eleventh-century Arabic love treatise, *Tawq al-Hamama,* or *The Ring of the Dove,* by the Andalusian jurist and theologian Ibn Hazm. This quotation surfaces in a chapter entitled "The Vileness of Sinning," and importantly, Ibn Hazm invokes those very Qur'anic verses discussed in the beginning of this chapter concerning the refrain:

> Let no man say, "I was in privacy." Even if he be entirely alone, yet he is within the sight and hearing of "the Knower of all secrets" [5:108], "Who knoweth the perfidious eye, and what the breasts conceal" [40:20], "and knoweth the secret and that which is even more hidden" [20:6], "so that there shall not be three whispering together but He is the fourth of them, nor five but He is the sixth of them, nor fewer than that nor more but that He is with them wherever they may be" [58:8]. "He knoweth all that is in the breasts" [57:6], "and he knoweth alike the unseen and the visible" [6:73]; "and they conceal themselves from men, but they conceal not themselves from God, for He is with them" [4:107]. Allah says, "And verily We have created man, and know all that his soul whispers within him, and We are nearer to him than his jugular vein; when two meet together, one sitting on the right and the other sitting on the left, neither uttereth a word, but beside him is a watcher watching" [50:15–17].[96]

Though Ibn Hazm seems almost to decry that there is no such thing as being "in privacy," declaring "[for even if one is] entirely alone, yet he is within the sight and hearing of the 'Knower of all secrets,'" he, in effect, declares that there is no self outside of or apart from a transparency of the self.

Conclusion

The significance of secrecy and revelation as markers of the self is rendered prominent in the Qur'an. Again, this may be due to incipient Islam's need to alter and reinvent the public self that was bound to honor/shame standards in mainly pre-Islamic Arabian culture—a self that premised virtue on only visible and known acts and deeds. To uphold a transparency of the self was, for the new religion, to propose an alternative conception of the self that was accountable to God for both secret and public acts and deeds.

All three Abrahamic religions, however, are characterized by themes concerning divine omniscience and human accountability. The belief in and recognition of "there is no hiding from God" and "there are no secrets kept from God" bear a psychical value for the believer in the Abrahamic religions that is related to the constancy of the presence of God. This psychical value, in turn, has profound moral and ethical implications regarding individual conduct and behavior. In the Qur'an, God does not just know; he sees, watches, and hears.[97] God has a panoptic gaze, for seeing and knowing are intimately linked in the Qur'anic lexicon of secrecy and revelation. This idea that nothing can be hidden from God, that God is all-aware and all-knowing and all-attesting, can be looked upon as having a tremendous psychical import for believers. Ana-Maria Rizzuto, a psychoanalyst who has written works on the psychology of religion, observes that "the constancy of the presence of God has psychological value . . . a child can deceive a mother, but an [adult] believer cannot deceive God; there is no hiding from God; [adults] feel this is the case and there is psychical value in this."[98] In the realm of religion, this "psychical value" also translates into moral and ethical values. The panoptic gaze of God functions to dissuade the believer from engaging in wrongdoing and, moreover, to hold the believer accountable for such wrongdoing if it transpires. Rizzuto acknowledges that "psychoanalysts may regard this [all-knowing, all-seeing God] as a component of the super-ego"—that is, the God who is all-aware and all-knowing and all-seeing is akin to the supreme sovereign or superpatrolman.[99]

Among the most acclaimed of hadith that address the panoptic gaze of God is the Hadith of Gabriel, in which the Prophet says that *iḥsān* is "to worship God as if you see Him, for if you not see Him, He sees you."[100] The following three elements (in order of priority) are specified by the Hadith of Gabriel as being constitutive to "the religion of the followers of Muham-mad": *islām* (submission, surrender); *imān* (faith); and *iḥsān* (doing what is beautiful).[101] What is relevant here is that Murata and Chittick, in *Vision of Islam,* employ precisely the aforementioned imagery of God as superpatrol-man in discussing the element of *iḥsān* in the Hadith of Gabriel:[102] "Here the Prophet focuses on the attitude and intention behind the outward activ-ity that is demanded by *islām.* His point is easily understood by thinking about the way we do things in everyday life. For example, the law tells you not to drive over the speed limit. Many people observe the law, but others observe it only because they are afraid there may be a patrol car lurking around the next bend. . . . Even if you do not see the patrol car, you can be sure that he [God] is employing devices that no radar detector will ever be able to foil."[103] Rizzuto argues that this view of an all-knowing, all-seeing God as a component of the superego does not have to be subscribed to by all. Linked with this notion of God's presence and gaze, she maintains, is that of God as witness amid our human need to "be seen, mirrored, and reflected" and protected, a need that is particularly acute when we are children:

> Most people studied liked it very much that "God is always there"
> as a potential presence for the lonely. With his need to be seen, mirrored,
> and reflected, the child of this age knows that he can lie to his parents
> and that they cannot know his thoughts. The child who feels that God
> is always there, knowing everything, is not truly alone in the privacy of
> his thoughts. His badness or his goodness may remain a total secret to
> the adults. God, however, is the only being to whom knowledge of the

inner self is attributed. Religion teaches children that goodness of heart pleases God and that he disapproves of bad thoughts. However dangerous this may be, it still provides a witness for the loneliness of that part of ourselves which Winnicott (1966) calls "the individual's non-communicating self."[104]

Rizzuto's idea that God is a witness is certainly implicit in the Qur'anic symbolism of secrecy and revelation. Likewise, Murata and Chittick recognize the importance of God as intimate witness when asserting that "not all activity is motivated by fear. It so happens that people do things out of love and the wish to be close to the object of their love."[105] The notions of God's presence, God's gaze, and God's face somewhat paradoxically bespeak of his immanence, a God who partly reveals himself to his creation, so that he may both witness and be witnessed.[106] Something of the complexity of this knot of issues is conveyed in a well-known Hadith Qudsī[107] that reads thus: "I was a hidden treasure, and I desired to be known; therefore I created the creation in order that I might be known."[108] God not only sees and witnesses but also wishes to be seen and witnessed; God is not just knower of the hidden but also desires to be known—the passive verb "to be known" is used twice in this saying. Ultimately, the import of the Qur'anic transparency of the self is in moral responsibility and accountability before God; but it is remarkable how intimately God's presence is bound with themes of human presence and openness.

There is no doubt, however, that the Qur'an sets forth the idea that a marker of the self (*nafs*) is its proclivity toward acts of concealment and revelation—the two always accompanying each other. The concealment and revelation are problematic when negative motives, such as deception, are linked with the self's concealment and/or when there exists a disparity between the inner and outer aspects of the self. Given God's omniscience, however, what is underscored is that in the context of the relation with the divine, one is always and constantly the object of God's awareness and gaze. Indeed, the Qur'an generally privileges a human consciousness that is self-aware and one in which the disparity between the inner and outer aspects of the self is at a minimum.

It is important to note the embodied quality of the human self and consciousness. There is also present the idea that the body—as a vessel for the self—is ultimately obedient to God. Therefore, on the Day of Reckoning and Judgment the human body is endowed with testimonial powers that can testify to the self's deeds. This Qur'anic imagery of the revealing/concealing embodied self has strong implications for understanding notions of self and subjectivity in early Arabo-Islamic ethics and love literature.

※※※※※※※※※※※※※※※※※※※※※※※※※※※※※※※※※※※

2.

Sharing and Withholding Secrets
God, Faith, and Worship in the Qur'an

> We should stop thinking of God as someone over there, way up there,
> transcendent . . . [but rather we might say . . .] God is the name of the
> possibility I have of keeping a secret that is visible from the interior but
> not from the exterior. Once such a structure of conscience exists, of being-
> with-oneself . . . once I have within me, thanks to the invisible word as
> such, a witness that others cannot see, and who is therefore at the same
> time other than me and more intimate with me than myself, once I can
> have a secret relationship with myself and not tell everything, once there
> is secrecy and secret witnessing within me, then what I call God exists,
> (there is) what I call God in me . . . God is in me, he is the absolute
> "me" or "self," he is that structure of invisible interiority that is called in
> Kierkegaard's sense, subjectivity.
>
> Jacques Derrida, *The Gift of Death*

Conceptions of the divine, as well as conceptions of faith, (un)belief, and
worship practices, as presented in the Qur'an are profoundly influenced by
and bound up with the idea of the secret. Furthermore, human secrecy in
the Qur'an has positive valuation in some ways. As remarked earlier, human
secrecy and revelation can have good or bad connotations in the Qur'an,
depending on the human intentions or motives for which they are employed.
This chapter again demonstrates how secrecy and revelation—albeit in a
positive context—function as markers of the self. In addition, the God-
human relation as set forth in the Qur'an is illuminated.

The Semantics of *al-Ghayb* (the Unseen)
The construction of God as the supreme knower and revealer of all secrets,
the one who knows par excellence, is perhaps the most effective strategy

employed by the Qur'an through which the deity himself is rendered the "central secret . . . [or the religion's] *mysterium magnum*."[1] In part, this is accomplished through the use of the concept of the *al-ghayb* (the unseen) in the Qur'an. There is constant reiteration in the Qur'an of the point that while God knows and sees all, he himself is unseen, invisible, and separate. Implicit in the recurrent claim that God knows the secrets of humans is the idea that human beings know *no* secrets of God—God is wholly Other, wholly mysterious.

Indeed, the term *ghayb* is crucial to understanding how richly the sacred discourse of the Qur'an defines the secret. In chapter 2 (Sūrat al-Baqara), the Qur'an stipulates that one of the requirements of faith is belief in the *ghayb* (who believe in the unseen, *yu'minūna bil-ghayb*):

> 2:2–4 This is the book
> in which there is no doubt,
> containing guidance for those who are mindful of God,
> who believe in the unseen [*bil-ghayb*], undertake prayer,
> and spend out of what we
> have provided for them.
> And who believe in the revelation
> sent to you, and in what was sent before you,
> those who have faith in the hereafter.[2]

Who are those "mindful of God"? The Qur'an provides a checklist: those who believe in the unseen (*al-ghayb*), observe prayer, and give to the needy.[3] I argue that there appear to be at least two primary uses of this term in the text: as that which refers to things related to the divine; and as that which, drawing upon the words of Jacques Derrida, refers to "a structure of invisible interiority" integral to Islamic practices of piety and worship.[4] Both these uses of the term *al-ghayb* generate ways in which secrecy in the Qur'an has a positive valuation.

The Divine *Ghayb*

Toshihiko Izutsu identifies the semantics of *al-ghayb* as a "major conceptual opposition discernible in the world-view of the Koran."[5] Two opposing dimensions characterize this world according to the Qur'an: the realm of the unseen (*'alam al-ghayb*) and the realm of the visible (*'alam al-shahāda*).[6] Only the latter realm is accessible to humankind, whereas God is the creator and knower of both realms.[7] Izutsu declares that consequently, "this distinction itself [between the two realms] is meaningful only in reference to the basic epistemological capacity of the human mind. It is, in other words, a distinction made purely from the human point of view, for, from the standpoint of God, there can be no *ghayb* at all."[8]

Izutsu maintains that the Arabic word *ghayb* had no explicitly religious connotations in pre-Islamic poetry.[9] The word is employed in pre-Islamic poetry to mean either "things that lie beyond the power of human perception in the most material sense" or "what is hidden in the heart, what is kept secret in the heart."[10] While later Muslim exegetes, such as the thirteenth-century Qur'anic commentator Fakhr al-Din al-Razi, may have drawn upon the pre-Islamic sense of the word, it seems that it acquired religious meanings specific to Islam as one of the Abrahamic faiths only as a subsequent development.[11] Edward Lane's *Arabic-English Lexicon* echoes Raghib al-Isfahani's classical Qur'anic lexicon concerning the religious meanings of the word.[12] According to Lane's *Lexicon,* the word's Islamic or religious cast embraces the semantics of "undiscoverable unless by means of divine revelation; a mystery, or secret, such as an event of futurity . . . a thing that has been hidden from men, and with which the Prophet has acquainted them, of the events of the resurrection and of Paradise and of Hell."[13] Religious meanings of *al-ghayb* are discernible in the definitions of Qur'anic commentators such as the tenth-century al-Tabari, who, for instance, enumerated things of the "unseen" in Q 2:2–4 above to include "heaven . . . and hell, resurrection, the day of judgment . . . as well as . . . the belief in angels, prophets, revealed scriptures, and recompense."[14]

In Q 2:2–4 above, the belief in the unseen (*al-ghayb*) is accompanied by, among other things, a belief in that which is revealed or "what has been sent down."[15] Fazlur Rahman suggests that, in the context of the Qur'an, a reply to the existential question Why (believe in) God at all? takes the form of a " 'belief in and awareness of the unseen' . . . ; this 'unseen' has been, to a greater or lesser extent, made 'seen' through Revelation for some people like the Prophet . . . , although it cannot be fully known to anyone except God."[16] Hence, what is essential is faith and belief in that which is first secret and hidden and then revealed. At times the Qur'an depicts God revealing something of the *ghayb* to believers, and at other times he is shown concealing it. In other words, "side by side with God's exclusive knowledge of the hidden there is another view, expressed in other verses, suggesting that God may occasionally confer some of this hidden knowledge on his creatures."[17] Indeed, the Qur'an portrays even spiritually elevated beings, such as angels, acknowledging that they do not know the *ghayb*. In 2:32–33 we read the creation drama involving the angels, Adam, and God. The angels are shown humbly proclaiming: "We have knowledge only of what you have taught us. You are the All-Knowing and All-Wise." God's reply to the angels underscores the construction of the deity as the supreme knower of all secrets and echoes the angels' admission of ignorance:

2:33 Did I not tell you I know what is hidden [*ghayb*] in the heavens
and the earth,
and that I know what you reveal and what you conceal?[18]

Moreover God, who is supremely omniscient, *chooses* to whom he reveals his secrets. There are profound connections here between the investiture of "knowing the hidden" and being divinely chosen or elect. In 3:42–44 the Qur'an shows God proclaiming that he is revealing something of *al-ghayb* to his chosen: "The angels said to Mary: 'Mary, God has chosen you, and made you pure: He has chosen you above all women. Mary, be obedient to your Lord, prostrate yourself and bow down with those who pray.' That is of the tidings of the unseen that we reveal to you." Likewise in 11:49, sandwiched between the narratives concerned with the prophet Noah, on the one hand, and the people of Ad, on the other hand, we find God declaring, "That is of the tidings of the unseen [*anbā'i al-ghayb*] that we reveal to you. Neither you nor your people knew them before now." In both of these verses the Arabic word *anbā'i* is used in conjunction with *al-ghayb*. According to Izutsu, the word *anbā'i* primarily has "the meaning of 'announcing' 'giving news of something' and yet it is not towards the future that the concept faces. In the Koran, the news brought by a Prophet is always news of the *ghayb* (the unseen world of God)."[19] In other words, it assumes an audience, both selected and select. It is noteworthy that the verb for "to reveal" employed in 3:42–44 (bearing the root *w-ḥ-y*) has (as does chapter 5 [Sūrat al-Mā'ida]) God almost always as the agent in the Qur'an, and the revelation is generally verbal.

God chooses to reveal the *ghayb* to certain of his messengers and prophets and not to others, and God's revelation of the *ghayb* is akin to his conferring secrets. Something of this concealment/revelation of the *ghayb* to his prophets or messengers is accentuated in 3:179, wherein it is proclaimed: "God will not leave the believers in the state in which you are, until he shall distinguish the evil from the good. And God will not disclose to you of the unseen, rather God chooses out of his messengers whom he will." The part of the verse that reads "And God will not disclose to you of the unseen" seems to be addressed to Muhammad, and hence, not surprisingly, he is portrayed as humbly stating his ignorance of this realm in several chapters:[20]

6:50 Say, "I do not say to you": I possess the treasures of God, nor do I know the unseen [*al-ghayb*] nor do I say to you I am an angel. I follow only that which has been revealed to me.

7:188 If I had knowledge of the unseen [*al-ghayb*] I should have multiplied all good and no evil should have touched me: I am but a warner, and a bringer of good tidings to those who have faith.

Some verses show other prophets and messengers hailing God as the one who knows par excellence precisely through their concession that they are ignorant of the *ghayb* (plural, *ghuyūb*). These verses are good examples of how the Qur'an, by constructing God as the knower of all that is hidden, renders him as the "central secret . . . [or the religion's] mysterium magnum"[21]:

> 5:109 [On] the day when God will gather the messengers and say:
> What reply was made to you? They will say: We have no knowledge: it is
> you who knows fully all that is hidden [*al-ghuyūb*].

In 5:116 we have a verse that conveys what Jesus says to God when asked why human beings took him for being divine: "He will say: 'Glory be to you. I would never say what I had no right to say. If I had said such a thing, you would have surely known it. You know all that is within me [*fī nafsī*] though I do not know what is within you. . . . It is you who know fully all that is hidden [*al-ghuyūb*].'" Here Jesus is shown delineating the difference between the divine and human precisely through the use of criteria linked with knowledge and knowing—he is shown venerating God by acknowledging that it is through God's omniscience that God is divine and he is *not*.

God's omniscience and omnipotence are further emphasized through a metaphoric phrase, "the keys to the unseen [*mafātīḥ al-ghayb*]," employed in Q 6:59. The phrase underscores the fact that one primary way that human inaccessibility of this "realm of the unseen" (*'alam al-ghayb*) is experienced is through what may be termed a "visual/perceptual incognition." There are resonances between this and the pre-Islamic meanings of *ghayb*, that is, "things that lie beyond the power of human perception in the most material sense."[22]

> 6:59 And with him are the keys to the unseen [*mafātīḥ al-ghayb*];
> none knows them but he and he knows all that is in the land and the
> sea. And there falls not a leaf but he knows it; nor is there a grain in the
> darkness of the earth nor anything green or dry, that is not [inscribed]
> in a clear record.

Here the *ghayb* variously embraces that which is hidden from human perception and cognition, whether it is what is concealed from the eye because it is deep within the land and sea or because it is that which transforms silently and/or invisibly (for example, a leaf falling or a grain buried in the darkness of the earth). God, and only God, creates this *ghayb* and has the means to allow access to this *ghayb*. In verse 6:60 no mention is made of the term *ghayb*, but together verses 6:59–60 again draw attention to how the Qur'an sets up parallels between God's knowledge of the internal workings of the vast, natural domain and his knowledge of the minutiae of hidden human recesses:

> 6:60 And he it is who takes your souls by night and knows what you have done by day: by day he raises you up again until that the appointed term may be fulfilled. Then to him is your return and he will inform you of what you have done.

God knows each human's interior condition day and night, and he knows the accounting that will unfold once the appointed term has been fulfilled.

Bil-Ghayb: A Structure of Invisible Human Interiority

There is an ambiguity associated with a cluster of Qur'anic verses using the phrase *bil-ghayb.* The ambiguity is inherent in some verses, most of which are in the Qur'anic chapters of the Meccan period and use the phrase *bil-ghayb* in conjunction with the verbs *khashiya* and *khāfa.* On the basis of this ambiguity, there is the question of whether the term *bil-ghayb,* which, for instance, is employed in chapter 2 of the Qur'an (that is, 2:3: "those who believe in the unseen"), also could be rendered thus: "those who believe [in the Lord] most secretly or inwardly, or in their innermost recesses." In other words, the phrase alternatively could refer to an invisible human interiority that profoundly colors conceptions of Islamic faith, worship, and reverence. Actually, understood thus, it has resonances with one of the meanings of *ghayb* as found in pre-Islamic poetry—the meaning of "what is hidden in the [human] heart" or "what is kept secret in the heart." Possessing this interiority, this hidden domain within the inner self, is constituent of belief and faith. This bespeaks the good secrets of human beings, and ones that God lauds. The parallelism between the *ghayb* of the heavens and earth, on one hand, and "that which is within human breasts," on the other hand (as seen in the verse below), lends itself to the assertion that the *ghayb* can be associated with this deeply embedded human interiority, with the innermost recesses of the human breast:

> 35:38 Indeed God is the knower of the unseen of the heavens and earth (*ghayb al-samāwāt wal-'ard*). Indeed he is knower of the recesses of [human] breasts (*'alīm bi-dhāt al-ṣudūr*).

As remarked, this ambiguity is found in verses using the phrase *bil-ghayb* in conjunction with the verbs *khashiya* and *khāfa.* The verb *khashiya,* considered to be a synonym of *khāfa,* embraces the following meanings according to al-Isfahani's classical Qur'anic lexicon: "He feared, or he dreaded; or feared with reverence, veneration, respect, honor or awe."[23] The following two verses from Meccan chapters contain the construct *khashiya bil-ghayb,* and below I provide three different recognized, English translations:

Yusuf Ali:

35:18 Nor can a bearer of burdens bear another's burden. If one heavily laden should call another to (bear) his load, not a bit of it can be carried (by the other), even if he were related. You can [merely] warn those who fear their Lord unseen and observe prayer.

36:11 You can warn only him who would follow the reminder and fears the Merciful unseen. . . .

M. Haleem:

35:18 No burdened soul will bear the burden of another; even if a heavily laden should cry for help, none of its load will be carried, even by a close relative. But you [Prophet] can only warn those who fear their Lord, though they cannot see Him, and keep up the prayer. . . .

36:11 You can warn only those who will follow the Qur'an and hold the Merciful One in awe, though they cannot see Him. . . .

A. J. Arberry:

35:18 No soul laden bears the load of another; and if one heavy-burdened calls for its load to be carried, not a thing of it will be carried, though he be near a kinsman. Thou warnest only those who fear their Lord in the Unseen and perform the prayer. . . .

36:11 Thou only warnest him who follows the Remembrance and fears the All-merciful in the Unseen. . . .

A close look at these translations raises several different questions. Regarding Arberry's translation "those who fear their Lord in the Unseen," what exactly is meant by fearing *in* the unseen? Is it that "the Lord" is "in the Unseen," or are the ones doing the fearing "in the Unseen"? Likewise, who or what exactly is the referent for Ali's term *unseen* in his translation "those who fear their Lord unseen"? Is the referent "the Lord" or those who are experiencing the fear? Haleem's translation is the least ambiguous: "those who fear their Lord, though they cannot see Him." Ali, in his notes concerning verse 35:18, clarifies that the phrase *bil-ghayb* refers back to "Lord" and means "Unseen" in the adverbial sense. He, like Haleem, understands the import here to be that "the man though he does not see God, so realizes God's presence in himself as if he saw him is of genuine faith."[24] However, it could be argued that the referent of the phrase *bil-ghayb* is "those who are doing the fearing," and as such, the phrase is suggestive of the presence of a certain invisible structure of human interiority.[25] Assuming such a referent, I provide an alternative translation:[26]

35:18 Nor can a bearer of burdens bear another's burden. If one heavily laden should call another to (bear) his load, not a bit of it can be carried (by the other), even if he were related. You can [merely] warn those who fear their Lord most inwardly and observe prayer.

36:11 You can warn only him who would follow the reminder and fears the Merciful most inwardly or secretly. . . .

Further light on the matter is shed by verse 57:25, which contains the construct *bil-ghayb* in conjunction with the verb *naṣara,* or "to help" (instead of *khashiya*). In this verse it appears that *bil-ghayb* is being used as a descriptive state to refer to the human action of helping God and his messengers. In other words, there are those who dedicate themselves secretly or invisibly to aiding God and his messengers. I have placed the word *unseen* next to the verb "to help" in the English translation, although in the Arabic it comes at the heels of the phrase "help him and his messengers":

> 57:25 . . . And we sent down iron in which is [material for] might warfare and diverse benefits for mortals and that God may know those who unseen help him and his messengers.

I interpret the verse to mean that the sincere person will help God whether he is seen or brought under notice or not.

If the phrase *bil-ghayb* necessarily describes only God or "the Lord," the meaning implied would be that there exist those who, despite the invisibility and hidden state of God, are thoroughly God-fearing; they are those who fear with awe their Lord, who, again, is hidden from the eyes; invisible, unseen, or unapparent. God's "Otherness" or alterity is made prominent in this meaning, and as conveyed by Derrida, it is God as *tout autre* that he is held in awe and fear: "God is himself absent, hidden and silent, separate, secret at the moment he has to be obeyed. God doesn't give his reasons. . . . Otherwise he wouldn't be God, we wouldn't be dealing with the Other as God or with God as wholly other [*tout autre*]."[27] This semantics of *bil-ghayb* dovetails with the other uses of the divine *ghayb* whereby God is rendered the "central secret . . . [or the religion's] mysterium magnum."[28]

If *bil-ghayb* refers back to the human agent, though, the semantics would shift to mean "one who is God-fearing deeply within, one who fears with awe his lord, a fear kept secret in the innermost recesses of the heart." I maintain that the phrase *bil-ghayb* in the aforementioned verses 35:18 and 36:11 could describe an invisible human structure of interiority characterized by a deeply embedded fear and reverence of God. The depth of this interiority suggests how deeply rooted the reverence is in these believers. Their faith in God is not worn outwardly but rather is profoundly embedded within their hearts. My interpretation resonates with the claims of the medieval exegetes, including the tenth-century al-Tabari and the thirteenth-century commentator al-Qurtubi. For instance, both gloss *khashiya al-rah-mān bil-ghayb* in 36:11 as meaning "one who fears and reveres God [even] away from the eyes of people."[29]

Interpreted as such, the expression *khashiya bil-ghayb,* with its import of a profoundly interior fear/reverence of God, often carries eschatological meanings, that is, only those who are truly, inwardly God-fearing can be warned. This would shed light on why most of the verses containing this phrase are from Qur'anic chapters of the Meccan period—Islamic studies scholars hold that the Meccan chapters are more eschatological in spirit and letter. A Meccan chapter containing an explicitly eschatological verse with this same construct is the following (the translations heretofore reflect my proposed alternative semantics):

> 50:33 Who feared the merciful most inwardly and came with a heart turned in devotion.[30]

Yet another verse that indicates an eschatological event is the following in chapter 21 (Sūrat al-Anbiyā'):

> 21:49 Those who fear their Lord most inwardly and regarding the hour, they are in dread.

Here the mention of the "the hour" refers to the ushering in of the Day of Judgment. The two kinds of fear (fearing in awe and dreading) mentioned in the verse have interconnections. Abdullah Yusuf Ali comments on these two kinds of fears (*yakhshūna* and *mushfiqūna*) along with making reference to a third, important type of fear (*taqwā*): "There is *khashyat,* the fear of God, lest the person who entertains it may be found, in his inmost thoughts, to be short of the standard which God wishes for him; this is also righteousness but in a less high degree than *taqwā* which is akin to love. And thirdly, there is the fear of consequences on the Day of Judgment (*ishfāq*); this also may lead to righteousness but is still on a lower plane."[31] All three of these uniquely righteous forms of fear embrace "an attitude of trembling before the power and majesty of God and the reality of the events to come at the end of time, including those signaling the coming of the 'hour,' the resurrection, the judgment and the final consignment."[32] This "awe-ridden trembling" specifically characterizes the semantics of *khashiya,* as is graphically conveyed through the following verse:

> 39:23 God has sent down the best discourse in the form of a book
> . . . from it or as a consequence of it, the skins of those who fear
> [*yakhshūna*] their Lord tremble.

My interpretation of the expression *khashiya bil-ghayb* as signifying an invisible human structure of interiority that concerns a deeply embedded fear and reverence of God is bolstered by this semantics of "trembling": so profoundly embedded is this form of fear that it can induce the very skins of those who experience it to tremble. In the verse below (also from a Meccan chapter), the mention of "forgiveness and a big reward" yet again evokes the events of the hereafter:

> 67:12 Indeed those who fear [*yakhshūna*] their Lord most inwardly [*bil-ghayb*] for them is forgiveness and a big reward.

These verses concerning the cultivation of a fear/awe of God within one's inner recesses, within a secret sanctum in oneself, have resonances with several pronouncements asking believers to pray or call upon God in secrecy, and in a low, hushed voice—not aloud. They include the following verses:[33]

> 7:55 Call on your Lord humbly and privately. . . .
> 7:205 And remember your Lord in your inner self with humility and reverence and without loudness in words in the mornings and evenings. . . .
> 17:110 Say: Call on God or on the Merciful—whatever names you call him, his are the most beautiful names. Do not utter your prayer aloud, or in a low tone, but seek a middle course.
> 19:3 Behold! He called to his Lord secretly.

This array of verses is indicative of how worship practices (for example, prayer or *ṣalāt*, remembrance or *dhikr*) are profoundly influenced by and bound up with the idea of the secret.

In sum one could argue that the phrase *bil-ghayb* is multivalent and both interpretations—the prevailing ones and my proposed alternative—are embraced by its semantics.[34] What is significant are the insights we have into how conceptions of divinity, faith, belief, worship, and reverence, as presented in the Qur'an, are substantially influenced by the idea of the secret. The prevailing interpretations make prominent God's alterity, while the alternative I propose draws attention to a structure of interiority and secrecy, an invisible human state. The cultivation of this interiority is one of the ways that human secrecy in the Qur'an has positive valuation. No doubt, this alternative meaning further illuminates the Qur'anic God-human relation.

Secrecy and Discretion in Charitable Giving

Charity, or charitable giving, also demonstrates how the secrecy of the self can be integral to worship. Moreover it too indicates that human secrecy and discretion in the Qur'an can have positive valuation. Charitable giving to uplift the poor and needy in Islam has much in common with the teachings of other religions, especially the biblical religious traditions. The Qur'an employs primarily two terms, *ṣadaqa* and *zakāt* (sometimes interchangeably), to convey a "conception of giving or setting aside a portion of one's wealth for others."[35] The word *ṣadaqa* bears the connotations of voluntary rather than obligatory giving, and in some Qur'anic contexts it is linked with themes of God's repentance, thus "suggesting its value for the expiation of sins."[36] As for *zakāt* (considered to be one of the "five pillars" in Islam), its centrality as obligatory giving is "underscored by the many times it is coupled with the commandment of ritual worship" and prayer (for example, 2:2–4).[37] Other terms that signify "giving" in the Qur'an include forms of the verb *nafaqa* (expend), which "occur primarily with the sense of expending one's wealth to please God."[38]

Repeatedly in various contexts, the Qur'an declares it meritorious to spend and distribute this wealth. Charity is at the forefront of some of the good, pious, and righteous purposes for which secret conferences may be held. According to 4:114: "There is no good in many of their secret conferences but if one enjoins a deed of charity [*ṣadaqa*] or goodness [*ma'rūf*] or peace-making and reconciliation among people, [secret conferences are permissible]." In other words three broad purposes for which human secrecy and privacy are allowed are charitable giving, bidding a good or honorable deed, and engaging in diplomacy and peace-making among groups or peoples in conflict with each other.[39] The Qur'an emphasizes that those who withhold their wealth are niggardly because an individual's wealth is considered a God-given bounty, and they will incur divine displeasure:

> 4:37 For God does not love those who are . . . niggardly and enjoin niggardliness on people, and conceal that which God has given them of his bounty. And we have prepared for the unbelievers a humiliating punishment.

Before the topic of secrecy and charity in the Qur'an is taken up further, suffice it to note that in the New Testament too there are several passages stressing the importance of giving charity in secret, especially in the context of allegations of hypocrisy made by Jesus with regard to mainly the scribes and Pharisees. These allegations imply that practices of piety in public can too easily be motivated by a desire for recognition and admiration. Indeed, chapter 6 of Matthew extends the need for secrecy from almsgiving to the worship practices of prayer and fasting:

> Matthew 6:2 So whenever you give alms, do not sound a trumpet before you, as the hypocrites do in the synagogues and in the streets, so that they may be praised by others. Truly, I tell you they have received

their reward. But when you give alms, do not let your left hand know what your right hand is doing, so that your alms may be done in secret; and your Father who sees in secret will reward you.

Matthew 6:3 And whenever you pray, do not be like the hypocrites; for they love to stand and pray in the synagogues and at the street corners, so that they may be seen by others. Truly, I tell you they have received their reward. But whenever you pray, go into your room and shut the door and pray to your Father who is in secret; and your Father who sees in secret will reward you.

Matthew 6:16 . . . But when you fast, put oil on your head and wash your face, so that your fasting may be seen not by others but by your Father who is in secret, and your Father who sees in secret will reward you.

It is interesting that variations on some of these verses from the New Testament filter into the early hadith (that is, sayings) associated with the figure of Jesus in the Islamic tradition. For example: "Jesus said: If it is a day of fasting for one of you, let him anoint his head and beard and wipe his lips so that people will not know that he is fasting. If he gives with the right hand, let him hide this from his left hand. If he prays, let him pull down the door curtain, for God apportions praise as He apportions livelihood."[40] According to certain prophetic hadith (hadith of Muhammad), the doing of good deeds in general ought to be carried out with privacy, discretion, and humility: "The Prophet said, 'He who lets the people hear of his good deeds intentionally, to win their praise, Allah will let the people know his real intention (on the Day of Resurrection), and he who does good things in public to show off and win the praise of the people, Allah will disclose his real intention.' "[41] Qur'anic verses establish a distinction between the secret and the public dimensions of spending one's wealth for charitable purposes. Some verses merely take note of the distinction between secret and open types of spending and laud both; no mention is made of one being better than the other. What is emphasized is that spending out of what God has provided is a good deed that is ranked very high, and as verse 35:29 below indicates, it is classed with the loftiness of "rehears[ing] the book of God and observ[ing] prayer":

2:274 Those who spend their wealth by night and day, secretly and openly have their reward with the Lord; on them [shall come] no fear, nor shall they grieve.[42]

16:75 God sets forth the parable of a slave who is owned, having no power over anything, and [the other] one whom we have bestowed well from ourselves, hence he spends thereof secretly and openly/publicly. Are the two equal? Praise be to God. But most of them know not.

> 35:29 Surely those who recite/rehearse the book of God and observe
> prayer and spend out of what we have provided for them, secretly and
> openly hope for a commerce that will never fail. . . .

In these verses two adverbials employed for the opposite of "secretly" (*sirran*)
are "openly, publicly" (*'alāniyatan*) and "publicly, loudly" (*jahran*). According to al-Isfahani's Qur'anic lexicon, the word *'alāniyatan* functions as an
antonym of *sirran*. Verbs pertaining to these two words are also found in the
Qur'anic refrain discussed in chapter 1 (for example, *'alana*, "to publish,
announce, make manifest, speak publicly," and *jahara*, "to proclaim, publish, be loud"), and both concern revelations of a verbal, public, open
nature.[43] Derivations of the word *jahara* are found in some Qur'anic verses
that discuss the importance of engaging in prayers and meditations using a
low, subdued voice, or in other words, not aloud or in a loud voice (*al-jahr
min al-qawl*). Verse 2:274 suggests that one of the meanings of the word
sirran in the context of charitable giving has the connotations of "invisibility
or not being seen [as in during the night]," for mention is made of those
who "spend their wealth by night and day, secretly and openly." Several
other verses corroborate this:

> 4:38 Nor those who spend their wealth to be seen by people, but
> have no faith in God and the last day. . . .
> 107:5–7 Who are neglectful of their prayers, those who [desire]
> to be seen, but refuse [to supply] assistance or neighborly needs.

Again the sacred text implies that those who desire to be seen doing good
deeds, especially the deed of spending in the way of charity, are governed by
motives that are impious. Th. Emil Homerin has pointed out how the role
of intention and motive in acts of almsgiving and other religious acts is
central.[44] Homerin, in a contribution on altruism in Islam, discusses how
practicing discretion and secrecy during charitable giving was seen as insur-
ing that one's motives were not tainted by pride, ostentatious display, and /
or hypocrisy: "to avoid ostentation and hypocrisy, donors should give alms
in secret to the extent, if possible, that they do not know who receives them,
while the recipient does not know who gave them."[45] Returning to verse
4:38, it suggests that people who desire to be seen lack faith in God and "the
last day," and in chapter 107 (Sūrat al-Mā'ūn) they are accused of being
"neglectful of their prayers and refus[ing] assistance."

Clearly then, God deems it more beneficial if individual acts of charity
are discreetly and secretly performed. For example, the verse below implies
that there is merit and goodness (*khayr*) in doing this:

> 2:271 If you disclose [acts of] charity [*al-ṣadaqāt*], it is well, but if
> you hide them, and make them reach the poor, that is best [*khayr*] for

you. He will remit from you from among your bad deeds. And God is well-informed of what you do.

Moreover various commentators suggest that the phrase "[God] will remit from you from among your bad deeds" (also translated as ". . . will act as an atonement . . . for you from among your bad deeds") indicates that there is a compensatory element inherent in these meritorious acts that offsets the negativity of one's bad deeds.[46] Of course, the hiding referred to in this verse concerns making secret one's acts of charity, and the verse indicates that it is not easy to simultaneously conceal one's acts of charity and ensure that the charity actually reaches those in need.

Seals and Locks upon the Heart

In this final section I examine the meanings and functions of secrecy in a selection of Qur'anic pronouncements on belief and unbelief. In other words, I explore the significance of secrecy with regard to the Qur'anic faith-belief system. There is a distinct psychology of belief and unbelief, of faith and infidelity in the Qur'an, and an analysis of the topic of secrecy and interiority in the sacred text allows for this psychology to emerge.

As seen already, the Qur'an shows God frequently proclaiming that he knows what human breasts conceal and reveal. This idea that God always knows one's inner self is, I think, closely bound up with a Qur'anic psychology of belief and unbelief. That God is always aware of what is concealed in one's breast and mind means that one is always an open secret before him, and it could be said that the best of the believers, according to the Qur'an, are those who consciously recognize and practice being adept secret-sharers with God.[47] It would follow, then, that a psychology of unbelief, or *kufr,* partly would be based on hiding things, on withholding secrets from God. It would be based on not only not confiding in and to God but also shutting God out—in psychological terms, on not being able to *internalize* God. Indeed, the principal Arabic root associated with unbelief (*k-f-r*) in the Qur'an originally meant "to conceal or cover something," and only later did it tropically acquire the theological meaning of "to disbelieve in or disacknowledge God." Not surprisingly then, the Qur'an identifies the covering and/or blockage of bodily organs, for example, "the sealing of heart," as a major trait of one who is a disbeliever.[48] Herein secrecy or hiding in the Qur'an acquires a negative cast when it is linked with deception or other impious motives. There is a whole series of Qur'anic verses that speak of the covering/sealing of the heart, ears, and eyes. To quote a selection of these verses:

> 2:6 As for those who have disbelieved, alike it is to them whether you have warned them or have not warned them, they do not believe.

2:7 God has set a seal on their hearts and on their hearing,
and over their sight/eyes is a covering, and there awaits them a mighty
chastisement.

6:25 And some there are of them that give ear to you, that listen
to you, and we put veils upon their hearts lest they understand it, and
in their ears a heaviness; and if they see any sign whatever, they do not
believe in it. . . .

17:45 And when you recite the Qur'an, we put between you and
those who believe not in the hereafter an invisible veil.

17:46 And we put coverings over their hearts lest they should
understand it and in their ears heaviness, and when you make mention
in the Qur'an of your Lord alone, they turn on their backs fleeing.

40:35 Those who dispute regarding the signs of God without any
authority coming to them, very hateful is that in the sight and in the
sight of those who believe; hence, does God set a seal upon the heart
of every proud and arrogant person.

47:24 Will they not then ponder the Qur'an? Or is it that there are
locks upon their hearts?

There are two verbs that are used for the expression "sealing of hearts" in
these verses: _khatama_ and _ṭaba'a_. The relevant meanings of these two verbs
can be distilled into two categories:[49] 1) Both verbs are concerned with
impressing a thing with the engraving of a signet and stamp; both are concerned with the production of an impression or effect on a thing from
another thing. 2) The primary signification of _khatama_ is the act of covering
over [a thing], but it can also tropically mean "securing oneself from a thing
and protecting oneself from it." The word used for "heart" is _qalb_, which, as
the lexica attest, also means "soul, mind, and intellect."[50] Izutsu too has
pointed out that _qalb_, as used in the sacred text, should be understood as a
psychological and mental capacity. The word _qalb_ is synonymous with the
Arabic word _ḍamīr_, which has the meanings "the heart; the recesses of the
mind or secret thoughts." Apposite here is the mention that the word _ḍamīr_,
or "conscience," is, in turn, a synonym for the Arabic word for "secret" (_sirr_).

The canonical tenth-century commentary of al-Tabari offers an exegetical
perspective on 2:7, specifically on the phrase "God has sealed their hearts,"
or _khatama allahu 'alā qulūbihim._[51] Al-Tabari presents the following two
significations for this phrase in 2:7: the first, based on a prophetic hadith, is
"that when sins pile up on the heart they lock it, and that when they have
locked it a seal from God is set on it, and an impress. The seal mentioned
by God . . . is like the imprint and seal on containers which are visible to
the eyes, the contents of which cannot be reached unless their [seal] is bro-
ken, and they are opened. In the same way, belief cannot reach the hearts of

those on whose hearts has set a seal, unless He breaks His seal and opens the band He [has tied around them]."[52] The second meaning of "God has sealed their hearts," or *khatama allahu 'alā qulūbihim,* is that "it is a message from God about their arrogance, and their aversion to listening to the truth they were summoned to, as when one says that a person is deaf to what someone says when he refuses to listen to it and arrogantly makes up his mind not to understand it."[53]

Both these significations draw upon the two categories of meanings spoken of earlier—the meanings associated with "sealing" (*khatama* and *taba'a*): 1) "to make an impress, to engrave"; and 2) "to cover over; to block or secure oneself from something." Behind the idea of "sins piling up and locking the heart," as set forth in the first signification, is a psychological concept concerned with the mental impress of repetitive or habitual behavior. Fazlur Rahman succinctly describes this concept thus: "if a person once does a good or an evil deed, his chances of repeating that kind of action increase and of doing its opposite proportionately decrease."[54] Some of the commentary reports consider this locking of the heart as the most serious condition—more serious than the sealing or staining of the unbeliever's heart.[55] Al-Tabari, in his exegesis of 2:7, relates a report ranking these various conditions of the heart (for example, seals, locks, and stains) in order of gravity: "The 'stain' is less serious than the 'seal' [*tab'*], the 'seal' less serious than the 'locks' . . . the 'locks' are more severe than all of these."[56]

The second signification that al-Tabari relates is that of "arrogance," which seals the heart. This is a form of narcissism and ingratitude. According to this signification, the various faculties of the self (feeling, perceiving, hearing) are covered over, blocked, and cordoned off from any sense of relationship with God. The narcissism referred to in this second meaning is conveyed in 40:35, which reads: "Those who dispute regarding the signs of God without any authority come to them, very hateful is that in the sight of God and in the sight of those who believe; hence, does God set a seal upon the heart of every proud and arrogant (*mutakabbir jabbār*) [one]." From a psychological perspective, this omnipotence of the self arises fundamentally from an inability of the heart/mind (*qalb*) of the narcissistic subject or unbeliever to relate to God, to allow for a sense of relationship with God. Implicit in this second exegetical signification of the phrase "God has sealed their hearts" is the use of the word *qalb* as primarily meaning the locus of human "affects" and "emotiveness." It follows, therefore, that since it is through hearing and seeing that human affects are mobilized, they too are blocked or sealed off. In addition to the idea of the sealing or blocking of the heart, we find in verses 2:7, 6:25, and 17:46 the mention of "on their hearing, and over their sight/eyes is a covering" or "in their ears a heaviness."

Clearly, both these significations of the phrase "God has sealed their hearts" (*khatama allahu 'ala qulūbihim*) as related by al-Tabari suggest connections between the metaphoric idea of the covering and veiling of the heart, on the one hand, and its blockage or sealing, on the other hand. According to another medieval Qur'anic commentator, al-Zamakhshari, "the word *khatama* or 'to set a seal' and *katama* 'to keep a secret' are cognate words or expressions since, in his words, 'when a man reassures himself of something by putting a seal on it, then he keeps it secret and conceals it so that no-one else can obtain entrance to it or learn anything about it.' "[57] We notice how in this exegetical comment on the word *khatama,* the preeminent meaning is "blockage so as to bar entry." Hence, in 47:24, which reads, "will they not then ponder the Qur'an or is it that there are locks on their hearts?," the symbolism of the heart as a door, a locked and sealed door, is powerfully evocative of barred entry, of avoidance, or to paraphrase Elaine Scarry, of disallowing God to enter within. Scarry, in *The Body in Pain,* has pointed out that in the biblical scriptures as well, "disobedience or unbelief or doubt . . . is habitually described as a withholding of the body, which in its resistance to an external referent is perceived as covered, or hard, or stiff."[58] Scarry observes that in certain passages of the Hebrew Bible, "the withholding of the body—the stiffening of the neck, the turning of the shoulder, the closing of the ears, the hardening of the heart, the making of the face like stone—necessitates God's forceful shattering of the reluctant human surface and repossession of the interior."[59] She asserts that in the Bible, "the failure of belief could be considered to be a failure to remake one's own interior in the image of God, to allow God to enter and to alter one's self."[60]

Scarry's point about the structure of unbelief being linked with "the withholding of the body" and with the barring of God from entry within is salient to the Qur'an. As is the case with the Hebraic-biblical tradition, in the Qur'an, withholding of the body represents a withholding of the *whole* self. It should be pointed out that "the Hebraic-biblical tradition . . . is [also] strongly holistic in its understanding of the human self."[61] Notions of body as understood in the Qur'an draw upon the Hebraic model—that is, the body is not separate from or exclusive of self and subjectivity; *soma* is not separate from psyche.[62]

Conclusion

The secrecy of the self acquires a highly positive value when it is linked with a human interiority that profoundly shapes conceptions of Islamic faith and worship. I have proposed that the term *bil-ghayb* introduces a Qur'anic view of the existence of this structure of interiority and secrecy through which genuine awe and worship can be cultivated and practiced. There is no opposition between the Qur'anic phenomenology of the "self as transparent" and this invisible human structure of interiority that concerns a deeply embedded fear and reverence of God. Keeping secrets from God is impossible, but sharing secrets with God is lauded. As remarked, the best of the believers, according to the Qur'an, are those who consciously recognize and practice being adept secret-sharers with God. In this chapter, I have also analyzed the utility of the term *ghayb* to the Qur'anic strategy by which God's alterity or "Mysterious Otherness" is rendered central. In the Qur'an, the content (or what the secret consists of) *does* matter, unlike the early Arabo-Islamic non-scriptural sources we examine, wherein it matters far less though is not entirely unimportant.[63] Conceptions of divinity, faith, belief, worship, and reverence as presented in the Qur'an are powerfully influenced by the idea of the secret.

Charitable giving is another way in which human secrecy in the Qur'an has positive valuation. The Qur'an recognizes that certain good deeds and worship practices should be done in secrecy and discretion. It implies that those who desire to be seen doing good deeds, especially the deed of spending in the way of charity, are governed by motives that are impious. In addition, among the three broad purposes for which human secrecy and privacy are allowable, charitable giving is the first mentioned.

Above all, the Qur'an privileges a transparency of self or porous self that allows for a relatedness with God. It privileges a consciousness that is self-aware. The opposite of such a consciousness is one that is blocked, sealed, and cordoned off and so does not allow for a relatedness with and belief in God. In the Qur'an, *kufr,* or unbelief, necessarily is linked with a set of meanings that have to do with a psychosomatics of hiding and suppression; that is, a psychology of hiding things, or withholding secrets from God. Unbelief, according to the Qur'an, is based on not confiding in God and shutting God out; in psychological terms, it is based on not being able to *internalize* God.

3.

Self as Cipher in Kitab Kitman al-Sirr (Book of Concealing the Secret)

Secrecy guards, therefore, not merely isolated secrets about the self but access to the *underlying experience of* secrecy.

Sissela Bok, *Secrets*

If, according to the Qur'an, it is God who is the supreme eavesdropper and watch guard (*al-raqīb*), our medieval Baghdadi Mu'tazilī theologian and ethicist al-Jahiz holds that what matters as much is the "watch guard within." His ninth-century work *Kitab Kitman al-Sirr wa-Hifz al-Lisan,* or *Book of Concealing the Secret and Holding the Tongue* (henceforth, *Kitman*), is the locus classicus on human secrets and secrecy in early Arabic writing and serves as the perfect transition that bridges the religious and literary conceptions of secrecy and selfhood. In *Kitman,* al-Jahiz, the Mu'tazili theologian and early 'Abbasid belletristic writer (*adīb*), who resided in Baghdad for much of his life, remarks: "How worthy is one whose words are countable and from whom no statement escapes unaccompanied by a ready guard [*raqīb*]."[1] Al-Jahiz's notion of "concealing the secret" (*kitmān al-sirr*) in *Kitman* ultimately embraces a discriminating, ethical self that constantly sifts through its own thoughts and potential utterances, its own intentions and actions.[2] This "watch guard within" has many resonances with the Qur'anic "transparency of self"; secrecy and revelation constitute a marker of both these conceptions of the self, and in both, the emphasis is on self-censorship and moral vigilance in thought, speech, and expression.[3] Another commonality between this watch guard within and the Qur'anic transparency of self is the idea that the body is implicated in the secret's disclosure. Hence, al-Jahiz's *Kitman* also sustains the embodied quality of the self—an embodied self that functions as cipher as outer signifiers attest to inner truths.

However, *Kitman* also signals departures from the Qur'an. The shift to *Kitman* from the Qur'an implies a change in focus from the God-human relation to primarily the interpersonal human relation. If not explicitly, at least implicitly Arabo-Islamic ethical and belletristic writings such as *Kitman* recognize that while it is impossible to keep secrets from God, *it is possible*— though very difficult—to keep secrets from *another human being*. Moreover, whereas God is not a revealer of one's secrets until the Judgment Day, a human being to whom one's secret is told can reveal the secret at any time. Hence *Kitman* shows a heightened anxiety over the revelation of the secret— *whether* it should be revealed to another and, if so, to *whom* it should be revealed. A by-product of this anxiety is the recognition of a distinction between one's own secrets and other people's secrets.

Audience and Context of *Kitman*

Al-Jahiz was an independent thinker, theologian, ethicist, and scholar whose treatment of subjects and written output were characterized by much range and versatility. According to the French scholar Charles Pellat, over two hundred authentic works are attributed to him, but only two dozen have survived intact.[4] Some of al-Jahiz's writings are devoted to analyses of human traits and emotions (for example, on arrogance, enmity, anger), examinations of conduct (for example, on keeping promises), and portrayals of character-types (for example, misers). His treatise *Kitman* squarely falls in this strain of *adab* trajectory—a trajectory that joins a larger one within classical Arabic belles lettres as a whole.[5]

Al-Jahiz was squarely a product of the ninth-century Baghdadi milieu. Before delving into *Kitman,* it is vital to address several elements in this Baghdadi context, including the Shu'biyya controversy and 'Abbasid court culture, which profoundly influenced his views on language and expression. These views, in turn, had an impact on his ideas regarding secrecy and revelation in *Kitman.*[6]

Al-Jahiz's views of language, more precisely the Arabic language, were powerfully shaped by the Shu'biyya debate that pitted Arabs against those with non-Arab (mainly Persian) backgrounds in the jockeying for power and privilege in the early 'Abbasid Empire. As Wen-Chin Ouyang points out, the complex processes of assimilation and acculturation were relevant to these power struggles: "Having lived in Baghdad for the latter half of his life, [al-Jahiz] was in touch with the thorny issues generated by the assimilation processes of Arab and non-Arab elements into Arabic-Islamic society, and the negotiations in the emerging Arabic-Islamic culture involving whether to assimilate or reject Greek, Persian, pre-Islamic Arabic and other influences."[7] Al-Jahiz chose to defend the Arab position and fashioned his religious beliefs regarding the relation of the Arabic language to the Qur'an in the context of this Shu'ubi controversy. Indeed, two of his major works—namely *Kitab al-Hayawan,* or *Book of Animals,* and *Kitab al-Bayan wa 'l-Tabyin,* or *Book of Eloquence and Exposition*[8]—"were in part written in response to the Shu'ubi attack on the literary and cultural heritage of the Arabs."[9] According to al-Jahiz, the Arabic language was unequaled in its linguistic richness and wealth, and its potential for rhetorical eloquence was unmatched by any other language:[10] "Because of the eloquence of Arabic and the beauty of its expression, God sent His best prophet amongst the Arabs, made his language Arabic and even revealed an Arabic Qur'an."[11]

No doubt this emphasis on eloquent Arabic speech as the divine revelation par excellence had an impact on early Arabo-Islamic ideas regarding the spoken Arabic word. It should also be mentioned that beginning with pre-Islamic poetry onward to Arabic poetry of the early Islamic period, the poetic genres of lampoon, satire, love poem, and panegyric were popular. The spoken word in general, especially recited poetry, was a powerful means of making or breaking names and reputations. Within this climate of the power of the spoken word, one would imagine that ideas concerning indiscretion and secrecy (as they related to an individual self) were being constantly negotiated, tested, and contested. Given such a climate, al-Jahiz's views of the Arabic language and expression arising from the Shu'ubi controversy served only to enhance his belief in the power of the spoken Arabic word. As Ouyang observes regarding al-Jahiz's position, "Defending Arabs and their language by ascribing *bayān* [eloquence] to them involves far-reaching consequences, for *bayān* is the literary quality attributed to the Qur'an, denoting its inimitability."[12] For al-Jahiz, among these consequences was the development of a distinctly theological cast to his theories and conceptions of speech, expression, rhetoric, and signification. As spelled out by James Montgomery: "A central feature of the *bayān* is the reciprocity of its function: communication is given by God to man in the form of the Arabic Qur'an (indeed God refers to the Qur'an as the *Bayān* on three occasions), and man must show appropriate gratitude to God by proper use of this gift."[13]

Occasionally al-Jahiz is rather ambivalent about the value and importance of human speech, and he proclaims at one point that "all evils of the world began with a word [*kalima*] which slipped out and brought protracted war."[14] Yet he deems speech to be "one of God's great gifts and substantial blessings" but a gift that has been misused by human beings.[15] A godly way to use speech would be "to use it in his remembrance and service,"[16] and in another work entitled *Tafdil al-Nutq* (*Virtues of Speech over Silence*), he declares, "you cannot convey gratitude to God, you cannot show it except through speech."[17] Divine speech also summons human beings to use their speech in this manner; for instance, the Qur'anic verse 93:11 proclaims: "And [of] the bounty of thy Lord, speak."[18]

Embedded in al-Jahiz's views is the recognition that while human Arabic speech can never mimic God's Arabic speech (which is uniquely perfect and inimitable), it can and must "be imbued with a religiously sanctified aura"[19] that demands its users approximate the superiority in eloquence and communication found in the Qur'an. As Montgomery observes: "The point of departure for the *Kitab al-Bayan wal-tabyin* was the growing realization in 'Abbasid intellectual and spiritual life of the ninth century that the *'Arabiyyah* of the Qur'an was itself holy and sacred and that, consequently, to compose in this language was to celebrate the Revelation."[20]

All these elements shaped al-Jahiz's analysis of secrecy in *Kitman*. It is likely that part of the audience intended for the treatise were those scholars interested in and contributing to discussions of the superiority of the Arabic language (that is, its theories of signification, rhetoric, poetics), including those following the Shu'ubiyya controversy and debate.

Al-Jahiz's views of speech and expression were also shaped by the milieu of ninth-century 'Abbasid court culture. Discretion, as understood within 'Abbasid courtly culture, undoubtedly colors his discussion of secrets and secrecy in *Kitman*. This is not surprising, given that, as Pellat has pointed out, he "acted as an advisor and apologist for the ['Abbasid] government."[21] Certainly, another part of his intended audience was probably 'Abbasid court functionaries, such as secretaries, scribes, chamberlains, and viziers.[22] Issues of discretion, tact, and diplomacy loomed large in the daily tasks and dealings of royal court officials such as the viziers, as they did for the court secretaries, or *kuttab,* who composed and wrote the court correspondence. Not surprisingly, another discourse in which the topic of secrecy is prominent includes the classical Arabo-Islamic encyclopedic works, or *paedia,* which were also composed and compiled for primarily the *kuttab,* that is, the court secretaries or "higher civil servants."[23] Consequently, this chapter also examines textual excerpts from these encyclopedic works:[24] Ibn Qutayba's ninth-century *'Uyun al-Akhbar* (henceforth *'Uyun*), al-Bayhaqi's tenth-century *al-Mahasin wal-Masawi* (*al-Mahasin*), the Andalusian Ibn 'Abd Rabbihi's tenth-century *Al-'Iqd al-Farid* (*'Iqd*), and al-Nuwayri's fourteenth-century *Nihayat al-Arab fi Funun al-Adab* (*Nihayat*). Nearly all of the central ideas and elements present in *Kitman* are found in these secrecy chapters (including the one by Ibn Qutayba, a contemporary of al-Jahiz).[25]

In *Kitman* the Arabic word *sirr* (secret) is defined in terms of both psychology and religion. Given this paradox of the Arabic word *sirr* having both intrapsychic and religio-ethical referents in this work, in this chapter I simply accept this paradox and "regard the dialectical tension between two perspectives as being inherent to the phenomenon involved."[26] The intrapsychic definition embraces the secret, or *sirr,* as an internal, valued possession of the self. As for the religious meaning, it defines "concealing the secret" (*Kitman al-sirr*) as the cultivation of the "watch guard within"— of which one key element is the use of morally and ethically disciplined, right speech. In *Kitman* and in his well-known work *Kitab al-Bayan* (*Book of Eloquence*), al-Jahiz views the clarity of individual eloquence and expression as ultimately a function of character and moral self-worth. This emphasis was, to some extent, shaped by al-Jahiz's deep interest in and examinations of theories of signification, rhetoric, and poetics in his writings such as *Kitab al-Bayan.*

Identity as Self-Censorship: Right Speech, Right Character

Throughout his treatise al-Jahiz emphasizes the moral and ethical interpersonal aspects of the process or activity of "concealing the secret," or *kitmān al-sirr.* The Arabic word *kitmān,* in this phrase, is derived from the root *k-t-m,* which includes among its meanings "to conceal [a secret], restrain; to hold [as a skin holding water]."[27] Importantly, a verb derived from this root is often used by the Qur'an in contexts in which an act of deception takes place and/or the content of the secret is morally or ethically negative.[28] It is striking, then, that in *Kitman* (as well as early Arabo-Islamic didactic and literary discourses in general), the oft-used phrase *kitmān al-sirr* (concealment of the secret) comes to acquire a positive meaning involving interpersonal, ethical comportment regarding secrecy and discretion.

According to al-Jahiz, a moral and ethical self that exercises discrimination and reserve with regard to the entirety of the speaking experience is practicing concealment of the secret. In the second half of *Kitman,* al-Jahiz ushers the reader into this conception of *kitmān al-sirr* by conveying a definition of *sirr* (the secret) that privileges concerns with morality (*ikhlāq*) as well as with ethics and virtues (*fudūl*): "All talk (*ḥadīth*), except what is pointless, is talk about people, (*dhikr al-nās*),[29] idle gossip, coarse and unseemly talk, delirium and raving, backbiting, slander and reproach. One of the sages said to his son, 'My son, man is nothing but talk, so if you can, be good talk.' Every secret on earth is nothing but a report (*khabar*) about a person or something concealed from a person."[30] Secrets are linked with interpersonal modes of communication (primarily speech related). In this definition, secrecy has connections with gossip, slander, and defamation of character.

Of significance is al-Jahiz's use of the Arabic term *khabar* (report) to define a secret. This oft-discussed term is especially important in Arabic-Islamic literary and historical discourses. It has a range of meanings, including "something disclosed and rendered public as well as something reported (that is, it is a form of hearsay)," and its mode of transmission may be oral and/or written. A *khabar* may consist of a news item, historical information, or an anecdotal tidbit. Al-Jahiz's use of this Arabic term to define a secret sheds light on how the idea of secrecy has links with the genre of Arabic biography (a genre for which the term *khabar* is crucial). Michael Cooperson, in his study *Classical Arabic Biography,* notes that when "secrets are reported" (that is, scandals) in a biographical account, an air of accuracy accrues to the account.[31]

That a secret is defined as a "report (*khabar*) about a person" assumes that it already has been told and publicized to one or more and presumably concealed from at least the person concerning whom it purports to "report." In other words, at its most basic, a secret is gossip, slander, or chitchat about others communicated between two persons and concealed from a third. Present in two Arabo-Islamic encyclopedias, namely the tenth-century *'Iqd* and the fourteenth-century *Nihayat,* is a variation of the two-liner pithy saying in which the one on the "receiving end of someone else's secret showcases his excellent ability to keep that secret." It foregrounds this definition in which the secret is conceived of as a news item or report (*khabar* or something close to gossip and slander, for instance): "It was said to another: 'How [good] are you at keeping a secret?' He replied: 'I turn away from or shun the news-bringer and I take an oath before the news-seeker.' "[32] This formula implies a reserve regarding what is spoken and what is sought in speech. It consists of the pithy, succinct interrogative for sizing up another person about that person's ability to conceal or keep a secret, but the equally pithy reply is something along the lines of "I don't accept news or secrets from others and I take a vow of silence before one wanting secrets from me." Through the reply, the respondent indicates that he removes himself from the circulation of this kind of news (neither giving nor taking it).

In *Kitman* al-Jahiz maintains that people love to talk about and publicize things; fondness for the giving and seeking of information is an aspect of human nature (*mahabbat al-ikhbar wal-istikhbar*).[33] According to him, this frequent give-and-take between people degenerates into negative kinds of talk: gossip, chitchat, slander, hearsay, faultfinding, backbiting, for example. What is crucial is that al-Jahiz implies that self, character, and speech are intimately related to each other. What one utters and the manner of how one speaks should be discriminating and dignified. As al-Jahiz would have it, ethical Islam is based as much on orthodicta (right speech) as it is on right practice (orthopraxy) or right belief (orthodoxy). The very title of *Kitman* links secrecy with the spoken word, and he begins and ends his work with this link. His opening foray into the subject is: "The two matters for which we chide you are: speaking at the wrong occasion [*wada' al-qawl fi ghayr maudi'*] and forfeiting a secret by broadcasting it."[34] The expression *wada' al-qawl fi ghayr maudi'* found in this statement can be translated literally as "placing speech in the inappropriate place." Improper and inappropriate "placing" of speech, that is, speaking the wrong words on a given occasion or in a given context, is equivalent to forfeiting or revealing the secret. Hence concealing the secret is a form of discretion that involves speaking only at the right occasion or context. This seemingly simple observation is critical. At the very least, it means that one must always pick one's words carefully and that one's words ought to be appropriate to the context or situation at hand. More injurious than the impact of inappropriate or wrongful speech on others is its impact on the self. Speech cumulatively molds and shapes character.

Behind this equivalence is a conception of the ethical and moral self as being constituted through modes of primarily verbal self-containment and discipline—modes that entail processes central to maintaining secrecy, that is, the processes of sifting and discrimination. According to *Kitman,* keeping the secret is a function of a continuous process of mental sifting and discrimination, and this process yields selective speech—selective in all manifold ways: in what is said, how it is said, how much is said, to whom it is said, when it is said, and why it is said. These processes of sifting, self-censorship, and discrimination are essential to how *Kitman* envisions the constitution of a moral and ethical disciplined selfhood. Al-Jahiz concludes *Kitman* by declaring, "From this and the similar things we have previously mentioned in this book we need only remember to preserve the secret and weigh the utterance."[35] *Kitman al-sirr,* therefore, consists of speaking purposefully and with discrimination. Some expressions that al-Jahiz employs are suggestive of a valuation of Arabic speech (perhaps reflecting his views arising from the Shu'ubi controversy). Speech is a precious property of the self. Speaking is a form of "expending" the self. There is speech that is well spent, and there is speech that is misspent; if the latter, one may be a spendthrift or a miser in one's misuse of speech. Speech that is to the point is speech that is well conserved and well guarded, and so secrets are kept. Conversely speech uttered without prior reflection and discrimination is speech misused and wasted, with secrets revealed. Al-Jahiz compares what he deems the nonbeneficial use of speech with "the two sins of the owner of a treasure." In the case of the first sin, the owner "was . . . necessarily guilty of withholding it even if he did not expend it sinfully."[36] In the case of the second sin, the owner was guilty of "spending [the wealth] in vain and depraved ways which would . . . make him guilty of dissipation."[37] The link between spending wealth and expending words again surfaces in a prophetic utterance, or hadith, quoted by al-Jahiz: *rahima allah 'abd anfaqa al-fadl min mālihi wa-amsaka al- fadl min qawlihi,* translated as "God is compassionate to a person who expends the excess of his wealth and withholds the excess of his talk."[38]

Yet another dimension of keeping the secret that al-Jahiz identifies is speech that aims at being proper and correct in content. The Arabic term *al-ṣawāb* is central to this dimension of the secret. The word means "a thing that is right, of what is said and of what is done" (it is an antonym of the Arabic word for "mistake," or *khaṭa'*, and a criterion in al-Jahiz's conception of eloquence, or *bayān* and *balāgha*).³⁹ Indeed, the primacy of disciplined, right, or proper speech in his ideas regarding *kitmān al-sirr* appears related to his preoccupation with the theory of "expression and eloquence" (*al-bayān*) as articulated in *Kitab al-Bayan* (*The Book of Eloquence*).⁴⁰ In *Kitab al-Bayan*, al-Jahiz expounds on the quality of moral refinement that must characterize the content of right speech. One detects here the influence of his religious beliefs regarding the *bayān* of the divine speech of the Arabic Qur'an. In the chapter entitled "On Eloquence" ("Bab al-Bayan"), al-Jahiz transmits sayings he adduces to support his belief that the clarity of one's eloquence and expression (*al-bayān*) is ultimately connected with self and character—a connection readily discernible in the ethical conception of *kitmān al-sirr*.⁴¹

Disciplining the Embodied Self

According to al-Jahiz, both verbal and bodily forms of reserve are linked with the practice of concealing the secret, or *kitmān al-sirr*. What al-Jahiz argues in *Kitman* (and what is generally emphasized in Arabic love literature) is the manifold ways in which the outer surface of the human body unintentionally betrays what the holder or owner of the secret desires to conceal. This has deep resonances with Qur'anic ideas regarding the body being implicated in the secret's disclosure—that is, the outer body reveals the secret in spite of the self's (deceptive) intentions to conceal. Al-Jahiz maintains that body language such as physical gestures, signs, movements, and symptoms will give one's secret away. The release of the secret may be triggered by several things, but the essential point is that this release often manifests itself through the signs of the human body's surface and body movements. In other words, the embodied self is implicated in the secret's disclosure.

Revelation inevitably occurs; it is the management of this revelation that constitutes "concealment of the secret," or *kitmān al-sirr*. According to al-Jahiz, this aims toward being a complete self/tongue/body form of discretion and reserve. He employs a brief elaboration of the Arabic word *ḥilm* (self-control) as a springboard to enumerate these diverse forms of reserve. To practice concealment of the secret and self-control (*ḥilm*), the following are some aspects of the self (*nafs*) that, according to al-Jahiz, must be managed correctly: "excessive desire for something sought, the intensity of longing and delicacy, multiplicity of complaints and regrets, quick shifts from pleasure to exasperation and exasperation to pleasure, and useless or pointless movements of the tongue and body."[42]

Indeed, references to the body and bodily organs are prominent in early Arabic accounts regarding secrets and secrecy. Al-Jahiz waxes eloquent in *Kitman* about the roles of the heart, breast, tongue, and skin in keeping and disclosing secrets.[43] An initial comment by him regarding where secrets may be found sheds light on the role of the heart: "The heart is a treasury [which guards] thoughts and secrets. It gathers [its contents] from the good and bad of the senses and from what cravings and desires generate as well as what wisdom and knowledge produce."[44] This intrapsychic definition of "secrecy" posits secrets as a form of abstract, inner property. Herein we obtain a glimpse into how *Kitman* defines "secrets" as a form of "internal property or possession." Ownership and exclusion are central to al-Jahiz's definition of "the secret" as "internal precious property." His use of terms such as *master/ owner of the secret* (*ṣāḥib al-sirr*) or *possessor of secret* (*mālik li-sirrihi*) corroborates this idea of sole ownership of the secret.[45] It is significant that the word *khizāna,* or "treasury," is used to describe the heart: it is a treasure chest, that is, a storehouse that guards contents, and furthermore this treasury is itself guarded within the cavity of the body's breast or the rib cage. The use of this word to describe the heart has strong implications for understanding the point that it is not so much the nature of the secret's content but that it is possessed and guarded that matters. In another short passage al-Jahiz observes that the heart contains "thoughts and secrets" and then comments on what he terms the "gathering or sifting function" of the heart: secrets are culled by the heart from what it sifts through of the senses, desires, and faculties of the intellect; in other words, secrets re selectively gathered from sensations, feelings and affects, impulses, thoughts, impressions, ideas, dreams, and memories.[46] Al-Jahiz seems to imply that there may exist unconscious forms of secrets (for example, memories, repressed content, forgotten material, dreams) as well as conscious forms (for example, a secret one deliberately and intentionally keeps). As shall be seen, these unconscious kinds of secrets are closely linked with ideas about the human body and body language in *Kitman.*[47]

An intricate psycho-religious formulation informs al-Jahiz's writing on the secrets of the self. The imagery of certain bodily organs plays an important role in it. More than a thousand years later, Sigmund Freud would launch a theory of the unconscious that had some parallels with this early Arab theorist's formulations.[48] According to al-Jahiz, an intrapsychic conflict that characterizes the core self is the tension between desire, passion (*al-hawa*),[49] and the intellect or reason (*al-ʿaql*). He identifies a "dominion of desire" (*al-daula lil-hawa*) and describes it as that which functions as "the incitement for broadcasting the secret and freeing the tongue in superfluous talk."⁵⁰ Nothing is more difficult, according to al-Jahiz, than "reining in one's nature and mastering the desires or passions."⁵¹ Only reason or the intellect binds or "shackles" the principal bodily organ that desire subjugates and through which it expresses itself—the tongue. Moreover, declaring that "the intellect is called a shackle and restraint,"⁵² he cites Qur'anic verse 89:5 ("Is there in that an oath for one with restraint/reason [*ḥijr*]?")⁵³ to support his assertion. The Arabic word *ḥijr* in this verse is derived from a root with the meanings "to hinder, deny access, prohibit, stop," and the word functions as a synonym for *'aql*.⁵⁴ Al-Jahiz implies that when desire or passion rules the tongue, there are "excesses in regard or attention [*fuḍūl al-naẓr*] which lead to excesses in speech [*fuḍūl al-qawl*]."⁵⁵

The imagery of the tongue crops up in the following kind of corporeal symbolism on which al-Jahiz often relies: two bodily organs set up in juxtaposition. One such juxtaposition is that of the breast (*ṣadr*) versus the tongue (*lisān*). Al-Jahiz maintains that the breast of a human being has a difficult time retaining and keeping all that it contains. In a passage that lays out a kind of mechanics of secrecy's contents, he observes: "It is part of the breast's nature (considered not as a bodily vessel but as a gathering agent) through a power of God which human beings do not understand that it becomes constricted around what it contains and finds what it bears heavy. [Hence] it feels relaxation in flinging out [its] . . . contents and [experiences] pleasure in moving them onto the tongue."⁵⁶ Using imagery that evokes the breast as not just a bodily cavity but a cavity that—through a divine power—stores and sifts its contents, al-Jahiz maintains that lightening the burden of the breast entails releasing or "flinging out [its] . . . contents" onto another organ, the tongue. There are distinct resonances, as we have seen, between this image of the breast as a holder and releaser of secrets and the Qur'anic image of the breast.

Al-Jahiz employs other juxtapositions of body imagery, in addition to that of the breast versus the tongue, to illustrate the theme of how difficult it is for the owner of a secret to keep it. In the following quotation, though there is no mention of the organ of the skin, it is significant that the phrase "he feels them in the core of his heart" is followed by a host of tactile sensations (creeping, itching, stinging, pricking): "Thus, anxiety overcomes him when he conceals a secret [*li-kitmān al-sirr*]. Disease and sorrow strike him. He feels them in the core of his heart like the creeping of ants, itching of a scab, stinging of bees, and pricking of needles, in proportion to the differing dimensions of self-control, composure and flightness. If he reveals his secret, it is as though he were released from shackles."⁵⁷ What seems to be conveyed is that the owner of the secret outwardly experiences the effects of concealment, that is, feels discomfort and dismay at skin level, and this outward discomfort (which may appear in the form of a rash or a scab, for instance) unconsciously reveals the distress of the "inner heart," which is what reveals the secret (a phrase in English—"the pricks of conscience"—conveys the same idea).

The theme of the secret's revelation draws on a whole array of body images to underscore the tension between retention and release of a secret. Indeed, it draws on the imagery of the body in its entirety, not just single organs such as skin or eyes. Emphasized again and again are the manifold ways in which the outer body unconsciously betrays what the owner of the secret desires to conceal.

Secrecy and the Vessel Function of the Breast

Al-Jahiz, in juxtaposing the "gathering" function of the breast with its tendency to become constricted, points to a conflict between the retention and the release that it experiences.[58] In the Qur'an and early Arabic love literature too, this imagery is characterized by a conflict between the retention and the expulsion of the secret. Al-Jahiz suggests that the breast functions as a kind of container or vessel of latent content. Apposite here is the mention that the Arabic word for "vessel" (*wi'ā'*) is derived from the verb *wa'ā,* meaning "to hold, to contain, to retain in one's memory, to know by heart."[59] If, as al-Jahiz suggests, the breast functions as a kind of vessel containing inner contents, then new content would always replace old content. In other words, the vessel form that originally contained the secret content would persist; only its contents would be released and replaced. This is a crucial point. The function of the breast as conserver of secrets would continue even after, as al-Jahiz notes, the breast released and transferred an existing secret onto the tongue.

Among the principal modern theorists who, like al-Jahiz, employ the image of the vessel in explicating the meanings and functions of the secret is Alfred Gross: "the secret, once surrendered, is lost only insofar as its *content* is concerned. The *vessel* which contained it endures, ready to be filled with new content. We see then, that in the study of the concept of the secret, one must differentiate between content and function; the hidden *content* of a secret is something different from the psychological state of *possessing* a secret."[60] Not surprisingly, there is a good deal of container imagery regarding the secret in *Kitman*. Al-Jahiz uses the Arabic word *wi'ā'* (vessel) when he comments on the breast's inclination toward constriction, and he again employs this same Arabic word in the following, rather humorous anecdote in *Kitman*: "[A jurist] used to harbor information beyond the comprehension of the common folk. When his breast became too constricted for it, he went into the desert. He dug a hole there, deposited an earthen jar or vessel [*wi'ā'*] in it, and then bent over that jar and told it what he had heard. Hence, he would ease his heart and think that he had conveyed his secret from one container to another."[61] The vessel function is evident in the repeated filling and emptying of the jurist's bodily cavity, that is, his breast. Upon his breast becoming full, the jurist transfers his secrets from one container (his breast) to another (the jar). After each act of transfer, he experiences relief. The jar will never disclose his secrets. This motif of depositing one's secret with things inanimate, mute, and hollow is also found in the ancient literatures of Greece and India.[62]

The classical Arabic encyclopedia *'Uyun* mentions a formula that ties in well with the discussions in *Kitman* of the constricted breast as a full vessel: "One [person] said to his brother, and [the latter] had [just] talked with him about [some] news: 'Put that in a vessel [*wi'ā'*] that does not have a leak.' "[63] Here the word *vessel* acts as a metaphor for the breast, and correspondingly, the symbolism of flowing/leaking suggests a breast that is releasing its secrets. Of course, an ideal vessel for keeping secrets is one that is sealed and does not have a leak (someone who is not prone to divulging confidences). In this same encyclopedia, *'Uyun,* there is a maxim that reads "Your secret is of your blood" (*sirruka min dammika*)[64] and also underscores the meaning of the secret as precious inner content. The same saying is accompanied by a small commentary in the *'Iqd* and *Nihayat*: "They said: 'Your secret is of your blood, so pay heed to see where you pour it [out].' They mean by this that perhaps in your secret's disclosure lies the spilling of your blood."[65] The saying and its commentary establish a link between the secret as the inner content of the heart or breast and blood as the inner liquid content of the body. Early Arabic love literature, as we will see, is replete with the imagery of flowing secretions—such as tears, saliva, and semen—and the symbolism of the flowing concerns the disclosure or betrayal of secrets. Blood is rendered as precious to one's physical life as the secret is to one's core self. The idea of the integrity of the outer physical body is linked with the idea of the integrity of an inner core self; both are to be preserved, and the preservation of one has to do with the preservation of the other.[66] The equivalences of secret = blood = valued inner content are even more clearly seen in a variant of the same saying in *al-Mahasin*: "Your secret is of your blood, so be watchful of whom you make the owner of it or whom you put in possession of it."[67]

Yet another passage in which al-Jahiz employs container imagery helps us to understand correspondences he makes between vessel = breast and inner content = breast's secrets as he draws upon 2:31–33 in the Qur'an:[68]

> For it was impossible for God to have taught him [that is, Adam] a name without teaching him its meaning, or to have taught him a meaning without creating for him the thing meant by it. A name without its meaning is but air or an empty vessel. Names correspond to bodies

and meanings to souls: thus a word is a body for the meaning, and a meaning constitutes a soul for the word. Had God given Adam the names without their meanings, He would have been giving him something inert and inanimate, insensate and useless. A word is only a name if it can bear a meaning, and if meanings can exist without names there are certainly no names without meanings. The word of God: "And He taught Adam all the names" indicates that He also taught him all the meanings.[69]

Here the container imagery generates an inner/outer dichotomy in al-Jahiz's conceptions of both the spoken language and the embodied self. This mapping of "body onto language" sheds light on how, in *Kitman,* revelation of the secret (the word being spoken) is also defined through the body (the body speaks and attests to the inner self, or *nafs*). Words have meanings just as bodies have inner selves; otherwise they are empty "vessels." If the breast is a kind of "vessel" that stores and sifts through secrets, an embodied self is necessarily a "full vessel" that must release secrets through spoken words and/ or the body's outer signifiers. In other words, the embodied self functions as a cipher.

> Even if the most level-headed, forbearing person subdued his tongue, protected his secret and decreased his words, he [still] would not be able to control the glance of his eyes, the appearance of his face, change of his [complexion's] color, his smile or frown when he remembers or thinks of the secret. It appears on his face and in his expression when present in his memory or when there occurs to him something comparable or when there arrives someone who has a stake in it unless he has [achieved the capacity for] strong dissimulation and exceptional restraint.[70]

Initially in this passage al-Jahiz draws attention to one key way in which he defines concealment of the secret (that is, a discriminating and disciplined use of speech, of which paucity of words is an important element). Then he goes on to present a dimension of the secret's revelation: body language. This passage surfaces in the context of a discussion of disclosure of other people's secrets rather than one's own secrets. As we shall see, a recurrent theme found in the treatise, indeed in Arabic accounts on secrecy in general, is that other people's secrets are much more difficult to keep than one's own, and inadvertent error and weakness play a greater role in the disclosure of the former. Yet in both types of situations, whether one is concealing one's own or other people's secrets, even "the most level-headed, forbearing person" who disciplines his tongue and preserves his secret is unable to check and control unconscious body language; physical gestures, signs, movements, and symptoms will give his secret away. Indeed, as Freud states below, all secrets become available precisely through bodily symptoms: "He that has eyes to see and ears to hear can convince himself that no mortal can keep a secret. If his lips are silent, he chatters with his finger-tips; betrayal oozes out of him at every pore. And thus, the task of making conscious the most hidden recesses of the mind is one which is quite possible to accomplish."[71] Only if one has long practiced "strong dissimulation and exceptional restraint" could one hope possibly to preserve the secret,[72] and by this, al-Jahiz does not simply mean a verbal reserve but rather a complete and total self/body reserve. It follows, therefore, that *kitmān al-sirr* aims toward being a complete, all-encompassing form of discretion and reserve. Al-Jahiz advises one to rely on a mixture of vigilance and caution in one's relations with others: "Be awake to these cicumstances and use critical thinking with all of mankind. Indeed it is related on the authority of the prophet (peace and blessings of God be upon him) that he said: Prudence is suspicion."[73] This advice surfaces in the context of a discussion of slipups, dropping of inadvertent hints, and second-guessing on the part of mainly the secret holder. Al-Jahiz cautions against this kind of second-guessing and instead promotes a "hermeneutic of suspicion" (*sū' al-ẓann*), which, according to the Prophet's dictum, is what constitutes prudence.

If the breast's God-given nature is to become constricted as a consequence of its suppressed, hidden content, it appears that the God-given nature of the tongue is to service this constricted breast by expelling its contents. Early in his monograph, al-Jahiz declares that "the tongue is merely an interpreter/translator for the heart" (*tarjumān lil-qalb*), or in other words, the tongue articulates the hidden "thoughts and secrets" of the heart.[74] How exactly this function of the tongue (that of interpreting the secrets and thoughts of the heart) differs from that of expelling or "flinging out" its contents for the breast is somewhat unclear. Perhaps a distinction between conscious and unconscious forms of secrets is implied: conscious secrets are those that are articulated by the tongue to a confidant, while ones that are "flung out" by the tongue from the breast are often of an unconscious nature, and their release too is somewhat involuntary. Hence, this latter function has a negative cast. From his description of how the tongue services the constricted breast, we see that the tongue can be a bothersome, dangerous, and harmful organ— its main fault being that it criticizes, slanders, gossips, and meddles. Al-Jahiz conveys general aphorisms and a few hadith concerning this destructive potential of the tongue: "The messenger of God (may God bless him and grant him peace) said: 'The Muslim is one from whose tongue and hand Muslims are secure.'. . . They said, 'The mortal area of a man is between his jaws.' . . . It was said, 'The tongue asks the other organs every day, "How are you?" They reply, "Fine, if you would leave us alone."' "[75]

We also find the idea of the constricted breast and its need to lighten itself in many early Arabic maxims and aphorisms connected with secrecy and revelation. One that al-Jahiz relates is: "It was therefore said proverbially about this state: 'The breast when it exhales is cured.'⁷⁶ As long as desire or passion (*al-hawa*), rather than reason or the intellect [*al-'aql*], remains in control, the breast persists in recklessly flinging its contents out and onto the tongue. Quick relief and 'a cure' are sought by unburdening oneself to an indiscreet person. A speedy 'cure' is sought through communication not with a trusted confidant but rather with 'another person who will not guard nor protect it [her or his secret].'" Al-Jahiz declares that telling or confessing something to oneself in private does not succeed in lifting the repression. "It (that is, breast's repression] is hardly cured, however, when a person tells something to himself in private . . . (*yukhatiba bihi nafsahu fī khalawātihi*)."⁷⁷ In other words, practicing something akin to introspection is not enough. Al-Jahiz implies that a kind of fleeting relief or cure will be found in self-disclosure that is to someone else, even if that person is indiscreet. Again, we discern the preeminence of the spoken or uttered word (albeit in a relational context) in al-Jahiz's writing on secrecy and revelation.

Al-Jahiz's assertion that a cure for the constricted breast stems from a self-disclosure that is relational raises the interesting issue of how his views contrast with modern Western perspectives on psycho-therapy. Sissela Bok, in discussing the merits of confession (in a general sense and not specifically Catholic confession) declares: "Confession may serve as a means for transforming one's life . . . this cannot easily be achieved through introspection alone. To seek out a confessor is, then to look forward for someone who can share one's burdens, interpret one's revelations, and show the path to release. Confessing may be a call for intervention and for help in reaching through to the layers of secrecy sensed in oneself or in the authority one confronts."⁷⁸ A thousand years subsequent to al-Jahiz's time, Carl Jung, the famous student of Freud and an esteemed psychoanalyst in his own right, expressed a belief in the therapy "of the secret by the secret." Jung clearly believed that genuine therapy had to occur in self-disclosure that is relational and interpersonal, that is, confessing to someone, and furthermore, he held that this confession of a secret must be met by absolute secrecy on the part of the recipient in order for the therapy to be effective.⁷⁹ Similarly, an idea that had a deep impact on Freud's career was that of the "talking cure."⁸⁰ The idea of the "talking cure" was based on the belief that passive internal content (that is, unconscious secrets) could exercise a great deal of influence latently and unconsciously over one's mind. According to this cure, when something is uttered to someone, when it is brought into consciousness by being spoken and communicated, its power over one fades.⁸¹ By contrast, al-Jahiz holds that a secret uttered to or shared with another is necessarily a secret publicized, and that this only transpires when desire rather than reason reigns over the elf. In effect, the desire to release and lighten the constricted breast produces a cure that is short-lived at best.

The Interpersonal Self: One's Own Secrets versus Other People's Secrets

Among the central points in al-Jahiz's *Kitman* and early Arabic writings on secrecy in general is that keeping one's own secrets must be distinguished from keeping other people's secrets. The main distinction between the two is that other people's secrets are far harder to keep, as emphasized by the following:

> If the breast of a man is constricted by his own secret [*sirr nafsihi*],
> the breast of one to whom he entrusts it is even more constricted.[82]

Al-Jahiz maintains:

> When a secret has gone beyond the breast of its owner and escaped from
> his tongue to a single ear, by that time it is no longer a secret. The breast
> of the second ear's owner is narrower, he is quicker to disclose it, more
> cavalier with it and more excuseable in speaking of it; any case against
> him is invalid. This is so even if the speaker is held to an oath, committed
> to keeping the secret and is an intelligent, disciplined and sincere
> friend.[83]

What then, al-Jahiz goes on to ask, if the speaker (that is, the "second ear") is unreliable and has not been commanded to keep the secret? Also, a person to whom a secret has been disclosed may divulge it out of some error or weakness rather than out of duplicity. However, no matter how serious the consequences of this person's divulgence are (end of blessings, war and bloodshed, dishonor, for example), the original owner of the secret is more blameworthy and culpable. Indeed a central and definitive feature of *kitmān al-sirr* is that it is the attempt at retention of a secret by the original owner of the secret. Again, we obtain a glimpse into how *Kitman* defines the secret as a form of internal property or possession.

The distinction between one's own secrets and other people's secrets points to the importance of the role of discretion as understood in the 'Abbasid courtly context. Many "secrecy works" or "secrecy chapters" in early Arabic encyclopedias that contain aphorisms addressing this distinction are sandwiched between chapters and/or sections concerned with the official duties of court chamberlains. For example, the following verse is found in three secrecy chapters in the encyclopedic sources of *'Uyun*, *'Iqd*, and *Nihayat*:

Do not disclose your secret save to yourself
For every confidant has a confidant. . . . [84]

One discerns here the idea of "do not reveal your secret to anyone, not even a confidant," for every counselor and confidant to whom a secret is revealed also, in turn, always has a counselor and a confidant. A related, yet differing notion, that a secret that goes beyond *two* persons is no longer a secret, is also found in all three of the aforementioned encyclopedic sources but is expressed in different ways in each. In *'Uyun,* a line of poetry suggests:

Your secret is what you share with [one] person
And the secret of three is not concealed. [85]

In other words one can share a secret with a designated confidant, but only with that sole confidant. The possession of a secret is transformed from being something within oneself to an interpersonal phenomenon that could enhance a relation between two individuals, but not beyond two. In *'Iqd* and *Nihayat,* a reference made to the *Kitab al-Taj,* a Persian work belonging to the "mirror of princes" genre, depicts an ancient Persian or Sassanian king advising his minister that "indeed the disclosure of the secret to one man is akin to the disclosure to two, and the disclosure to three is like the disclosure to a group."[86] Moreover, lines from the *Nihayat,* by the famous 'Udhri Arab love poet Jamil, echoes this idea:

[Do] not allow your secret and my secret to [reach] a third [party]
Every secret that goes beyond two is forfeited.[87]

Al-Jahiz repeatedly emphasizes the point concerning how other people's secrets are even more difficult to keep than one's own secret. To have confided in someone is to have virtually broadcast one's secret. Other people's secrets are more easily disclosed because the prohibition associated with them (that is, "don't tell the secret I shared with you") invites transgression. It invites transgression since, according to al-Jahiz, the forbidden is more easily transgressed and a prohibition is more easily violated. Indeed, he maintains that "one of the greatest aids in making a secret public [*izhar al-sirr*] is to ask for a pledge [from the person to whom it is told] and warn against publishing it . . . for a prohibition entices since it is an imposition of labor. Patience with this imposition is hard. It is hazardous, and the self [*nafs*] is fleeting and changing, passionately fond of revealing the secret and desirous of liberation."[88]

Actually both premodern Muslim and modern Western writers insist that a secret revealed is no longer a secret. The Muslim Andalusian theologian and belletristic writer Ibn Hazm, author of the famous eleventh-century love treatise *Tawq al-Hamama* (*The Ring of the Dove*), is emphatic on this matter:

"for the one to whom the lover's secret is entrusted will generally act in one of two ways: either he will mock his opinion, or he will publish his secret."[89] In this regard, the modern theorist of secrecy Georg Simmel too declares: "It is therefore said quite correctly that the secret known by two is no longer a secret."[90] Indeed, Simmel maintains that the struggle not to reveal another person's secret "alone is designated as secret."[91]

Discretion, as understood in the 'Abbasid courtly context, is also at the heart of some of al-Jahiz's statements on the dangers of having confided one's secret to someone else. In these statements he uses master-slave metaphors: one remains the master by retaining the secret, whereas releasing it reduces one to slavery. One who has revealed his secret (that is, the original owner) "has made himself a servant to another, [and has chosen] . . . slavery without [being led into it by] captivity or coercion." Such a person becomes a slave to and subject of the person to whom he has released his secret.

Less metaphorically al-Jahiz also addresses links between secrecy and power when he observes that the secrecy of royalty and the elite classes is often violated by subordinates in age and rank—servants and "common people." Those who have power have secrets, and those who do not have power acquire power through gaining access to the secrets of the powerful. "Most often those who spread people's secrets are their family members, servants, dependents, offspring and those over whom they [have] control and authority. When a caliph entrusts his subordinate with a secret which could harm him, it is most likely not to be concealed."[92] According to al-Jahiz, envy is linked with the desire by commoners to reveal the secrets of the royals. Telling "royal" secrets, or the secrets of superiors, becomes a kind of revenge against those one envies due to their elevated social and economic rank.

While al-Jahiz recognizes that there is a human need for self-disclosure and self-expression, he staunchly maintains that even if one finds an ideal person to whom one can tell one's secret, his or her ability to keep it is much less than that of the original owner of the secret; this is why he maintains that even if relief and a cure are to be experienced (for the constricted breast) through disclosure to someone (rather than to oneself), they are not lasting. It is a situation in which passion rather than the intellect reigns over the tongue. He goes so far as to suggest that when it comes to confidential communication, messengers who are compensated are more reliable in conveying and purveying secrets than even a reliable friend: "What we have tried out and discovered is that one informed privately of something achieves in broadcasting and publishing it more than a messenger entrusted with the task of delivering the message who is praised and rewarded for his action."[93] As for the qualities of an ideal confidant, he offers advice on choosing such a confidant at the end of his work. Al-Jahiz insists that the mind and heart both matter in the ability to inspire and establish trust: "Do not depend for your secret on a man whose acumen and intelligence you praise without also admiring his capacity for affection and his sincere counsel."[94] He expounds on this further by citing a verse:

> Not everyone bestowed with intelligence gives you sincere advice
> and not everyone bestowed with [capacity for advice-giving] is intelligent.[95]

What is essential is that both types of qualities—those concerned with intelligence and with sincerity—should be present in a counselor. An intelligent person may be able to share wise words but not have one's best interests in mind, whereas a sincere person may have one's best interests in mind but not be able to steer one wisely.

In his *Risalat al-Ma'ad wal-ma'ash* (*Epistle of the Hereafter and This Life*), al-Jahiz suggests that from among one's friends, at least one should be designated as a confidant:

> You may have recourse to one man for his opinion or suggestions, make another the faithful repository of your secrets, look to another again for energy and vigour, and rely on yet another for devoted hard work: each has his part to play in the role assigned to him. . . . Be heedful and considerate with each one, whether of exalted or more lowly station, rewarding them when they do well and admonishing them when they fall short, so that they may know that your eye and ear are always on them. Keep each one in his place and do not involve him in matters outside his province, and you will find that your affairs will prosper and they will all serve you faithfully.[96]

Al-Jahiz clearly assigns importance to the need to have a confidant, that is, a friend who can "hold one's secrets," and importantly, he suggests that this friend should be there only for this role. In this regard as well, modern social scientists echo al-Jahiz. For example, Carl Sulzberger declares, "To the many definitions of friend could be added, 'the person to whom we may tell all, with impunity.'"[97]

Conclusion

In both the Qur'an and al-Jahiz's *Kitman*, self and subjectivity are constituted through the concealing and revealing of secrets. As remarked earlier, there are strong resonances between al-Jahiz's conception of "watch guard within" (that is, the ethical and moral self constituted through self-censorship), on one hand, and the Qur'anic "transparency of self," on the other hand.

For al-Jahiz, as ethicist and theologian, the task at hand is to perfect the inner self, the watch guard within, because inevitably the self's outer, physical signifiers attest to inner moral life. What is vital, according to al-Jahiz, is the management of the self-censorship inherent in the process and work of "concealing the secret," or *kitmān al-sirr*. How well contained is the revelation that sooner or later occurs? This is the supreme challenge to the ethical and moral self that exercises *kitmān al-sirr*. Arguing that through modes of self-discipline and containment (involving verbal and bodily forms of reserve) the self practices concealment of the secret, al-Jahiz renders this practice most meaningful within the earthly context—a context involving interpersonal relations, self-presentation, and ethical conduct.

While the religious view deeply informs al-Jahiz's composition of *Kitman,* his analysis and discussion of secrecy are not framed in terms of religious concepts. According to al-Jahiz, concealing/revealing the secret (*kitmān al-sirr*) is conceived more in terms of a process, more in terms of an interpersonal mode of ethics. Given his courtly audiences, al-Jahiz's emphasis on both moral vigilance and discretion in expression is set within the context of the here and now; he conceives of the practice of *kitmān al-sirr,* like the art of *al-bayān,* to be a goal to be strived for by anyone belonging to early Arabo-Islamic culture and society—whether a caliph, a jurist, or a teacher.

In the next several chapters, we shift to a consideration of eminently literary texts. The shift to early Arabic love literature from *Kitman* implies a change in focus from the concept of the secret to the trope of the secret, but it does not imply a substantive change in the links between selfhood and secrecy.

※ ※

4.

The Rhetoric of the Secret

Love, Sexuality, and the Body

He that has eyes to see and ears to hear can convince himself that no
mortal can keep a secret. If his lips are silent, he chatters with his finger-
tips; betrayal oozes out of him at every pore.

> Sigmund Freud, "Fragment of an Analysis of a Case of Hysteria"

Why, in a study devoted to secrecy, is there a section on its significance in
love literature?[1] First, it should be recognized that the topic of secrecy concerns human relations, what psychoanalysts call "object relations."[2] The issue
of boundaries is central to this topic. In a way, a study of the secret and
secrecy is an examination of boundaries, the self's inner boundaries as well as
those between the self and others. Of course, love relations are an especially
important type of interpersonal bonds. Georg Simmel devotes a good portion of his influential work "The Secret and Secret Society" to the analysis
of the relevance of secrecy to a form of intimate relations, that is, marital
relations.[3]

In this book I argue that diverse Arabo-Islamic discourses (ethics, *paedia*,
scripture) identify secrecy as a marker of the self. Hence, the second reason
I examine love literature is because early Arabic love literature also emphasizes the role and function of the secret in its representations of the self and
self-other relations. The very rhetorical qualities of this poetry are significantly enhanced by the paradoxes associated with notions of self, body, and
sexuality. It is precisely to this enhancement that the critic Andras Hamori
alludes when, in discussing the Arabic love poetry of the courtly al-'Abbas b.
al-Ahnaf, he observes: "The secret no doubt has social realities behind it, but
it is also an element in the rhetoric of paradox in love poetry; providing for
contrast between inside and outside, feeling and behavior."[4] In the 'Udhri
Arabic romances or love stories that I examine, secrecy and revelation are

present not only in their rhetorical and verbal textures (for example, tropes, metaphors used) but also in their semantic aspects (for example, import of the story motifs, plot incidents, and stratagems of deception that occur in them).

This paradox to which Hamori refers is, first and foremost, a feature of the secret itself. A defining trait of secrecy, paradoxically, is that it is always accompanied by revelation. In other words, secrecy and revelation are inextricably linked, and it is this very inextricability that is a marker of self and subjectivity in a range of early Arabo-Islamic discourses. Subsumed under this overarching theme of the inextricability of secrecy and revelation is another one of how the body inevitably reveals what the owner of a secret desires to conceal. The role of the body is conveyed through the imagery of body organs, especially the juxtaposition of body organs. The template for understanding this contrariness of secrecy is the human body: a matrix for the conserving and yielding tendencies in secrecy and revelation can be found in bodily functions. Repeatedly in Arabic writings on secrecy one comes across the idea of a correspondence between the integrity of the physical body and the integrity of the core self. Preserving the wholeness and soundness of the physical outer body is akin to preserving the secrets of the inner core self. Paradoxically, though, the embodied self both keeps and gives the secret away. Indeed I would argue that partly it is this emphasis on body that enables the passage of Arabic love literature's treasure trove of themes, motifs, symbols, and rhetoric into Islamic asceticism and mysticism, with their concomitant concern with bodily effacement and deprivation.

Early Arabic love literature of various genres propounds the theme of how secrecy inevitably accompanies revelation (whether the two occur simultaneously or in an alternating fashion). Hence, this paradox to which Hamori alludes is discernible not just in Arabic love poetry but also in other love-related genres (for example, romance, love treatise) and at various levels in these discourses—such as at the levels of theme, character, and genre.

Furthermore, secrecy and revelation are gendered in the 'Udhri romances: themes of indiscretion and notoriety are linked with the subjectivity of the male poet-lover, whereas motifs of secrecy are associated with the female beloved. As we shall see, the etymology of the Arabic word for secret, *sirr,* supports this gendering of secrecy and revelation, for it indicates a nexus between male sexuality and revelation, on the one hand, and female sexuality and concealment, on the other hand.

Sexuality and Gender in Early Arabic Definitions of *Sirr* (Secret)

Recall that the most commonly employed Arabic word for "secret," *sirr,* has contrary meanings of "something concealed or suppressed" as well as "a

thing that is made manifest or disclosed."[5] According to the classical lexicons, the word *sirr* is multivalent. This is evident in its linking of the internal
world of thoughts and emotions with the sexualized body. *Sirr* means "the
heart or the mind" as well as the "external generative organs" (that is, "the
penis of a man . . . and the vulva of a woman").[6] This is an extremely
important link that can be interpreted in several different ways. First, it
suggests that sexual organs are the manifested bodily signs of internal feelings, thoughts, and desires. Second, the choice of the sexual organs as the
manifest signs with which the inner is linked is suggestive of the degree to
which secrecy is fundamentally concerned with intimacy, love, and sexuality.
Third, the link between the inner bodily organs (that is, the heart and mind)
and the outer organs implies the dialectic of secrecy and revelation; what the
heart conceals, the outer body reveals, and what the body reveals must be
kept covered, that is, the external signs of the body must be concealed. When
the body is gendered male, the dialectic of secrecy and revelation is conveyed
through the contrast of the inner organs with the external male sexual
organ—what the heart conceals, the visible male body reveals. Again, we see
how secrecy invites revelation, and this revelation implies concealment.

    Sirr also means "marriage" as well as "adultery" and "fornication." One
can envision how these dual aspects subsume the notion of the inextricability
of secrecy and revelation. Marriage is the secret concealed, and adultery is
the secret revealed. The ritual of marriage initially consists of publicizing an
intended sexual union—in Islam, it is this publicity that confers legitimacy
on the union. Once consummated, however, the conjugal union becomes
something concealed, or secret from the public. Adultery or fornication, on
the other hand, is a transgression of the marital bond of secrecy; hence, it is
the secret revealed. However, adultery is also the sexual union concealed or
hidden because it is not socially and legally sanctioned, and the clandestine
nature of the relation accentuates its illegitimacy.

    Gender associations in this etymology indicate a strong nexus between
concealment and female sexuality. As noted earlier, *sirr* means both the hidden "female genitalia" and the visible "male organ." The derivation *sirriyya*
means "a free woman with whom one has sexual intercourse secretly," or a
prostitute, and a *surriyya* is a "female concubine-slave." The fifth and tenth
forms of the verb *sarra* mean "to take to oneself a concubine-slave." Hence,
"secret" is also defined as a female paramour who is to be hidden, especially
if the sexual relation with her is illicit. In the 'Udhri romances, as we shall
see, the secrecy of the female body is intimately linked with female chastity.
Actually some Qur'anic references to female modesty and chastity are literally references to the concealment and protection of female genitalia.[7] The
veiling and concealment of a woman's body are explicitly linked with the

preservation of her chastity. Given the inextricability of secrecy and revelation (that is, a secret is not a secret until it is revealed), in the 'Udhri romances female chastity is inevitably violated (that is, the divulgence of a beloved as secret occurs). Gender dimensions in the etymology of the word *sirr* also suggest that female secrecy is connected with female guile and deception as well. Women are to be kept secrets, and they keep secrets.

The Inextricability of Secrecy and Revelation

There are three paradoxes.

Paradox of Love

A well-circulated definition of love *('ishq)* during the early Islamic period described it as a hidden spark that is ignited into flames. The ninth-century Muslim philologist al-Asma'i, having camped among the Bedouin Arabs in order to gather linguistic data, conveys the following description about love: "I asked a bedouin Arab about love [*'ishq*] and he said, 'It is too sublime to be seen and it is hidden from the eyes of mortals, for it is concealed in the breast like the latent fire in a flint, which when struck produces fire, this fire remaining hidden as long as it is left alone.' "[8] Love was defined as both the concealment and manifestation of certain signs. Actually, in early Arabic culture a secret love was considered a profoundly true love, or a true love was deemed a secret love. Love consisted of the suppression of that which was defined as expression and the expression of that which was defined as suppression. For example, the writer Ibn Dawud, who authored the ninth-century love treatise entitled *Kitab al-Zahra* (*Book of the Flower*), partly defined love as the manifestation of certain signs and symptoms and yet paradoxically insisted on true love being the concealment and suppression of these very symptoms. According to the Andalusian Ibn Hazm, in his famous eleventh-century love tract *Tawq al-Hamama* (*The Ring of the Dove*), the signs are bodily symptoms, outward manifestations of an inner, hidden experience of love. A sign itself is understood as an outward form with a latent meaning. Among the traits of a discerning individual was the ability to detect and interpret this visible evidence of love.[9]

Secrecy is pivotal to the ethics of love, as articulated by Ibn Dawud in his love treatise. The significance of discretion and chastity in love permeates the whole work, which includes chapters with titles such as "The path of patience is remote, and the concealment of love is difficult" (*tariq l-sabri ba'idun wa-kitmānu l-hubbi shadīd*) and "One whose patience is overtaken, manifest is his secret" (*man ghuliba sabruhu, zahara sirruhu*).[10] According to the ethics articulated in love treatises such as the ninth-century *Kitab al-Zahra,* it was incumbent upon the receiver of a secret to conceal it, in part because a secret told or revealed to one was considered an expression of intimacy, and therefore, disclosure of another's secret was betrayal of the worst kind. In fact, it was incumbent upon the receiver of a secret to conceal it according to the ethics of love, as expressed by love theorists such as Ibn Dawud.

A famous but not so authentic Hadith al-'Ishq (prophetic saying concerning passionate love) also provides a window into how, in early Arabic culture, a secret love was considered a profoundly true love. A fairly well-circulated text of this hadith is quoted in Ibn Dawud's love treatise *Kitab al-Zahra*: "He who loves passionately, remains chaste, conceals [his love], and then dies, dies a martyr."[11] The Arabic verb for "conceals" in this hadith is *katama*—secrecy and passionate love are rendered equivalent here. Also of interest are the close syntactic and semantic links between chastity (*'affa*) and concealment (*katama*): suppression of speech about love (that is, not talking about it) is linked with being chaste.

Ibn Hazm's work *Tawq al-Hamama* (*The Ring of the Dove*) includes several chapters on the art of concealing and revealing in matters of love. This ethically oriented treatise on love, which acquired renown among Arab Muslim scholars in both the Islamic East and the West during the medieval age, may also be regarded as a manual on the art of discretion or keeping secrets. Ibn Hazm enumerates the varieties of love in his chapter entitled "al-Kalam fi Mahiyyat al-Hubb" ("Concerning the Nature of Love"), and among the kinds of love he mentions, one is defined as "the love that is based upon a shared secret which both [lovers] must conceal."[12] Not ranked as high as other kinds of love, this love (along with other kinds), he concludes, "comes to an end when . . . [its] causes disappear."[13] Yet, Ibn Hazm shows his awareness of the paradox of defining love as both concealment and revelation when he begins a chapter entitled "Of Concealing the Secret" with the following declaration: "One of the traits of love is holding the tongue [*al-kitman bil-lisan*]; the lover will deny everything if interrogated, feign a show of perseverance and make it seem that he is extremely continent and a bachelor. Despite this, the subtle secret will out [the subtle secret refuses, *ya'bi or ya'ba al-sirru al-daqiq*]."[14] Love itself is an inborn capacity of the self, and the inextricability of love's secrecy and revelation functions as a marker of self and subjectivity. Perhaps Ibn Hazm, more than other love theorists, was aware of this paradox of love being defined as both the concealment and manifestation of certain signs. However, the paradox characterizes the entire discourse on love in early Arabic love literature, especially in Arabic romances such as *Majnun Layla*. In the tenth-century courtly culture in which 'Udhri romances such as *Majnun Layla* were compiled and recorded, there was a strong connection between the ideals of love and secrecy.

To Speak or Not Speak of Love?

Even though true love was deemed a secret love, all the great lovers were those who spoke about their love—that is, poets. The "most famous of the famous" love poets in early Arabic culture was Majnun, the character in the Arabic romance associated with his name, the 'Udhri love story of *Majnun Layla*. To the extent that he is a historical character, Majnun is a famous early Arab poet and tribal nobleman named Qays bin al-Mulawwah, born in the Hijazi region of the Arabian Peninsula during the latter half of the seventh century.[15] The word *majnun* was his nom de plume or *laqab,* meaning the "madman" or the "one obsessed." The love of Majnun for Layla is rooted in childhood, when they used to tend the flocks of their families:

> I fell in love with Layla when she was just a child with ringlets,
> When no sign of her breasts had yet appeared to playmates.
> Two children tending the lambs.
> Would that we never had grown up, nor had
> the lambs grown old.[16]

After a brief period of courtship between them, during which Majnun publicly serenades and declaims indiscreet poetry about his relation with Layla, her family bars him from seeing her. Afraid that he might lose her, Majnun asks for Layla's hand in marriage but is flatly refused by her father. Thereafter numerous other suitors from her tribe propose marriage to her; ultimately she accepts (or her kin accept) a proposal from a rich man (Ward ibn Muhammad al-Uqayliyyi) from a distant tribe. Majnun consequently loses his mind, leaves society, and retires to the wilderness, but he continues to recite beautiful poetry about her, which circulates in the region.[17] Even after Layla is married, the lovers continue to have trysts when her husband, Ward, is away, and in several anecdotes it is related that her husband and her lover engage in verbal jousts with each other over the issue of Majnun's continued public declamation of poetry about her. Majnun, however, remains in the wilderness of the desert and one day is found dead among the rocks by a tribesman who had sought him out for his poetry. Upon hearing news of his death, Layla's father expresses regret over his harsh treatment of Majnun and attends his funeral.

All the great lovers in early Arab culture were those who publicly articulated their love, and hence, not surprisingly, Majnun is described primarily in terms of his eloquence in recited poetry and conversation throughout the romance. It is mentioned that he was the best in the art of conversation and "the most comely, elegant and brilliant in the poetry of the Bedouins."[18] Another narrative describes his eloquence in the context of his courtship of Layla: "When Majnun first fell in love with Layla, he used to sing her praises often [*kathīr al-dhikr lahā*] and visit her at night. The Bedouins used to regard as acceptable that youths or lads converse with lasses. When her family came to know of his love for her, they banned him from visiting her."[19] In part, lovers were poets because there was a well-acknowledged connection between poetry and courtship in early Arabic culture.[20] The Arabic verb *khataba* means "to orate" as well as "to woo."[21] The word *jamala* means both "to rhetorically embellish" and "to flatter." Indeed, the pre-Islamic ode's love prelude is suggestive of a model of masculinity in which men cultivated the art of composing and publicly reciting poems and odes praising women. A man could boast, as does the pre-Islamic poet al-Muraqqish the Elder, of his ability to compose and declaim odes—each in praise of a different young woman:

> And many the smooth-cheeked maiden,
> brought up in luxury, long-haired, long-necked. . . .
> Have I toyed with for a time in my youth,
> and thorough-bred she-camels have visited her [with my messages],
> and odes have been made by me in her praise.
> Those were people! As oft as I wore out one tie [of love],
> there occupied me a new one . . . in its place.[22]

Language was the medium through which male desire expressed itself and sought satisfaction. A man's linguistic prowess was the main credential that established his status as a lover. A man's desire was articulated through the eloquence of his own language. Furthermore, the articulation and revelation of love were a recognized motif and rhetorical element.[23] In early Arabic love literature, love poets are shown competing with one another in a motif of "publicizing love and concealing it." A passage found in the biography of the Umayyad love poet 'Umar ibn Abi Rabi'a corroborates this. The passage provides a list of poetic devices and conventions, rhetorical elements, strategies, and motifs in which 'Umar excelled and surpassed his male rivals. A brief excerpt of this list reads: " 'Umar ibn Abi Rabi'a surpassed people and outclassed his rivals . . . in the matter of the facility of his poetry. . . . He publicized love and he concealed it [*wa 'alana wa asarra*] and he hid it and he revealed it and he coined examples of sayings of revelation and its concealment."[24] In fact, the romances portray Bedouin women celebrating and capitalizing on the acquisition of such a rhapsodizer, as the following quotation from Ibn Hazm's famous love treatise *The Ring of the Dove* demonstrates: "I have read in some Bedouin tale [*akhbār al-'arab*] that their women-folk do not feel satisfied and convinced that a man is really in love with them, until his romantic feelings become public knowledge and are completely divulged; he must advertise and broadcast his attachment, and sing their praises for all to hear. I know not what to make of that, considering they have such a reputation for chastity: what chastity does a woman in fact possess, if her greatest desire and joy is to be notorious after this fashion?"[25] Ibn Dawud faulted male poets such as Majnun for their tendencytoward indiscretion and revelation, and Ibn Hazm, living more than a century later, expresses puzzlement, in the quotation cited above, over why Bedouin tales and stories show the women as being very fond of this publicity. It is likely that his use of the term *Bedouin tale* refers to stories and romances such as *Majnun Layla,* for as a member of eleventh-century Andalusian courtly society, he clearly would have had access to diverse literary and scholarly works produced during the earlier Umayyad and ʿAbbasid periods.

Moreover, many of the ʿUdhri romances of the Umayyad and ʿAbbasid periods are characterized by the thematics of an inner feeling of youthful love and desire that cries out to be heard and yet remains a secret. Jamil, another ʿUdhri poet, offers eloquent testimony of this when he recites:

> I spend my day bewildered by love,
> at night my soul embraces her soul in sleep.
> Is there a respite for me in love's concealment or would
> revelation be an antidote for me,
> were I to reveal her?[26]

Here too we discern the paradox to which Hamori alludes. The poet wonders whether concealment or revelation of the secret of his love would afford him some relief. Evidently the lover's task of keeping the secret is experienced as taxing and burdensome. This keeping of the secret, which consists of young love and infatuation, is characterized by an intrapsychic conflict between suppression and expression. To shed light on this conflict further, we turn to a poem by Ibn Hazm in which he describes how the lover regrets that his tears betray his secret, while at the same time he experiences anguish over having to hide his secret:

> The tears of passion flow
> and flow again
> The veil of love, I know
> is rent in twain . . .
> How long, how long must I
> this secret hide
> which I cannot deny
> nor lay aside.[27]

Then he observes: "This however only happens when the instinct for concealment and self-protection [*ṭabʿi l-kitmān, wal-taṣawun*] conflicts with and overcomes the lover's natural disposition [*ṭabʿi l-muḥibb*]; the victim caught

ﻥ

between two raging fires, feels utterly bewildered."[28] Ibn Hazm would sym-
pathize with Jamil's desire in the aforementioned verse to express his love;
he seems to suggest that it is an aspect of the lover's natural disposition, and
yet he understands the inclination toward suppression of this secret love.
What Ibn Hazm means by "the instinct for concealment and self-protection"
is clarified through his observation in the same chapter: "It is possible in the
early stages to delude those lacking in finer sensibility; once Love has firmly
established itself, however, that is entirely out of the question."[29] Present in
this observation on the hidden quality of love in its infancy is an important
psycho-social function of the secret, self-protection. Georg Simmel's landmark essay "The Secret and Secret Society" also points out that secrecy "is
the suitable social form for contents which still (as it were) are in their
infancy, subject to the vulnerability of early developmental stages."[30] Ibn
Hazm foregrounds precisely this in another of his poems, in which he relies
on the imagery of a lamp to illustrate this:

> Has thou not seen, and learned by it,
> How, when a lamp is freshly lit,
> The flame burns feebly, and one puff
> To put it out is quite enough?
> But when the wick is well alight
> And blazing broadly through the night,
> To puff and puff will only go
> To fan it into fiercer glow.[31]

Poetry That Transgresses What It Posits

Paradox is further discernible in the following narrative (with several subsequent variants) transmitted by al-Isfahani in the introduction to the *Majnun
Layla* romance: "I was told that the sayings of Majnun and his poetry were
forged by a young man from Bani Umayyah who was in love with his pater-
nal cousin. He loathed revealing what was between him and her and so, he
fashioned the account of Majnun, recited the poetry which people [al-nās]
relate as Majnun's and attributed it to him."[32] Whatever the credibility of
this narrative, we confront the peculiar case of a youth concerned about
secrecy and discretion in his love affair and producing a poetic persona
whose undoing is precisely love's indiscretion. In other words, *Majnun Layla*
is a remarkable example of a "tale of . . . revealed love," spun by a poet
whose concern was supposedly *not* to reveal his love. His revelation, in turn,
induces concealment, for the story's dissemination occurs through the device
of the pseudonym. Secrecy invites revelation, and disclosure necessitates concealment. Love is first constructed as a secret between the two lovers and
then as revelation to the public—the same youth who views it as a secret
love desires to speak about it and to compose verses about it. Hence, his

ingenious compromise; he revealed his love by not revealing it. He manufactured a "fictive" love story and its accompanying poems that both concealed and expressed his true love.

The *Majnun Layla* romance is a love story, the core of which is characterized, in R. Howard Bloch's words, by "a logic of poetry that transgresses what it posits."[33] Bloch, in his important book on medieval misogyny, draws attention to a similar paradox, as it exists in medieval, courtly French poetry. In a chapter arrestingly entitled "The Old French Lay and the Myriad Modes of Male Indiscretion," he notes:

> Here we encounter a contradiction every bit as powerful as the paradox
> of virginity: that love only exists to the degree that it is secret; that secret
> love only exists to the degree that it is revealed; and revealed, it is no
> longer love. At the center of the courtly code of discretion and of almost
> every tale of so-called hidden love lies the logic of the poetry that
> transgresses what it posits, and not, as has been asserted . . . a conflict of
> good versus bad lovers. . . . For if love must be kept secret to exist, then,
> as in the case of the virgin, there can be no speaking of it that does not
> imply its transgression.[34]

The analogy between a "secret love" and virginity that Bloch makes in this quotation is pertinent to the romance of *Majnun Layla*. Just as love must be kept secret to exist, so too must virginity be kept secret to exist—"there can be no speaking of virginity that does not imply its transgression."[35] In the first half of *Majnun Layla*, the motif of "love revealed" concerns virginity and not adultery. That is, unlike what is found in the courtly French poems that Bloch examines, initially it is impugnment of female chastity rather than disclosure of female infidelity that constitutes the unacceptable in *Majnun Layla*. Yet, both medieval Arabic and French love poems are characterized by "a logic of a poetry that transgresses what it posits,"[36] and in both, the transgression takes the form of male indiscretion.

Bloch's phrase "the logic of the poetry" suggests that there is something inherent to the suppression of poetic language (secret) that logically entails its expression (revelation). He recognizes this when he asks, "does this not mean that there is something specific to the secret that autonomously uncovers . . . that which language, or at least courtly language, cannot hide?"[37] He tends toward identification of the paradox, mainly on the level of genre (poetry). Yet this paradox is present in the entire Arabic corpus to which the romance of *Majnun Layla* belongs. *Majnun Layla* is a romance belonging to the 'Udhri corpus of love tales, known for their portrayals of ostensibly chaste and thwarted love affairs, in which a poet-lover loses his beloved precisely because of his impugning her chastity.

To speak of matters concerning virginity and sex was not against poetic convention. As J. C. Burgel, in his article entitled "Love, Lust, and Longing," notes: "But the permissibility for poets to say things at variance with a high moral standard . . . [was] expressly stated by an early writer on poetics. In his *Naqd al-Shi'r*, Qudama ibn Ja'far says that a fine love poem does not necessarily imply a poet's personal experience or conviction, and he must also not be reproached if what he says in his poems is morally reprehensible. What is demanded from him is not so much truth and morality as good poetic style and suggestive description."[38] So why is Majnun punished for speaking about these things in our romance? The response may be that the romance of *Majnun Layla* foregrounds a particular kind of tension: pre-Islamic Bedouin poetic conventions versus emergent Muslim social norms and conventions. What was permissible as poetic convention was impermissible according to prevailing social conventions. In the romance, the opposition between love and society is actually an opposition between the poetic rhetoric of love relations and their practice in the nascent Islamic society. According to the view of many critics, Majnun's error is, as Michael Dols, author of *Majnun: The Madman in Medieval Islamic Society,* broadly words it, his "public display of love, his *tashbīb*—the rhapsodizing about a beloved woman and one's relationship to her."[39] If this is the case, *tashbīb* would have to be cited as the cause for the loss of beloveds in all the 'Udhri love stories, because 'Udhri poetry is nothing if not the performed rhapsody about a lover's relationship to his beloved. All the 'Udhri poets publicly identified their beloveds and publicly recited verses about their love for these women. In the love story of *Jamil Buthayna,* too, the poet's serenading of Buthayna contriutes to the demise of the love affair.[40]

Yet, it is not *tashbīb* as mere rhapsody of a beloved that destroys Majnun but rather *tashbīb* with satirical connotations, for which the literary antecedents are to be found in the pre-Islamic love prelude (*nasīb*). Since the lady of the love prelude was an object that was both desired and sometimes scorned, elements of satire became intertwined with rhapsody in the prelude.[41] Jean-Claude Vadet maintains that this combination of serenade and satire sorely tried early Islamic society's values concerned with female chastity and matrimony.[42] Thus, Majnun loses Layla not simply as a result of a "public display of love" but because his *tashbīb* revealed a satirical disregard of emergent Islamic social values associated with chastity and matrimony. An example of this *tashbīb* (mixed with satire, or *hijā'*) is found in the passage cited below from the romance of *Majnun Layla,* which exhibits an exchange between Majnun and the beloved's husband:

> [Word] reached Majnun . . . that Layla's husband had spoken of
> him, reviling and cursing him as well as saying: Has Majnun's temerity

reached [such a degree] that he claims Layla's love and parades her name? Then [Majnun], in order to enrage him, recited:

If there is among you a husband of Layla it is me—by the Lord of the
  Throne
I have already kissed her mouth eight times.
And I swear by God that I have seen her,
when twenty of her fingers were [wrapped] around my back.
Is it not an incomparable catastrophe that she was married to that dog
and not granted to me?[43]

Here Majnun openly declaims poetry in which he advertises sexual secrets about his beloved, Layla, ostensibly so as to insult and antagonize her husband. Lover and husband engage in a verbal joust with each other whereby one publicly divulges female secrets and the other publicly issues obscenities. The mention of Layla's "twenty fingers" in this poem refers to both fingers and toes. The phrase "twenty of her fingers were [wrapped] around my back" evokes a graphic image of the beloved with her fingers and toes entwined around the lover's back. The reference to her mouth having been kissed not twice, not thrice, but rather eight times conjures up a sexually laden image. Majnun panders Layla's secrets in retaliation for being made the public target of her husband's invectives.

How the Body Reveals the Secret

I return to Hamori's point regarding how the secret is an element in the "rhetoric of paradox" characterizing Arabic love poetry. This paradox is conveyed through the theme of the body ineluctably revealing what the secret's owner desires to conceal. The juxtaposition of exterior versus interior body organs is one significant way that this theme of the body's revelation is conveyed; such juxtaposition also conveys the "contrast between inside and outside, feeling and behavior." Precisely this juxtaposition of exterior versus interior body organs is found in diverse Arabo-Islamic discourses, including Islamic ethics and the Qur'an. Such body symbolism makes prominent the notion that the body is implicated in the secret's disclosure, that is, that the outer body reveals the secret in spite of its owner's intentions to conceal. This notion recurs throughout early Arabic love literature. In addition to the symbolism of body organs, however, there is also the role of bodily gestures, symptoms, reactions, sounds, ailments, and bodily modes of dressing—all of these are employed in this theme of how the body reveals what the owner desires to conceal.

Another important way that this theme of the body's revelation is conveyed is through metaphors that express a correspondence between the revelation of the secret and somatic excretions. One finds many bodily metaphors, such as tearing eyes, sealed hearts, emaciated bodies, and leaking skins. The imagery and symbolism of bodily fluids and secretions is especially strong. The body both sets up the binary of inside and outside and, paradoxically, subverts this boundary. The exterior body reveals what the inner self desires to conceal.

The psychoanalyst Alfred Gross has discussed how the "secret [is] comparable to a private possession (from which others are excluded),"[44] and this induces him to consider the link between the secret and a body organ: "The secret is also more closely identified with its owner than other possessions; it perishes with him and thus, is analogous to such corporal 'possessions' of man as his head, his heart or his hands."[45] We have seen how, in diverse Arabo-Islamic discourses, including those of the Qur'an and Islamic ethics, the heart is identified as the organ that stores secrets. Moreover, according to Gross, the parallel between the secret and a body organ allows for a correspondence, in the human unconscious, between the revelation of the secret and somatic excretions: "This leads us to ask whether there is not in our unconscious a complete identity between the secret on the one hand, and the body excretions (respectively the organs of secretion) on the other. It may be noted at once that such a hypothesis is supported by the etymology of the Romance languages; in Italian, the secret is called *il segreto* and in French, *le secret*. The literal meaning of the Latin word *secretum,* from which these words are derived, means 'that which has been secreted,' or 'secretion.'"[46] In other words, according to Gross, "the secret and secretions are closely connected with each other in the unconscious"; however, he emphasizes that "only the *content* of the secret may be identified with the secretions."[47]

Tongue That Conceals versus Eyes That Reveal

A juxtaposition often seen in Arabic love literature is that of the tongue that conceals and the eyes that reveal. In Islamic ethics, as is evinced by *Kitman,* the tongue is an organ of revelation, but in Arabo-Islamic love literature it conceals.[48] Eyes, an external organ, are almost always paired with themes of disclosure and revelation. An illustration of this is found in Ibn Hazm's love treatise. Two chapters in *The Ring of the Dove* (the first entitled "Of Concealing the Secret" immediately followed by "Of Revealing the Secret") are devoted to the subject of secrecy. Quoted again, the first paragraph of his chapter entitled "Ṭayy al-Sirr," or "Of Concealing the Secret," reads:

> One of the traits of love is holding the tongue [*al-kitmān bil-lisān*]; the lover will deny everything if interrogated, feign a show of perseverance and make it seem that he is extremely continent and a bachelor. Despite

this, the subtle secret will out [the subtle secret refuses—*ya'bī al-sirru al-daqīq*]. Love's fire [will] blaze in his ribs but will be visible and manifest in his gestures and in the expression of his eyes; they will creep out into the open, like fire among coals or water through dry clay. It is possible in the early stages to delude those lacking in finer sensibility; once love has firmly established itself, however, it is not possible.[49]

Here the various traits associated with love—holding the tongue, denial by the lover if he is interrogated, and the feigning a show of perseverance—are all contrived acts that entail suppression. At least two of these traits are due to the tongue's concealment (*kitmān bil-lisan*): holding of the tongue and the denials of the lover. The heart enlists the tongue in order to conceal through a combination of denial, a noncommittal attitude, and outward composure. Yet, Ibn Hazm declares, "for all that, the subtle secret will out"—that is, in spite of, or perhaps because of, these forms of forced retention, the secret ousts itself. By grammatically making the word *sirr* (secret) an active subject such that the secret takes on a life of its own, he indicates the inevitability of revelation or the secret's escape—it refuses to be suppressed and "will out." In this very use of grammatical and rhetorical devices, Ibn Hazm offers an example of what Hamori identifies as the "rhetoric of paradox." Through the juxtaposition of suppression with expression, we discern the tension between retention and release of the secret. Ibn Hazm demonstrates that the male lover's conscious enterprise of concealing the secret paradoxically fails because his bodily signs reveal it. The stages of love have a bearing on this. During the early stages of love, when the lover's conscious and unconscious content is "less burdensome," he may voluntarily and intentionally conceal his love. However, with love's maturation and growth, revelation is inevitable.

Exactly how does the secret's revelation occur? It occurs through the involuntary expression of the lover's external body language, through his gestures and the expression of his eyes (the Arabic in the paragraph above is *ẓuhran fil-ḥarakāt wal-'ayn*). The contrast between internal feelings and outward motions is accentuated. The two important terms are *gestures* (*ḥarakāt*) and *eye* (*'ayn*).[50] The first word, *ḥarakāt*, appears again just a few sentences later on the same page in Ibn Hazm's treatise, when in defending love's revelation (note the paradox of such a defense in a chapter concerned with concealment of love), Ibn Hazm states: "Love itself is an inborn disposition; man can only control those motions [*ḥarakāt*, which can also be translated as 'gestures'] of his members which he has acquired by deliberate effort."[51] Ibn Hazm argues that there are certain kinds of bodily movements or gestures over which one has conscious control and others over which one does not. Movements of the appendages or limbs—motor movements that

are learned and practiced—can be controlled. Other kinds of bodily movements or gestures—such as facial changes (for example, frowning, blushing,
twitching)—are not always within one's control, and it is these that give the
lover's secret away. Ibn Hazm echoes al-Jahiz, who nearly two hundred years
earlier, in *Kitman,* also maintained that "the most level-headed and forbearing person" who disciplines his tongue and preserves his secret is unable to
check and control visible, external body language: physical gestures, signs,
movements, and symptoms will give his secret away. Ibn Hazm employs
kinetic images of two of the four natural elements in describing the lover's
revelation: "[it] will creep out into the open, like fire among coals or water
through dry clay."[52] The "burning flames, flowing water" perhaps symbolize
the disorder of the four bodily humors induced by love.[53]

Among the expressions used by Ibn Hazm to describe the eye is the
phrase "the self's well-polished mirror."[54] The eye reveals in two ways: eye
movements and the eye's tears. It is eye movements that disclose in the
aforementioned quotation. This juxtaposition of eye movements (revelation)
with the heart (concealment) is also found in romance.

Heart That Conceals and Eyes That Reveal

In the romance of *Majnun Layla,* a passage describing an initial meeting
between Majnun and Layla depicts her as openly flirting with other men by
conversing with them while ignoring Majnun. She does this deliberately
because she wants to gauge his feelings for her; in other words, she deliberately baits and tests him so as to discover whether he really feels love for her.
To know his inner, secret feelings, she has to pretend to conceal a secret from
him—so she is shown whispering a long secret to a rival male (*wa sarrathu
sirāran ṭawīlan*), then bidding this rival to leave, followed by a searching gaze
directed toward the seated Majnun.[55] Indeed, Majnun immediately reacts:
the color of his countenance changes.

Paradoxically, Layla uses secrets to uncover her lover's secrets. The contrasts and disparities between outward conduct and inner feelings are made
prominent in this anecdote. Outward behavior can be full of contrivances,
as is Layla's act of flirtation; apparent behavior can be deceptive. Yet, precisely because of these disparities between the outer and inner, precisely
because feelings and emotions belong to the self's inner realm, Layla is
shown as wanting to know these hidden feelings of her suitor, Majnun. This
scene reveals an important insight regarding the significance of secrecy in
love relations—Layla is shown as desiring to know her beloved, perhaps to
know him fully. She is depicted as wanting to know his hidden feelings,
moods, and consciousness—in other words, to know his secrets. In all relations, however, even love relations, there are limits to one's own ability to
know and, in a sense, possess the beloved other. Simmel too remarks on

this: "One can never know another person *absolutely,* which would involve knowledge of every single thought and mood. Nevertheless, one forms some personal unity out of those of his fragments in which alone he is accessible to us."[56]

Again what subverts this binary of the outer and inner is the body. The body's signs and gestures break down this binary of outer and inner as the body makes the secret public (Majnun's complexion changes). The role of the body's disclosures is further emphasized through what transpires next: after engaging in the pretense of whispering secrets and eliciting a reaction from Majnun, Layla then manages to have a private moment or two with him, during which she recites a verse to him. The romance presents two versions of her recitation. The first is

> In front of people, both of us appear
> to hate each other,
> and yet each is steadfast with his friend
> Our eyes tell us what we desire
> and in our hearts beats a latent love.[57]

The other version is

> In front of people, both of us appear
> to hate each other
> and yet each is entrenched with his friend
> The secrets of the glancer are not hidden
> when the eyes disclose what they conceal.[58]

Here again the juxtaposition of the organs is prominent. The heart is an organ that functions as a repository for guarding secrets, and the eyes are a means of disclosure. The eyes inform and disclose, and they do so through glances and other movements.

A pretense of antipathy, an outward behavior feigning loathing (that is, her whispering secrets to a rival and excluding Majnun), is juxtaposed against an inner emotion of love. The verses show how this posture of antipathy toward each other (concealment) that Layla speaks of (and enacts) is constantly being undercut by the sign language of the eyes (for example, glances of the eyes). Each verse is characterized by rhetoric of the secret (with the language of what is shown and hidden, revealed and concealed); each is replete with the vocabulary of secrecy and revelation.

Layla's secret recitation to Majnun, in turn, provokes a very public and physical display from him. Again, we have two different accounts of his reaction. The first is that "when he heard these verses, he moaned violently and fell into a swoon. He remained thus for a while, and they splashed water on his face until he regained consciousness."[59] According to the second account: "he fainted, and then he arose having lost his mind. [And then] he began to wear not[hing] . . . except rags and to walk [around] . . . naked."[60] The loss of control over senses, body, mind—all function as metaphors for revelation of the secret. He blatantly and publicly displays his secrets. Actually, moaning and swooning are among the bodily symptoms that are considered to define love. In Ibn Hazm's text, as in many of the Arabic medieval tracts on love, there is an entire chapter on the signs of love or outward manifestations of a hidden experience of love, and moaning and swooning are audible and visible somatic signs of love. Indeed, Majnun's rapturous loss of control (moaning, fainting, losing his mind) is rather climactic—a *petit-mort* in the sexual sense,[61] and so one is not surprised to find the symbolism of his nudity.

Signs of the Skin versus Heart's Secret: Emaciation and Wasting Away

Another popular metaphor for the secret's revelation in Arabic love literature is the emaciated, thinning body of the male lover. The entirety of the outer body—with the flesh falling away, pallid skin color, bony look—is deemed a sign of love and, therefore, the secret's disclosure. As remarked earlier, early Arabic writings on secrecy establish congruence between the integrity of the core self and the integrity of the physical outer body. One vivid example of this in the Arabo-Islamic encyclopedic literature is the following verse concerning how slanderers damage "one of sound skin" (*adīman ṣaḥīḥan*):

Do not disclose your secret except to yourself
For every confidant has a confidant
Indeed those that deceive people
Do not leave behind an unblemished surface.[62]

Found in three secrecy chapters in the sources of *'Uyun, 'Iqd,* and *Nihayat,* the verse implies that if one's secret is disclosed to another, the disclosure inevitably sullies one's reputation. In other words, disclosure of the core self's secrets is symbolized as a marring of the outer skin—a marring in the form of any mark, blemish, wound, or even cut of the skin (suggestive of the idea captured in the English phrase "marring of one's reputation"). The well-known Andalusian love poet Ibn Zaydun composed a verse that embraces this somatics of the secret or how the outer body reveals the inner secret:

By God, what harmed me was not my wasting away
Rather what harmed me is that through [this] wasting away, my secret was publicized
Were my affair—in the hiding of love—in my hand
The body would not have known what was in my heart.[63]

Here there is a juxtaposition of the outer skin versus the inner heart—the visible, outer, wasted away skin and body juxtaposed against the inner, concealed treasury of love's secrets, that is, the heart. Of course, the links between love and sickness as well as between love and malady have a long and rich history in Arabic literature, the antecedents for which in part are from Greek and Hellenistic sources.[64] However, what the lover laments is not his love sickness but rather that this sickness has—in the form of a wasted, thinning body—publicized his love. He implies that this disclosure is beyond his conscious control and declares that were this matter under his control, "The body would not have known what was in my heart." He clearly acknowledges that the secret's betrayal occurs through the physical body.[65]

In Ibn Hazm's love treatise there is an entire chapter entitled "Of Wasting Away." In it he discusses how a range of the lover's symptoms and signs concerning wasting away, such as keeping the head cast down, groaning, facial complexion and color, and staring eyes, offer "visible evidence of his miserable condition."[66] "Wasting away" (*al-ḍana*), according to Ibn Hazm, is a sign of unrequited love or of some deprivation in love; he considers it the necessary consequence of somehow being barred from union with one's beloved. Relevant here is the mention of the related metaphor of the grieving, invisible lover also found in Arabic love literature —that is, "the lover is said to be wasted by grief, to such a point that he vanishes."[67]

Corporeal metaphors such as weeping eyes, wasted bodies, leaking skins, and the like all represent the secret's disclosure, that is, love's revelation. In the romance of *Majnun Layla,* one finds verse in which equivalence is established between the two metaphors of tearing eyes and wasted body. Majnun proclaims:

> No troop of genies possesses him, they say [about me], nor any touch of
>   madness,
> save the lies that he invents.
> My eye's tear is the evidence of my passion
> [and] love for her is wasting away the flesh from my bone.[68]

Both metaphors, the "eye's tear" and the wasting away of the flesh, are love's evidence; both are the outer body's display of the secret. Also from *Majnun Layla* is the following:

> The memory of her has worn away the flesh and then my bones,
> like a chisel which carves a piece of wood to make an arrow.[69]

The essential point is that the embodied self both keeps and gives the secret away. The site for secrecy's retention and release, fundamentally, is the body, as 'Umar ibn Abi Rabi'a declares:

Love for you, O Layla's folk, is my slayer
[It's] through my body that love's revelation and concealment occur
No love is there more supreme than my love for you
Save slaying myself or going mad.[70]

Body Secretions

Repeatedly in Arabic writings on secrecy one comes across the idea of a congruence or correspondence between the integrity of the core self and integrity of the physical body. Preserving the secrets of the inner core self is akin to preserving the wholeness and soundness of the physical outer body. This correspondence has yielded other important parallels and links—for example, the link between the secret as liquid content of a vessel, on the one hand, and the inner liquid content of the body, on the other hand. Indeed, the flowing of bodily liquids and secretions in general, secretions such as tears, saliva, and semen, functions as a metaphor for the secret's revelation. An important dimension of this is the special "inside-out" quality of the flowing secretion or liquid; the flowing of secretions crosses the boundaries of the body, and moreover, tears flow from the inside of ducts to the outside of the face, and blood flows from the inside of an artery or vein to the surface of the skin. This "crossing over" of the inner-outer boundary of the body lends a certain power to the function of secretions as metaphors for the secret's revelation.

As already mentioned, the eye—an organ of secretion—is an important organ of revelation in Arabic literature. That love's revelation is conveyed through the metaphor of the tearing eyes is commonplace in Arabic literature. Many examples exist in *The Ring of the Dove;* Ibn Hazm remarks in his chapter on "The Signs of Love" that "Weeping is a well-known sign of Love," and on the same page he has a poem on this:[71]

For when the man by love possessed
Conceals the secret of his breast
His tears the guarded truth betray
And bare it to the light of day.

The juxtaposition of the eye versus the breast is intensified through the imagery of the eye's secretions, that is, tears. The concept of the secret's betrayal occurring through the outer body's signs, symptoms, and gestures (here, the outer eye's flowing secretions) is assimilated with the concept of love's signs and symptoms. Love, the secret par excellence, is revealed by the external body.

Besides tears, other bodily secretions and liquids that are associated with the secret's revelation in *The Ring of the Dove* are saliva and blood. In the chapter entitled "Of Correspondence," Ibn Hazm is concerned with the exchange of epistles between lover and beloved. After noting that "the letter is sometimes the lover's tongue,"[72] he observes that for the lover to know that the letter has been delivered to his beloved, and is being held in her hands, brings much pleasure to the lover, for it "is a consoling substitute for an actual sight of the object of his affection."[73] It seems that the reverse is also true: receiving a letter from the beloved and "gazing fondly upon it, delights him fully as much as a lovers' meeting."[74] What is interesting here is how material objects, such as the letter—given that they are part of an intimate courtship exchange between lover and beloved—acquire a corporeal significance. Symbolically they are transformed into bodily parts of the lover that the receiving party can see, touch, smell, and hold. Also, these objects-*cum*-bodily-parts function as the tokens of the lover's inner secret; they function as visible, tactile evidence of the lover's concealed and inaccessible self. Again, it is no coincidence that the organs that are analogized with the secret are mainly organs that secrete, such as the eyes (secrete tears), the tongue (secretes saliva), or the skin or epidermis (secretes perspiration). The imagery of tears and saliva is present in the following excerpt from Ibn Hazm's treatise: "As for the watering the ink of the love-letter with one's tears, I know of a man who did this regularly, and his beloved repaid him by watering the ink of her missives with her saliva."[75] Associations between the flowing of blood and the secret's revelation are especially strong in Arabic writings on secrecy. Blood is not a secretion, ut it is the vital inner liquid of the body. In the following excerpt by Ibn Hazm, blood symbolism powerfully renders the letter as visible, tactile evidence of the lover's inner secret and self: "I once saw a letter written by a lover to his beloved: he had cut his hand with a knife, and as the blood gushed forth he used it for ink, and wrote the entire letter with it. I saw the same letter after the blood had dried, and would have sworn that it was written with a tincture of resin."[76]

As seen, Arabic writings on secrecy construct a link between the secret as content of a vessel and blood as content of the body. The dictum "your secret is of your blood" is found in many secrecy chapters in Arabo-Islamic encyclopedias, and it evokes the meaning of "secret" as precious internal property of the core self. Just as blood is the precious biological source and sustainer of one's body, likewise the secret is a precious psychological support to and sustainer of one's core self.

In these love epistles, the symbolism of bodily secretions and liquids—whether in the form of saliva, tears, or blood—is the somatic expression of the emotions and inner worlds of those who are secretly or covertly exchanging these letters. They are the love content of the body. The revelatory and affective significance of the letters marked by these secretions is intensified through their physical or material contact with the bodily fluids. Furthermore, the give-and-take of these items bearing the secretions of the lovers (for example, saliva) is substitutive of the possibly prohibited contact between the lovers. Clearly, these revelations are not unintentional; in other words, they are not revelations against the will of the secret-holder. In a chapter entitled "Of Contentment," we witness the use of secretions in yet another context of exchange between lovers—that of gift giving. Ibn Hazm describes the practice and then offers a little verse on the matter:

> As for exchanging chewed toothpicks, or masticate after it has been used,
> that is a frequent practice of lovers who have been barred from meeting.
> I have a little poem to the point:[77]
> Her spittle, as I verily
> Believe, is Life's own fount to me . . .

That the exchange of "chewed toothpicks" is a ritual often resorted to by "lovers who have been barred from meeting" suggests again that the give-and-take of items bearing these secretions (for example, saliva) is substitutive of the prohibited contact between the lovers; hence, the exchanged items acquire a distinctly erotic-sexual significance.

The symbolism of bodily liquids and secretions such as tears, blood, and saliva occurring in these contexts of intimate exchange can also function as a disguise for genital secretions. It should be recalled that encoded in the very etymology of the Arabic word for "secret," *sirr*, is the connection between secrecy and the genital organs. What Freud has observed regarding secretions in the context of dream symbolism may also be relevant to the literary sphere: "The genitals can also be represented in dreams by other parts of the body: the male organ by a hand or a foot and the female genital orifice by the mouth or an ear or even an eye. The secretions of the human body—mucus, tears, urine, semen, etc.—can replace one another in dreams . . . what in fact happens is that significant secretions, such as semen, are replaced by indifferent ones."[78]

Arabic writers and Freud consider the secret to be irrepressible. Both suggest that there are connections between secrecy and the unconscious. Both often couch the revelation of the secret in terms of corporeal expressions. At the very least, Freud was implying that somatic secretions and the revelation of the secret are linked—a link that is clearly represented in early Arabic love literature. How the presence of bodily secretions such as blood and other fluids works as a disguise for sexual secretions is evident in the following excerpt from one of the tenth-century 'Udhri romances, *Kuthayyir 'Azza:*

> Kuthayyir (the lover) said: I went for pilgrimage one year, as did
> 'Azza's husband with her. No one from [among] us was aware of his
> companion's [presence]. On the way, her husband commanded her

to purchase butter with which to prepare food for the folk of his traveling entourage. She began to go around the tents, tent by tent, until she came to me not knowing it was my tent. I was making arrows. When I saw her, I kept cutting, while I was gazing at her, distractedly until I cut my [flesh down to the] bones several times. I did not feel anything [even though] my blood was flowing. When that became obvious, she came to me and gripped my hand and began to wipe the blood off it with her gown. I had a churn of butter and I made her swear to take it. So she took it and brought the butter to her husband. When he saw the blood, he asked her for information concerning it and she concealed it, until he swore she must tell him the truth and so she did. Then he hit her and swore that she must revile me to my face. So she stopped before me, having him with her, and said to me, weeping: "O son of a whore" and then they left.[79]

Kuthayyir's gaze at the beloved 'Azza causes him to wound himself.[80] Here, through the lover's gazing at his beloved, he wounds or cuts himself, and because he is so smitten with his beloved, he continues to inflict a wound on himself as his gaze remains fixed on her. Kuthayyir's flowing blood here acts as a metaphor for his love's revelation, but the other secret in this passage is the bloodstain that his beloved 'Azza tries to conceal. 'Azza stains her gown with Kuthayyir's blood because, while he is oblivious to his wound, she is not, and in trying to stem the flow of blood and wipe it, she stains her gown. It is Kuthayyir's hand that she grips in wiping the blood, and if, in keeping with Freud's observation, the male organ can be symbolized by a hand or a foot, the lover's blood may function as a disguise for semen. The bloodstain could also symbolize the loss of her virginity. In either case, we see why she tries to hide the bloodstain from her husband. The husband reacts to the bloodstain thus: he asks his wife to explain its presence, and she in turn conceals the stain until he forces her to talk and tell him the truth. The lover's blood literally mars the beloved's chastity, signified by the bloodstain on 'Azza's gown. That the garment, her gown, is stained is important: by staining the gown that clothes and conceals her body, he marks and mars her body.

Female secrecy is exposed through the male lover's revelation. The bloodstain becomes the emblem of her unchastity, and the narrative relates that when her husband asks her to explain its presence and she conceals it (that is, the account of her interaction with Kuthayyir) until he forces her to talk and tell him the truth. In one of the epistle exchanges earlier quoted, a lover also is portrayed as having cut his hand (read: phallus) with a knife (just as Kuthayyir is depicted here) and of using the blood from his wound as ink for his letter to the beloved.

In a passage from the love story of *Majnun Layla,* as in the aforementioned quotation, there exists the role of a symbolic commodity (butter,[81] or
samn) in the triangulated exchanges:

> I said to Qays ibn al-Mulawwah before he went mad: What is the most
> wondrous of things that has struck you in your passion for Layla? He
> said: Guests stayed with us [one] night and we did not have anything to
> eat. So my father sent me to Layla's father's abode, saying to me: Ask of
> him for food. I went to him and stood [outside] his tent and called out
> to him. He said: What do you want? I said: We have guests with us
> tonight but we have no food, so my father sent me to ask you for some
> fare. He said: Layla, get out for him that churn and fill his vessel with
> butter. She took it out, and I had with me a wooden cup, and then she
> began to pour the butter in it while we conversed. The conversation
> distracted us while she poured the butter. The cup became full and we
> did not realize it, and the butter flowed until our legs were [immersed]
> in [a pool of] butter.[82]

Here the connection between the flow of butter and the flow of conversation
(that is, an exchange of secrets between the two lovers) is unmistakable—
again, the flow of a fluid acts as a metaphor for revelation and exchange of
the lovers' secrets. Apposite here is the mention that the Arabic word for "to
pour," *ṣabba,* used in this passage also means "to love another one," and
ṣabbun means both "pouring of a liquid" and "loving another." It could be
argued that the imagery of butter here has a symbolic connection with a
genital secretion—perhaps with semen. However, this is partly disguised
through the association of the vessel, or "wooden cup" (the Arabic is *qaʿb,*
and here I am reminded of al-Jahiz's use of "vessel" symbolism), with Majnun, the male lover, and the act of pouring with Layla, the female beloved.
Although it is not entirely clear which genital secretion (female or male)
is associated with which fluid (butter, blood, tears, or saliva) in these
exchanges, that the latter are functioning as symbolic disguises for genital
secretions seems certain. The second half of this narrative, which parallels
the first part, constructs a scene in which fire and the nudity of the lover's
body act as metaphors for revelation in language. An excerpt of the anecdote
reads: "[Majnun] said: I arrived at [Layla's father's home] a second night
seeking fire while wrapped in a cloak of mine. She [Layla] brought out fire
in a rag for me and gave it to me and we stood there conversing. When the
rag burned out, I tore a piece of my cloak and lit it instead. When this
burned out, I tore another [from my cloak] and kindled the fire with it [and
this continued] until there did not remain [anything] of the cloak on me
save what concealed my genitals. I had no sense of what I was doing."[83]

Night and light, female secrecy and male revelation—these are made prominent in this scene. The exchange of words (language) between the lovers is
made simultaneous with the burning of fire as well as with the denuding of
the male lover's body.[84] Burning of fire and barring of body here act as
metaphors for love's revelation. The burning of the cloak is suggestive of the
stripping or falling away of his outer bodily organ, that is, his skin, and the
baring of his outer body acts as a metaphor for the secret's revelation. Eventually Majnun is left naked save what covers his sexual organs. The fact that
only the latter remain concealed further draws attention to his nudity, but
again, his indiscretion, that is, his self-revelation and loss of control, ultimately exposes and destroy female secrecy. Layla is both the spark that
ignites his desire and the night that is unveiled by his passion.

Conclusion

In early Arabic love literature, especially 'Udhri romances such as *Majnun
Layla,* self and subjectivity are marked by secrecy and revelation. At times
secrecy is deployed because it confers protection on what it keeps. Sometimes
it is deployed because it conceals a sexual taboo. Another key reason that
secrecy is deployed is because, at times, preciousness inheres in its contents
(for example, love and intimacy) and secrecy confers (added) value on these
contents. A. C. Spearing claims in *The Medieval Poet as Voyeur* that there
exists a "preciousness that comes from shared secrecy itself."[85] He argues that
"instead of secrecy between lovers being the consequence of externally posed
barriers, such as the disapproval of parents or surveillance by a jealous husband or wife, it may even be the other way around: external barriers 'have to
be imagined in order to make secrecy necessary and thus to make a specially
intense kind of private experience possible.' "[86]

Secrecy is deployed in these romances chiefly for rhetorical reasons; it is
precisely because it invites or generates revelation. A defining trait of secrecy
paradoxically is that it is always accompanied by revelation. This trait is also
found in the Qur'an and early Arabo-Islamic ethical and didactic texts such
as *Kitman.* This inextricability of secrecy and revelations, in turn, generates
its own paradoxes that constitute the trope of the secret in early Arabic love
literature—paradoxes embracing motifs regarding self, subjectivity, body,
and gender relations. One such paradox is how love is defined as both expression and suppression. Another is the paradox of how a true love is defined as
a secret love and yet all the legendary lovers in early Arabic literature are
those who speak about their love. Another is the enigma of how the body
inevitably reveals what the owner of a secret desires to conceal. Michel Foucault, in his *History of Sexuality,* makes the following remark: "What is peculiar to modern societies, in fact, is not that they consigned sex to a shadow
existence, but that they dedicated themselves to speaking of it *ad infinitum,*

while exploiting it as *the* secret."[87] From this observation, what is of relevance to the early Arabic romances and other love-related genres under examination is his point that love and sex are constituted as "*the* secret" only to allow their disclosure as secret. Yet, with the establishment of Islam in the late seventh century came ensuing social changes in courtship, marriage, notions of female chastity, and gender relations that rendered this disclosure of love and sex as "*the* secret" increasingly unacceptable. In pre-Islamic Arabia it was acceptable for a man to serenade and publicize a female beloved through verse as well as to boast of one's love adventures, but with the arrival and spread of norms and values associated with Islam, this became suspect.

※ ※

5.

Toward a Literary Archaeology of the Private and the Secret

Among the worst of people in the eyes of God on the Day of Judgment is the man who communicates a secret to his wife and she communicates a secret to him, and then he divulges and publicizes her secret.

Hadith from Sahih Muslim

In his book *Forbidding Wrong in Islam,* Michael Cook observes that "history relates that in early tenth-century Baghdad the Hanbalites would challenge men and women seen walking together in public; if they did not get a satisfactory answer, they would beat the offender and hand him over to the chief of police."[1] Couples out in public who "looked as if they might be unmarried" were prime candidates for being accused of wrongdoing.[2] Indeed, our tenth-century Arabic love literature sources suggest that the very existence, not to mention the privacy, of the heterosexual, unmarried couple *as couple* is challenged. The romance considered in this chapter, that of *Majnun Layla* (like the entire 'Udhri corpus of romances), is thought by some scholars to originate in the Umayyad age in the late seventh and early eighth centuries. The pseudobiographical material on the main character of the romance, Majnun, suggests that to the extent that he is a historical character, he is a famous early Arab poet and tribal nobleman named Qays bin al-Mulawwah born in the Hijazi region of the Arabian Peninsula during the latter half of the seventh century.[3] However, it is important to note that the renditions examined in this chapter are from the tenth-century work *Kitab al-Aghani,* or *Book of Songs,* by the Baghdadi courtier Abu al-Faraj al-Isfahani.

    In part, the tensions and strains associated with the privacy of the couple appear to be a function of the 'Udhri literature's portrayal of changing norms regarding marriage, courtship, gender relations, and love as early Arab society slowly made the transition from a pre-Islamic to a nascent Islamic ethos.

Susan Crane regards romance as "the medieval genre in which virginity, courtship, marriage, lineal concerns, primogeniture, and sexual maturation are most fully at issue."[4] In the 'Udhri stories, there are tensions between two different systems of conjugality that bear certain similarities to those identified by W. Robertson Smith in his landmark study *Kinship and Marriage in Early Arabia.*[5] For instance, in the *Majnun Layla* romance, the bond between beloved and lover is nonconjugal, but aspects of it seem similar to a type of semiconjugal, amorous relation that Smith claims existed in ancient Arabia. In pre-Islamic Arabia, what was considered extramatrimonial was simply not established, primarily because, as both Smith and Gertrude Stern have argued, matrimony was not standardized. In other words, the 'Udhri romances delineate tensions between a then newly institutionalized form of matrimony, on the one hand, and, on the other hand, the vestiges of another, far less fixed and defined, older form of conjugal relation, variously identified by Smith as *ṣadīqa* or *mut'a*.

W. Robertson Smith maintains that early pre-Islamic Arab conceptions and practices of marriage were characterized by variety and flexibility. Among the Arabs, the meanings of the term *marriage* (*nikāḥ*) include "the large class of cases in which a woman only received occasional visits from the man on whom she had fixed her affections."[6] He links this class with *ṣadīqa* (another term for them is *mut'a* or *mot'a*) marriages, one of two types of marriage identified by him. According to Smith, *ṣadīqa* marriages had a different, looser standard of chastity than the second type, dubbed by him as "marriages of dominion."[7] Apparently *ṣadīqa*-type marriages eventually disappeared with the establishment of Islam (late seventh and early eighth centuries), and "marriages of dominion" came to replace them in the new Islamic ethos. Smith maintains that though Islam gave certain freedoms to women, it allowed for the establishment of this latter type of marriage, a type that ultimately limited women's liberties far more than the older *ṣadīqa* type did: "[In the marriage of dominion], the wife who follows her husband and bears children who are of his blood has lost the right freely to dispose of her own person; her husband has authority over her and he alone has the right of divorce. Accordingly the husband in this kind of marriage is called, not in Arabia only, but also among the Hebrews and Aramaeans, the woman's 'lord' or 'owner' (*ba'l, ba'al*)."[8] He declares that "wherever this name for husband [*ba'al*] is found we may be sure that marriage is of the second type, with male kinship, and the wife bound to her husband and following him to his home."[9] Smith implies that, in pre-Islamic Arabia, the *mot'a* semiconjugal relation was not illicit and that it was publicized in verse. Consider the following passage from Smith's well-known ethnography:

> This is the case which is so constantly described in Arabic poetry; the
> singer visits his beloved (who may often be a married woman) by stealth

and often she belongs to a hostile tribe. It is usually assumed that such relations were simply illicit, and that the poets boast of them as in all ages poets have boasted of guilty amours. But it must be noted that though the lover ran a risk in seeking to approach his beloved, the relation was generally a matter of notoriety, openly celebrated in verse, and brought no disgrace or punishment on the woman . . . indeed the secrecy which a man is obliged to observe in approaching his mistress is a mere matter of etiquette, his visits being really quite well known . . . the kind of relation which the Arab poets are never weary of describing fell under the category of *mot'a*.[10]

However, in our tenth-century literary evidence, as represented by the 'Udhri romances, emerging Islamic norms deemed this kind of heterosexual relation and its flexible standards of chastity suspect and even illicit, and moreover, they deemed their disclosure in poetry as socially taboo. In light of this, I am led to consider the possibility that in the *Majnun Layla* romance (and other 'Udhri romances), a kind of *mut'a* or *ṣadīqa* tie is juxtaposed against a *ba'al* marriage or "marriage of dominion."

Kernels of sociohistorical realities, therefore, are discernible behind the themes of indiscretion that play a big role in the 'Udhri romances under consideration. No doubt it is not easy to discern these, because, as Andras Hamori rightly observes, "the poets of 'Udhri love are shadowy characters, their biographies full of conventional narrative motifs. It seems quite impossible to separate history from fiction."[11] To make matters more complicated, the 'Udhri romances, in all likelihood, are "the romantic creation of the early 'Abbasid age, projected backwards in history at a time when biographies of Bedouin poet-lovers were a popular form of entertainment literature in Baghdad."[12] In a sense then, these romances are twice removed from history. Yet, that they are so consistently characterized by depictions of "love gone awry" suggests that there are social dimensions to these portrayals.

I tend toward a paradigm in this chapter that explains and examines representations of privacy and secrecy in Arabic love literature in terms of social realities and practices. In scholarly work on European courtly love literature, two paradigms exist for the study of secrecy. Some critics have argued that there are social realities behind the secret and that an approach that ties secrecy's literary conventions to social practices is the most defensible.[13] The other paradigm reflects a shift toward understanding and explaining secrecy not in terms of social realities or practices but rather in terms of psycho-literary factors. A. C. Spearing, in *The Medieval Poet as Voyeur*, comes closest to expressing the views prevalent in this second paradigm—a paradigm that influences my analysis.[14] In this chapter, while I privilege the paradigm holding that there are social realities behind the secret, I also pay attention to how, in certain textual exempla, both these aforementioned paradigms are applicable to the material at hand, namely the poetry and prose of the 'Udhri romances.

Conceptualizing the Private and the Secret

To paraphrase and modify somewhat Danielle Regnier-Bohler's remarks in her chapter on "Imagining the Self" in George Duby's work on private life, I turn to early Arabic love literature and employ it "as evidence in a 'literary archaeology of the private and the secret.'"[15] The vocabulary of both privacy and secrecy is relevant to our study of Arabic love literature.[16] What differentiates privacy from secrecy? Not all that is private is secret, whereas that which is secret is necessarily private. Secrecy and privacy may overlap, as pointed out by Sissela Bok: "Privacy and secrecy overlap whenever the efforts at such control rely on hiding. But privacy need not hide; and secrecy hides far more than what is private. A private garden need not be a secret garden; a private life is rarely a secret life."[17]

What is prominent in the definition of privacy is the issue of unwanted access. Bok writes that privacy is "the condition of being protected from unwanted access by others—either physical access, personal information, or attention. Claims to privacy are claims to control access to what one takes . . . to be one's own personal domain."[18] Certainly, the notions of privacy as a condition or the right or claim to privacy have a modern, primarily Western ring to them. Yet, Bok's point that "privacy need not hide; and secrecy hides far more than what is private" is relevant to early Arabic love literature. Moreover her use of vocabulary such as "access" and "domain" points to how conceptions of privacy have physical spatial dimensions, and in early Arabic love literature, too, the private as it is imagined, interrogated, and depicted is not without spatial dimensions. As we shall see, inaccessibility is not defined just in terms of physical space, but in Bok's definition of privacy, notions of personal space and territoriality play a large role: "To be sure, the boundaries of this space are differently envisaged according to culture and personality and imagination; but recent work in the social sciences shows that most individuals do conceive of certain near-physical boundaries enclosing their bodies, some of the space immediately surrounding them, and at times certain objects and living beings."[19]

Early Arabic love literature is characterized by the symbolism of public and private spheres, but these spheres are defined not so much by their spatial dimensions (for example, whether they are open, guarded, or enclosed) as by the extent to which they are peopled or not. In other words, privacy is not defined by territorial spheres but rather in terms of domains that are peopled or vacant or anything in between. Hence, issues of uninvited and/or intrusive access do loom large: To what degree are there unwanted gazes or looks? To what extent is one's speech overheard? To what extent is one alone? To the extent that domestic spheres are where one's own kin, especially one's female kin, dwell, they are rendered private spheres because the issue of intrusiveness does not arise. Conversely, that which is public consists of spheres and/or spaces that are filled with people (*al-nās*) who are strangers or nonkin—spheres in which inevitably one talks and gossips, one is talked to and gossiped about, one sees and is seen, and one hears and is (over)heard, for example. What is most salient to these configurations of public and private are behaviors deemed outside of Islamic law—including illicit or even improper sexual behaviors.

Talal Asad has observed that a study of boundaries and rights in Islamic law suggests that there are no spheres of private and public; rather, what is pertinent, according to him, is the "need to explore the different configurations of behaviour: legally mandatory, approved, legally indifferent, disapproved or legally prohibited."[20] This resonates with Michael Cook's claim that there was no notion, in early Islam, "that certain kinds of behaviour are inherently private, and as such immune to public scrutiny."[21] Cook discusses this claim in relation to the individual Muslim's duty of "commanding right and forbidding wrong" (*al-amr bi'l-maʿrūf wa'l-nahy ʿan al-munkar*).[22] Insofar as our very definition of spheres of private and public rests on the degree to which they are peopled, what Cook and Asad have to say is relevant to our sources because, after all, one cannot have people without behaviors or vice versa. It could be said that the ʿUdhri corpus of romances exemplifies the hazards and problems associated with behaviors that came to be deemed socially "disapproved or legally prohibited." In other words the ʿUdhri corpus of romances exemplifies the hazards and problems associated with secrecy's opposites: slander, indiscretion, scandal, notoriety, and infamy. It is tenable to view them as examples of literature about socially and legally unacceptable behavior according to rising Islamic norms—irrespective of whether we associate these norms with the presumably late seventh-century literary context of the romances and/or the tenth-century compilation of the romances. Early ʿAbbasid culture and literature consecrated the main characters of these romances as legendary poets and lovers, and yet, legendary though they may be, they also exemplify the dangers and problems inherent in legally and socially unacceptable conduct and behavior. Within the literary context of these romances, tese poets acquired fame but lived on the margins of society.

A question posed by A. C. Spearing, "how does private *become* public?," bears a certain utility for this chapter: the modes by which the private becomes public actually help us to delineate what was deemed worthy of being kept private and secret. Hence, this question can be employed as a springboard for constructing a literary archaeology of the private and secret

in the 'Udhri romances.[23] For Spearing, a critic of early European love literature, the private regarding love life in medieval European narratives was
made public through looking: "the private becomes public by being seen,
and it can be seen because of the gaps in the boundaries between the two
spheres [private and public]."[24] By contrast, in Arabic love narratives it is
primarily through talk and gossip and its counterpart, listening and/or (over-
)hearing, that the private becomes public. Speech and sound are integral to
how private becomes public. This is especially relevant to the 'Udhri
romances, wherein it is through the recitation and circulation of mainly
poetry and news reports (*khabar*) that private becomes public. The main
characters in these romances are poets, and therefore, recited and performed
poetry is essential in how issues of secrecy and privacy play out in them.
Hence the private becomes public through the circulation of poetic language
as well as through talk and gossip, through eavesdropping. It also becomes
public through the disclosures made by subordinates and servants. The presence of imagery of day and night, light and darkness contribute to how
seeing, looking, or spying aided the private in becoming public. Moreover
gender dimensions are pronounced in how the private and the secret regarding love and romance were made public. Almost consistently, women are
paired with concealment and men with revelation. Perhaps this is because
women were considered private property or as possessions. Yet, in addition
to being kept as secrets, women also kept secrets.

As suggested, it is impossible to assess the meanings of secrecy and privacy in Arabic love literature without first recognizing the prominence of
gossip or, to borrow Bok's terminology, "speech networks" in it. The question then becomes: just how does private *become* public in the 'Udhri
romances (especially the love story of *Majnun Layla*)?

The Private Becomes Public through Gossip

The symbolism of gossipmongers and rumor mills looms large in Arabic love
literature. The antecedents for this are to be found in the pre-Islamic love
prelude (*nasīb*), in which one often finds images of gossip networks that
trade personal information. These networks appear to have multiple functions: relaying information, entertainment, facilitating social rituals, and
offering avenues of personal advancement, among others. Talk in the form
of the spoken word is almost everything and everywhere in Arabic love
literature—talk that courts, informs, maligns, praises, advertises, bemoans,
boasts, curries favor, and so forth. The literary texts alert us to the presence
of informal and formal agents of communication and performance whose
stock and trade are the spoken word; there is the presence of poets, gossips,
singers, publicists, narrators, preachers, and others.

Gossip would be one such form of communication or "speech network" referred to above. From a modern theoretical perspective, Bok argues that it would be reductionist to summarily dismiss gossip as being only negative— "cheap, superficial, intrusive, unfounded, even vicious."[25] According to her, it can be all of this, but to limit its semantics to only this would "be to overlook the whole network of human exchanges of information, the need to inquire and to learn from the experience of others, and the importance of not taking everything at face value."[26] Her definition of "gossip" can be employed as "informal personal communication about other people who are absent or treated as absent."[27] Furthermore, Bok offers a three-part classification of harmful gossip: "gossip in breach of confidence, gossip the speaker knows to be false, and unduly invasive gossip."[28] The third category, unduly invasive gossip, is relevant to the several poems discussed below.

Pre-Islamic Ode: Motifs of Gossip in the Love Prelude

The pre-Islamic Arabic ode's love prelude often contains images of gossip networks that trade personal information concerning matters of conjugal and sexual intimacy. Frequently the imagery involving such networks constructs an opposition between the "couple" and the external social group. In the lines from poems below, there are gender dimensions to concealment and discretion: it is with the females that they are associated. The first two poems are by the pre-Islamic poet 'Alqamah b. 'Abadah and are found in the renowned eighth-century anthology entitled *The Mufaddaliyat*.

A heart quick to thrill when touched by Beauty has drawn thee far, although Youth has sped long since, and grey hairs invade thy brow

It fills all my thought with Laila, distant though now her home, and matters of weight stand twixt us, obstacles manifold.

In comfort she dwells—no speech with her is for me to gain: a guard waits before her door, forbidding all visitors.

When as forth her husband fares, no secret of his she tells; and when he again comes home, yea, sweet is his home-coming.

But what boots the thought of her to thee who are so far away? the well where she draws is dug to serve her in Tharmada

Nay, deem me not scant of wit, untaught in Love's Mysteries. . . .[29]

In this first poem, speech or conversation with the beloved is equated with access to her, and the poet realizes that this will not be possible because of the guard waiting before her doors. The barrier of the guard is but one of the obstacles and hindrances to his imagining a meeting with the beloved. Another is that of the conjugal bond: his beloved is now a wife, and "no secret of his [her husband] she tells" while he is away. We note that this motif highlights how gossip or talk is conceived of that which transgresses, in Spearing's words, the "preciousness that comes from shared secrecy [of an intimate bond]."[30] Here, the bond is the marriage between husband and wife, and talk is conceived of as conversation with one, outside of the bond, about an absent spouse. In other words, the mention of the husband being away is central to this motif of gossip and slander: especially during his absence, she does not betray her conjugal bond through talking with other men, for such talk or conversation would be perceived as scandalous and a betrayal of her husband's secrets. The association of secrecy with the marital bond lends an intensity to it: because she tells no secret of his, when he again comes home, "yea, sweet is his home-coming." Both motifs, that of gossip and that of external guards, interlock with one another in this poem.

In another of 'Alqamah's odes, there is no explicit reference to gossip or guards, and yet the motif of gossip seems to be implied in the poet's ruminations concerning whether his beloved Salma has kept their love bond hidden from others. A modern translation is employed here:

> Is what you came to know,
> given in trust,
> kept secret? Is her bond to you
> broken, now that she is far?
> Does a grown man weeping
> tears without end for those he loved,
> the dawn of parting,
> receive his fair reward?[31]

The love prelude begins with the mention of the secrecy of the love between the poet and the beloved. The poet wonders whether she can preserve this secrecy now that they are apart. Secrecy and the preciousness of the love relation are equated. Again, what Spearing recognizes as a "preciousness that comes from shared secrecy itself" is relevant to 'Alqamah's evocation of this secret love.[32] In another pre-Islamic ode's love prelude, we again discern the motif of gossip:

> . . . And women white like the moon or statues stately to see,
>   that softly carry around great cups filled full with wine—
>
> White women, dainty, that shoot the hearts of men [with their eyes], fair as
>   a nest full of ostrich eggs betwixt rock and sand.
>
> Kind words they speak, and their limbs are soft and smooth to the touch,
>   their faces right, and their hearts to lovers gentle and mild.

> Low speech they murmur, in tones that bear no secrets abroad;
> they gain their ends without toil, and need no shouting to win.[33]

Traditional pre-Islamic imagery is employed to describe the women (for example, "white like the moon," "fair as a nest full of ostrich eggs"). Discretion here is linked with desirable, socially constructed feminine traits—the women are characterized by softness, kindness, and discretion and thus "gain their ends without toil." They speak in "low" voices; they do not engage in loud or shouting tones—in other words, they do not speak in a manner that allows the private and secret in their lives to be heard or overheard, and hence, they "bear no secrets abroad."

In the following poem by al-A'sha, we have an example of a different kind of pairing between women and discretion. Here, the motif of gossip embraces the ideal of the woman who will not seek other people's secrets rather than one who will not reveal secrets:

> She's not one of those
> whose neighbors hate to see her face.
> You won't find her,
> ear to their secrets, listening.[34]

It is through overhearing or listening that the private and the secret are represented as potentially becoming public. The presence of these motifs and themes of gossip, talebearers, guards, and barriers aids setting up a dichotomy of the couple versus the larger social group.[35] Frequently women are shown as protecting the secrecy of the couple, whereas men are depicted as undoing this discretion, as revealing this secrecy whether it is through their speech, bodily gestures, or actions. The couple's secrecy is constantly being transgressed by the males and upheld by the females.

Motifs of Gossip in the 'Udhri Romances
Recall that the main characters in these romances are poets and that the role of recited and performed poetry is pivotal to understanding the meanings of secrecy and privacy in them. Indeed, the dichotomies of private versus public were collapsed in the performance and reception/circulation of 'Udhri poetry: this poetry purported to be about matters deemed private and secret (emotions, trysts, love relations, female beloveds, among others), but it was intended for general, public consumption and was consumed on a large scale. What is noteworthy is that the private and secret become public through what is heard. The following excerpt from the tenth-century *Kitab al-Aghani* version of the romance of *Qays Lubna* illustrates all this. It also provides a good example of how the genre of the 'Udhri romances has embedded in it kernels of sociohistorical realities: for example, the connection between recited poetry and the music scene in the urban center of

Medina during the Umayyad period, with the mention of the names of actual historically prominent singers and musicians such as al-Gharid, Ma'bad, and Malik. These musicians are depicted as singing Qays's poems at public performances; these love songs are the 'Udhri poems of Qays set to music:

> Qays's affair acquired fame in Medina and al-Gharid, Ma'bad,
> Malik and their cohorts sang his poems. There remained no noble or
> commoner who did not hear this [music]. [Then Lubna's] husband
> went to her and reprehended her concerning this and said: You have
> scandalized me with your notoriety. She became angry and declared:
> Listen! By God, I did not marry you out of love nor for what you have,
> and nor have you been deceived by my situation. . . . He refrained from
> replying to her and [instead], to placate her, he began to bring to her
> singing-girls from the city that sang Qays's poetry before her. Yet, this
> only increased her misery and she did not cease weeping hot tears when
> she heard something of that [song].[36]

This anecdote suggests that through the recitation and circulation of primarily poetry and news reports (*khabar*) in public places and gatherings in the city of Medina, the private becomes public. Poetry had a large circulation because of its connections with music. In any case, these love songs were immensely popular and heard by people of various social ranks and classes, ranging from the elite to the general public. Importantly, the link between sung 'Udhri poetry, on one hand, and gossip and public scandal, on the other hand, is made prominent in Lubna's husband's angry complaint to her: "[He] reprehended her concerning [the fame of Qays's songs] and said: You have scandalized me with your notoriety." That Lubna's name and aspects of her love relation with Qays have become part of public networks of entertainment causes problems for her spouse. Although he reproves his wife for "permitting" her name to be bandied about, it is likely that Lubna's husband married her as a consequence of her fame and star status as Qays's beloved—a status achieved through previous "songs" and poems about Lubna publicly circulated and celebrated among their respective tribes and others. Private homes were another locus for the performances of these songs, as depicted in the example of Lubna's husband inviting singing girls to sing Qays's poems at their encampment in order to mollify her. Perhaps this indicates that the performance of these "songs" and poems was socially acceptable in a home but not in public places. Lubna's "weeping hot tears when she heard" Qays's songs about her is suggestive of her pleasure—albeit bittersweet—in hearing these words describing her. Hence, in the 'Udhri romances, though the female beloved / wife is often depicted as being deeply pained and angered by the poet-lover's revelation of his desire for her, she also enjoys and benfits from the publicity her name acquires as a consequence of the spread of love poetry about her. In fact, as we saw in the previous chapter, Ibn Hazm, in his famous eleventh-century love treatise *The Ring of the Dove,* pointed out this very feature: that these romances portray Bedouin women as celebrating the acquisition of such a rhapsodizer and capitalizing on this acquisition.

In the love story of *Majnun Layla* too, it is what is heard (for example, recited poetry, scandalous gossip, and news) that looms large. In this romance, the lovers learn of key events in each other's lives through circulating news and reports. Within the economy of romance, the ups and downs of the lovers' lives constitute news, and such bits of news spread quickly. Evidently a primary way people had of being informed was through networks of gossip, talk, and through circulation of poetry and news. Certainly, this resonates with claims made by Sissela Bok regarding the meanings and functions of gossip and other networks of human communication. For instance, the story shows that Majnun learns of Layla's marriage to the wealthy Ward through networks of gossip and news:

> Subsequently, a bit of this news was related to [Majnun]—news that he was unable to verify. So he recited:
>
> I prayed a prayer, not unaware . . .
> And my Lord is a seer of what is hidden in the breasts [of human beings]
> If you had only presented the coolness of her upper teeth to [one] poorer
>   than me, indeed I am an impoverished one.
> The news that she has married has spread,
> Will a bearer of good tidings bring to me [news] of her [37] *divorce*?

In the phrase "a bit of this news was related to [Majnun]," the word for "news" is from the root of *namīma,* which essentially means "gossip." The poem also includes a variation on the Qur'anic theme of God as all-seeing and all-knowing. The poet is depicted as not being "in the know" about his beloved (others have concealed secrets from him), and yet, he appears to be consoled by the recognition that what is hidden will be revealed, especially other people's secrets that are never hidden from God. In this context, however, he bemoans that another man has attained his beloved.

The Private Becomes Public through Poetry and Song

Viewing the 'Udhri corpus as an example of literature about socially disapproved and even illicit behavior becomes more tenable when we recall that Majnun loses Layla not simply as a result of a "public display of love" but because his "serenading," or *tashbīb,* revealed a satirical disregard and violation of newly emerging Islamic values associated with female chastity and matrimony. Therefore the romance frames the dire consequences that follow from social behavior and conduct that are outside the norm.

An important narrative describing the inception of their affair implies that Majnun was publicly declaiming poetry about his beloved and that it was through hearing of this poetry that her family initiated the breakup of their bond: "When Majnun first fell in love with Layla, he used to sing her praises often and visit her at night. The Bedouins used to regard as acceptable that youths or lads converse with lasses. When her family came to know of his love for her, they banned him from visiting her."[38] While it appears to have been socially acceptable among the Bedouins—including those of pre-Islamic times—to have unmarried young men or youths visit and converse with unmarried young women in private, the use of the past tense in the passage signals that this kind of thing was becoming less the norm in the early Islamic period. As we shall see, the controversy over the declamation of Majnun's love for Layla is linked with these issues of visitation and private conversations with her. Several passages describe Layla as having been veiled right after the rise of publicity and scandal. It is possible that female seclusion may have been a puberty rite, especially since the romance shows her being veiled at the time of the lovers' maturation. However, there are numerous references throughout the romance indicating that Majnun lost his beloved because of an onslaught of publicity concerning the love relation (and that her being cloistered from him may have had to do with this publicity). For example Majnun's father is depicted telling his son's sad tale, and in it he remarks: "When his and her business was disclosed, her father resented having to marry her to him [especially] after their matter had been publicized—so he married her to another." Yet another romance passage begins by proclaiming: "When the matter of Majnun and Layla became public and people were reciting his verses about her, he proposed to her . . . and Ward ibn Muhamma al-Uqayliyyi [also] proposed to her."[39] Clearly the role of what was deemed scandalous poetry about Layla contributed to his being banned from seeing her and, furthermore, from being able to marry her. She marries another (named Ward), and the news of this marriage is hidden from the poet by her family.

These pivotal scandalous verses are revealed in a dramatic scene (appearing at the end of the story) that consists of a visit by another Qays (not Majnun), named Qays ibn Dharih, to Layla, the beloved of Majnun. Qays ibn Dharih is another 'Udhri love poet and is both a fellow poet and rival to Majnun. Actually he visits Majnun first, whereupon he is asked by the latter to convey his greetings to Layla. When Qays goes to see Layla for this purpose and conveys Majnun's regards, Layla bursts out in anger and declares (it should be noted that Layla's nom de plume is Umm Malik):

If I had known you [Qays ibn Dharih] were his messenger, I would not have welcomed you! Tell him from me: What about your saying,

> A night, in the valley of al-Ghayl, O Umm Malik, refused,
> To give you, anything other than [except] a true love that does not lie . . .
> Indeed, you have caused an echo to resound, O Umm Malik
> Which goes wherever the wind takes it.

Tell me about this night of al-Ghayl, which night was it? Have I ever been alone with you [that is, Majnun] in the Ghayl or elsewhere, day or night?[40]

In response to Layla's display of anger at Majnun, Qays tries to defend his fellow poet and console her by asserting: "Indeed people have interpreted his verses in a manner not intended by him. Don't be like them. He [only] related that he saw you the night of the Ghayl Valley and you stole his heart. He did not mean you harm."[41] These verses of Majnun (that is, "A night, in the valley of al-Ghayl, O Umm Malik, refused . . .") seem to have resounded—like the echo to which they refer—and caused a sensation among tribespeople, spreading gossip about Layla in the verses far and wide. Qays attempts to console her, urging her to ignore people's gossip and distortions and claiming that "actually, what he was relating was that he saw you the night of al-Ghayl and you stole his heart; he meant no harm to you."

Yet, as the "night at al-Ghayl" incident suggests, Majnun was not just publicly celebrating and professing his love for Layla to people but also was disclosing information about their (perhaps private) meetings and thereby scandalizing her in the community. He evidently was composing and publicly reciting verses about Layla, the content of which he must have known would besmirch her reputation and cause him to be banned from seeing her, let alone marrying her. The implication, also present in the verses, of the lovers having been alone during a night wreaked havoc on their reputations, especially that of Layla. Indisputably the most immediately damaging consequence of these verses was the impugning of Layla's virginity. As is evident from Layla's reaction, the mere hint in the verses of her having been alone with Majnun (not to mention any exchange of intimacy between them) had imperiled her reputation as a virgin. Gossip about her was being fueled by the implications of her being alone with Majnun, especially the implications regarding her chastity. The verb *khalā* (used by Layla in her retort) primarily means "to be alone" or "to be alone with someone" but also means "to speak in private with" someone. The word *khalwa* (a derivation) most closely approximates the notion of privacy in our Arabic sources. This very word is employed in al-Jahiz's *Kitman,* wherein he emphasizes that "telling something to oneself in private" (. . . *yukhaṭiba bihi nafsahu fī khalwatihi*) does not succeed in lifting the sense of burden experienced in keeping a secret. Significantly, in the 'Udhri romance of *Kuthayyir 'Azza* too, the beloved named 'Azza perceives her reputation to have been besmirched by poetry allegedly composed by her lover, Kuthayyir. Moreover, in this romance too, the culprit verses concern language that is suggestive of the beloved having "been alone" with her suitor. Unlike the *Majnun Layla* romance, in which there is never any direct exchange between the lovers themselves regarding Majnun's slanderous verses, this story portrays 'Azza confronting the poet and declaiming the culprit verse to him. After 'Azza recites this verse, she poses a question almost identical to that framed by Layla in the narrative quoted above: "Have I ever been alone with you in a tent or outside of one?"[42] Kuthayyir responds by denying that he ever uttered this verse.

The semantics of *khalā* links the privacy of space with the privacy of speech, and there is a gender dimension to this: to speak in private to an unrelated member of the opposite sex is akin to being alone with the same person. Again, while in Bedouin pre-Islamic Arabia this may have been acceptable, the semantics of *khalā* in the 'Udhri romance suggests that emerging Islamic values and norms increasingly deemed this kind of behavior socially unacceptable. "According to a number of Hadith cited in this connection, when a man and a woman are alone together, the third present is Satan. When the Prophet was asked, 'What if they are good people?' he replied, 'Even if they were the Virgin Mary and John the Baptist!' "[43] Apposite here is the mention that even the etymology of *sirr* in the early Arabic lexicons suggests that intimate speech between an unwedded man and woman, when occurring in private, shades into the adulterous and/or illicit. The Muslim commentators cited in the early Arabic lexicons indicate that not just intercourse but even conversation and discourse between an unwedded man and woman about something intimate, when concealed, when occurring in secret or privacy, acquire adulterous qualities. They adduce the Qur'anic example 2:235, which states: "God knows that you will make them an offer of marriage . . . but do not make secret promises to them." What is being discouraged in this verse is the secret broaching of marriage proposals with widowed women before the end of a prescribed waiting period after the first husband's death. Apposite here is the point that al-Tabari and other commentators, in their interpretations of this verse, equate the word *sirr* with *zinā'*, or adultery. It seems that this interpretation occurs not just to underscore the point about not discussing marriage with widows before the end of the waiting period, but also because the phrase refers to an exchage between an unmarried man and woman that is secret and covert. Hence, intimate, private speech between an unwedded man and woman shades into the adulterous.

Returning to the love story, the added factor of the lovers having had a secret and intimate verbal exchange intensified the scandal. As will be discussed shortly, the romance demonstrates that private and secret encounters and conversations between the lovers are fraught with tension and fear. Qays ibn Dharih, whose voice carries interpretive authority in that he is a fellow poet of Majnun, suggests that the semantic import of the verses was totally contrary to the public's interpretation of them. Majnun simply meant that upon merely seeing his beloved during a night in the valley, he "refused all" (in other words, insisted on nothing) to his beloved except "a true love that does not lie." Yet, by introducing into public discourse verses that easily lent themselves to misinterpretation regarding his beloved's chastity, Majnun gravely impaired her reputation and occasioned his own downfall. If the use of the word *night* in the verse is interpreted literally (and in the excerpt above, both Layla and Qays do interpret "night" literally), its usage in connection with the poet-lover and his beloved could refer to a night during which he dreamed about his beloved or a night during which he saw her in passing (as Qays argues) or a night during which he met with or visited her (as Layla questions). Evidently the public at large (that is, *al-nās*, referred to by Qays in his defense of Majnun) selected the most provocative interpretation out of many for this verse—that is, they interpreted it to mean that the lovers were alone together sometime during a night.

The romance foregrounds a misinterpretation of the poet's use of the word *night* in his verse as the cause for the loss of his lady. It appears that the public interpreted the word *night* literally. This is strange since the verse easily lends itself to a nonliteral reading of this word, especially since "night" is personified ("A night . . . refused"). However, the public went further. They not only interpreted a possibly metaphoric term literally and selected a most provocative interpretation for the verse but also assumed that the culprit verse represented the poet's personal experience. Thus, a combination of a "vulgar misreading" of poetic tropes and misassumptions regarding the relation between poetic language and reality wreaked havoc on Layla's reputation, as is evident from the intensity of her reaction. By foregrounding this disjunction between literary and popular interpretations of the said verses, the romance demonstrates a tension between Bedouin literary conventions, especially regarding love poetry, that dictated the use of tropological language, and social norms (of early Islamic society) that inevitably misread this language. That Layla challenges the veracity of Majnun's verses (specifically regarding the representation of her virginity) suggests that she too is not judging poetic expressions and revelations by criteria different from nonpoetic ones. She exhibits anger not over the very act of Majnun's poetic declamation or over its circulation but rather over the "falseness" of gossip generated by them. In her study on secrecy, Sissela Bok identifies several forms of gossip that are "especially reprehensible," and one is "gossip the speaker knows to be false";[44] it is this type that is salient to the romance of *Majnun Layla*. Yet, the two issues, of course, are related—it is because the verses have been introduced into the public domain that he issue of their veracity arises in the first place.

Paradoxically at times the 'Udhri romances indicate that poetry could also aid in preserving the secrecy and privacy of couples. As depicted in these romances, selecting the right place and especially the right time were key issues in the arranging of private encounters and conversations between the lovers. Simply put, there was a need for secret trysts. Secret trysts required their own secret codes and communication strategies, and not surprisingly, the medium for these codes is often poetry. The following passage from the romance of *Jamil Buthayna* illustrates, quite realistically, just how tricky it was to find the right time and place for a private meeting. Anxious because he cannot remember the place for an upcoming tryst he has with Buthayna, Jamil persuades his bard and fellow poet Kuthayyir to visit his beloved's tents in order to confirm this appointment. Before he dispatches Kuthayyir, he describes to the latter his last meeting with Buthayna, and among the things that he relates is that it occurred while his beloved's maidservant was washing a dress. Kuthayyir then broaches to Jamil an idea concerning how he may be able to use this bit of information to indirectly elicit a response from Buthayna when he is there:

> Kuthayyir said to him: How do you feel about my acting out some
> verses, when I go to her encampment, in which I mention this clue
> if I am not able to be alone with her? He [Jamil] said: That is the right
> thing. So he sent him to her. . . . Then Kuthayyir set out until he was
> lodged with them. Her father said to him: What do you have to offer?
> He said: Three verses occurred to me, so I would like to present them to
> you. He said: Bring them. Kuthayyir said: So I recited them to him while
> Buthayna was listening:
>
> > Then I said to her: O 'Azza, my friend was sent to you as a
> > messenger—the one entrusted is the one dispatched—to establish
> > between you and me a tryst and so that you may command me
> > what I should do in this matter.
> >
> > My last tryst with you was the day you met me in the bottom-
> > most valley of al-Dum while the robe was being washed.
>
> He said: Then Buthayna slapped the side of her tent curtain and said:
> Beat it! Beat it! Her father said to her: What is the matter, Buthayna?
> She said: While folk are sleeping, a dog, from behind the hill, keeps
> harassing us. Next, she said to her maidservant: Get us firewood from
> al-Daumat so that we may slaughter and stew a sheep for Kuthayyir.

Then, Kuthayyir said: I am in too much of a hurry for that. He went to Jamil and informed him, and Jamil said: The tryst is in al-Daumat. She [Buthayna] remarked to Umm al-Husayn and Layla, daughters of her maternal aunt, with whom she was on intimate and trustworthy terms: Indeed, I perceived that Jamil was behind what seemed like Kuthayyir's serenade. So Kuthayyir and Jamil set out until they came to al-Daumat and Buthayna arrived with her companion. They were together until dawn broke.[45]

As an unmarried man and woman, Jamil and his beloved Buthayna cannot be alone, and therefore they have arranged a tryst. Again, because they cannot be alone, they cannot even confirm the tryst's date. In order to confirm this date, Jamil has to rely on his crony and bard Kuthayyir, but even Kuthayyir cannot be alone with Buthayna for the private exchange of a few words. Hence, he has to use declaimed poetry to surreptitiously communicate with her while her father is present. Ostensibly he addresses the father, but really he is "secretly conversing" with Buthayna through coded language. Also, Kuthayyir creates a form of intimacy between himself and Jamil's beloved, Buthayna, merely by invoking his beloved, 'Azza, as a mirror for Buthayna. By poetically rendering 'Azza as a stand-in for Buthayna and by presenting himself as the stand-in for Jamil, Kuthayyir succeeds in drawing Buthayna's attention to the matter at hand. Certainly, the poetic charade enacted by Kuthayyir allows for the confirmation of Jamil's tryst with Buthayna. Secrecy and revelation are inextricably linked in this passage, and consistent with the contrariness of the word *sirr*, here Kuthayyir's telling or revelation of a secret to Buthayna implies the concealment of it from her father. The secret is never let out fully; it is revealed only in gradations to the parties concerned, and again, its revelation occurs through poetry, through its recitation and its being heard. The tidbit of Jamil's information regarding a dress being washed is successful in communicating and signaling the message to Buthayna, and she, in turn, replies to Kuthayyir (and Jamil) through ostensibly addressing her maidservant while employing her own coded language (but not in the form of verse).

Private and Public: Nighttime Subterfuge and Espying Servants

As just seen, in the 'Udhri romances, private encounters, and conversations between the lovers are fraught with tension and conflict. Consider the following quotation from Regnier-Bohler: "Fiction reveals how difficult it was to find the right time and place for private conversation. The texts generally portray these difficulties realistically."[46] Only during the night can the lovers be together without excessive risk. In other words, there is no right time or place for conversation during the day. Incidents from all the 'Udhri romances, including the romance of *Majnun Layla,* depict these difficulties. What is salient in these incidents is not a "personal domain or sphere" but rather, as Talal Asad has argued, certain kinds of behaviors: talk in private between an unmarried man and woman, meetings in private between un-wedded men and women, and so forth.

The next passage from the romance of *Majnun* Layla depicts this quite effectively. Time is made prominent for the secrecy of the encounter; *where* Majnun and Layla meet and converse is rendered less important. The passage contains an element rarely present in the romance, the involvement of the lover's mother. At her behest, Layla secretly leaves her tribal quarter to visit Majnun.

> When Qays ibn Mulawwah's mind became disordered and he abandoned food and drink, his mother betook herself to Layla and said to her: Indeed, Qays' love for you has robbed him of his senses and he has forsaken sustenance. If you were to go see him . . . I think his sanity would return. Layla then said: Not during the day, since I do not trust what may happen to me at the hands of my clan, but during the night— [yes]. So she went to him during the night and related to him: "Qays, your mother claims that you went mad because of me and that you have left food and drink. Fear God and have mercy on yourself." He began to weep and then he recited:
>
>> She said: "You have lost your mind over me" I said to her Love is greater than what [afflicts] the madmen;
>> One entrusted with love, the possessor [*sāḥib*] of love, does not recover from it for eternity,
>> Whereas the madman is only felled by it for a time.
>
> Then she wept with him and the two conversed almost until dawn, when she bid him farewell and departed.[47]

Both conversations and encounters—the one between the mother and the beloved and the one between lover and beloved—occur secretly. Clearly, the more hazardous one is the second, as quite realistically framed by Layla's comment regarding the need for secrecy and invisibility during the visit: "Not during the day, since I do not trust what may happen to me at the hands of my clan, but during the night— [yes]." Once they meet, the nature of their interaction is suggestive of a secret and private intimacy: they both weep and converse, he recites poetry, she admonishes him and invokes his mother. Intimate converse, intimate speech, and discourse are made part of the coupling. In spite of the risks involved, the lovers converse until dawn.

The imagery of servants who conceal and/or reveal the secrets of their masters and mistresses looms large in how the private is made public in early

Arabic literature. This issue is also discussed in *Kitman* by al-Jahiz, who maintains that the privacy and secrecy of royalty and the elite classes are often violated by subordinates in age and rank, servants and common people. According to him, those who have power have secrets, and those who do not have power acquire power through knowing the secrets of the powerful.

From the 'Udhri romance of *Jamil Buthayna,* the following excerpt depicts the lover Jamil visiting his beloved Buthayna during the night—a time more conducive to privacy and secrecy. However, he is exposed by a maidservant of Buthayna's father and brother. The narrative then describes how Buthayna's father and brother, in turn, hide and spy on the lovers. In the end, the lovers engage in dissimulation to fool the beloved's male kin and to preserve their privacy.

> A maidservant of Buthayna betook herself to her [Buthayna's] father and brother and said to them: Jamil is with her tonight. So they came to her with swords under their gowns. They saw him seated off to the side from her, talking to her and complaining to her about his sorrows. Then he said to her: O Buthayna: Wouldn't you like to reward me for my ardent and passionate love for you? She said: With what? He replied: With what happens between lovers! She said to him: O Jamil, is that what you desire? By God, you have been far from [such a thing] with me in the past! Were you to again suggest [such] an impropriety, you would never see my face again! He then laughed and said: I only said this to know what your reaction would be to it. Were I to know that you would grant it to me, I would know that you would grant it to others too, and had I seen you compliant toward it, I would have struck you with the sword I am holding in my hand. . . . Thereupon, her father said to her brother: Let us go. It is not necessary after today for us to forbid this man from meeting with her. So they went away and left the two of them.

This narrative illustrates how difficult it was for an unmarried man and woman to have a private conversation. In addition to physical barriers that prevent access to the beloved, there are servants (female and male) who are paid to guard her. J. C. Burgel has observed that it would seem that Jamil "made a serious proposal but sensing either the coy reserve of Buthaina or the presence of her guardians, or the one well as the other, he withdrew into the 'Udhrite guise or pose."[48] The narrative is suggestive of the inability of the male guardians of the beloved to look beyond the obvious and visible. In other words, while the private may have been made public through the spying of servants, the secret has not been revealed. The secrecy here is the inner world of the lovers, which is in part constituted by their shared secrets as a couple. The 'Udhri romance narratives too contain the imagery of the servant or slave who spies. More often the servant is portrayed spying on behalf of the guardians of the female beloved rather than on behalf of the poet-lover.

Another narrative excerpt from the romance of *Jamil Buthayna* that showcases the role of the tattle-tale servant has a daytime setting. It is the imagery of both the daytime and the servant that exposes the lovers (further underscores how the night was associated with secrets of the lovers, privacy of space / not being seen or heard, illicit bonds). The anecdote begins with Jamil, the lover, being on the lookout for his beloved Buthayna. When he spots her with a bevy of her friends and female cousins, including one by the name of Umm al-Jusayr, he hides in some forage and pelts them with pebbles to signal his presence to his beloved. The narrative relates that thereupon

> [Buthayna] arose and went toward Jamil and admitted him to her tent. They talked for a long while, then he reclined and she lay down beside him and sleep stole over them until dawn came when her husband's servant came to her with a morning draught of milk. . . . [The moment] he saw her sleeping with Jamil, he ran pell mell to inform his master. Layla [Buthayna's maternal cousin] saw him [running] with the draught of milk and knowing the situation with Jamil and Buthayna, she delayed [the servant] making it seem as if she was inquiring after his well-being. [In the meantime] she dispatched a slavegirl of hers to warn Buthayna and Jamil.

When the slave girl wakes the lovers up and warns them, Buthayna has Jamil hide under a pile of provisions, and the narrative continues thus:

> Buthayna went to sleep as she had been before and Umm al-Jusayr lay down beside her. Then Layla's slavegirl went back to her [mistress] and told her of what had transpired whereupon Layla permitted the servant she had been delaying to proceed to his master, taking with him the draught of milk. He went to him and announced: "I saw Buthayna sleeping with Jamil next to her!" Nabih went to [his wife's] brother and father, took them by their hands and apprised them of the situation and, then all of them proceeded to Buthayna, and [found her] sleeping [soundly]. They lifted the coverlet on her and—lo and behold—Umm al-Jusayr was sleeping next to her. Buthayna's husband was [highly] embarrassed and he cursed his slave.[49]

The women join together to conceal the love relation while the men try to expose it. The narrative frames a competition between a male-male bond (that is, male slave and husband) and a web of two or three interlocking all-female relations. It depicts the male pair as attempting to expose a love relation (between Jamil and Buthayna) that, if it is not outright illicit, borders on being illicit, while the female network is shown to be intent on concealing it. The act of divulging the secrecy of the couple galvanizes same-sex loyalties in this narrative.

In this next incident too, the lovers meet covertly during the night. Again, the imagery of a servant is present in the narrative, but this time the servant girl helps to preserve the secrecy and privacy of an illicit, adulterous relationship. It occurs after the beloved Layla is married, and unlike the one above, it is suggestive of a sexual intimacy between them.

> Layla's husband and her father departed due to a matter that took the tribe away to Mecca during the night. Then Layla sent her slave-girl to Majnun to extend an invitation to him. So he stayed at her place for a night and she made him leave at daybreak, saying to him: Come to me each night as long as the tribe is away. He [regularly] came to her place until they [father and husband] returned. Concerning the last night of their tryst, when she bade him farewell, he recited:

> Enjoy Layla, indeed you are an owl . . .
> that each day draws nearer to its death.
> Enjoy until the riders return, [for] when they return,
> Forbidden to you is her speech (*kalāmuhā*).[50]

Several elements are noteworthy: Layla takes the initiative to invite him; she uses a messenger (her slave girl) to convey the invitation; the main authority male figures being deceived are the father and the husband of the beloved; and the lovers meet clandestinely at night more than once. Also, the equivalence between (verbal) converse and (sexual) illicit intercourse is discerned in the following verse: "Enjoy until the riders return, [for] when they return, / Forbidden to you is her speech." These verses are certainly to be included among Majnun's risqué verses; yet, here again the poetry transgresses that which is private and secret through its recitation and circulation. In these verses, the lover surrenders to a desire to covertly enjoy his experiences with Layla while he can, until her husband and father return. As for the reference to the owl—in pre-Islamic poetry the owl's cry represents the soul of an unavenged man. Avenging the blood of one wrongly slain was very much a part of pre-Islamic tribal custom. Indeed, an aspect of the law of vengeance—which according to Joseph Schacht was adopted from pre-Islamic custom into Islamic law[51]—was the legal right on the part of the family of the slain to be compensated in some shape or form by the slayer and/or his kin. The symbolism of the owl in the aforementioned verses is appropriate given the fact that Majnun's blood-vengeance right (that is, his family's entitlement to compensation were he to be slain by Layla's folks) has been rendered legally obsolete by the provincial authorities—a matter further discussed in the next section.

It should be mentioned that it is the love prelude of the pre-Islamic ode that contains the antecedents for this motif of the illicit, adulterous, and risky encounter between the 'Udhri lovers. Imagery of the covering and veiling of women, of women in curtained tents and howdahs (women not only kept and revealed secrets but also were to be kept secret) abounds in pre-Islamic Arabic poetry, and this imagery partakes in the motif already identified: that of the secret encounter and meeting, even one that shades into the adulterous. In the selection from the well-known ode below by the famous pre-Islamic poet Imru l-Qays, paradoxically secrecy and accessibility are associated with the "curtained quarters" and the "egg" therein (an egg being something concealed and protected by a shell):

> Many an "egg" of the curtained quarters,
> whose tent none dares to seek,
> I took my pleasure with her,
> unhurried.
> I stole past guards
> to get to her, past clansmen
> Eager, could they conceal it,
> to slay me . . .[52]

The night allows the lover access, and it is the night's darkness again that ensures their secrecy and privacy as a couple. The presence of "guards" and "clansmen" symbolizes the barriers to this access; the guards are on the lookout. Certainly, the forbidden quality of the love (the "egg" is pregnant and presumably wedded to another) heightens its intensity. Carl Sulzberger's observation regarding the "dual attraction of forbidden fruit and secret knowledge" is relevant to this poem and to much of early Arabic love literature: "One does not have to seek far, in literature or in real life, for evidence that the emotions engendered by secret amours usually far outstrip the sensations experienced in open and legitimate marital situations. The fact that it is forbidden leads us to keep it secret, so that the whole situation is endowed with the dual attraction of forbidden fruit and secret knowledge."[53] This tabooed quality and the intensity that it lent to a possibly secret romantic encounter are seen in a love poem by 'Umar ibn Abi Rabi'a, a poet from the Umayyad period. The mere mention of the enemies (that is, the family guardians) and the accompanying imagery of the curtained beloved in the poem accentuate the inaccessibility of the beloved:

I offered greeting and made myself sociable, fearful that an enemy
see my position or one secretly harboring hatred see my movement
   And she said while lowering a side of the curtain: verily my family is
with me, so [instead go] talk to one who is not on guard
   I said to her: I don't have a lookout for them, but [as for] my secret,
there's no one who can carry and guard it like me.[54]

'Umar 's lady friend is not averse to suggesting that he go elsewhere to seek
intimacy, for she remarks, "my family is with me, so [instead go] talk to one
who is not on guard"—here again we discern an equivalence between private, secret converse and (sexual) intercourse. Assuming this equivalence, the
absence of speech (secrecy, discretion) implies chasteness. This sheds light
on why 'Umar here seems less concerned with being detected by the enemies
or kin than with underscoring to his beloved his ability to keep secrets—an
ability he claims is unmatched.

The Private Becomes Public through Spatial Trespass

Pertinent to the consideration of how the private becomes public in the
'Udhri romances is the portrayal of spatial trespass or forced entry. As mentioned, among the pre-Islamic Arabs, models of conjugality embraced practices in which a woman may have received sporadic visits from the man for
whom she had reserved her affections.[55] The depictions of spatial trespass in
these romances are suggestive of these kinds of practices, and they alert us,
once more, to how the tensions and strains associated with the privacy of
the couple appear to be a function of the 'Udhri literature's portrayal of
changing norms regarding marriage, courtship, gender relations, and love as
early Arab society made the transition from a pre-Islamic to an incipient
Islamic ethos.

   A few principal passages exemplify this motif of trespass, including the
romance of *Jamil Buthayna*. According to the *Kitab al-Aghani* version, Jamil
fell in love with Buthayna when he was a lad, and upon reaching manhood,
he proposed to her but was refused because of the infamy of his poetry about
her. Buthayna is then married to another man, but Jamil continues to
covertly visit her until her family importunes the lover's father to persuade
his son to stop his clandestine meetings since her husband was becoming
increasingly agitated over them. The romance goes on to relate that after the
refusal: "[Jamil used] to come to her secretly and then she was married.
Thereafter, he used to surreptitiously visit her in her husband's house until
Dajajah ibn Rib'i was appointed governor over the Wadi al-Qura. They
complained about [Jamil] to him and he ordered him to not visit her at her
home and empowered them to shed his blood with impunity if he resumed
visiting her."[56] Some fifteen pages later, a variant of this narrative appears in
which her kin are shown pleading with the provincial governor to take action

against Jamil because "He lampoons [them], stealthily visits their homes, and publicly declaims amorous verse about [their] women."[57] Each of these would be contrary to what I would consider emerging Islamic-oriented norms of privacy, that is, slandering men's reputations through lampoons, invasions of domestic spheres where women dwell, and moreover, the besmirching of female chastity through publicly declaimed love poetry. Another account containing the motif is the following:

> The sultan[58] empowered the tribesmen of Buthayna to shed Jamil's
> blood with impunity if they found him having trespassed their homes.
> He was wary of them for a period, then they discovered him with her.
> [But] they [both] absolved him and blamed him. [The truth is that] they
> were averse to have him become enmeshed in a war between them and
> his people . . . a war over the matter of his blood, [since] his tribe was
> more powerful than . . . [them]. So they reiterated their complaint of
> him to the sultan, and he aggressively pursued him. [Jamil] fled to al-
> Yaman and stayed there for a while.[59]

The reference to "shed[ding] blood with impunity" (*fa-ahdara dammahu lahum*) in the narratives means that Buthayna's tribesmen have waived the legal obligation of having to pay Jamil's kin compensation if they were to kill him. This did not deter Jamil from his behavior. Moreover, as the passage points out, Buthayna's tribe did not take advantage of this waiver because they recognized that their slaying of Jamil may instigate an unequal battle. It is important to note that through the waiver action of the ruling authorities, the narrative constructs as a kind of legal right the tribe's "self-defense" against the lover's acts of trespass into the private spheres of their homes.

In the romance of *Majnun Layla,* certain overtures toward reconciliation are made by dignitaries and notables who take pity on Majnun's plight once he has been banned from seeing his beloved, Layla. In response, Layla's folks categorically reject any form of resolution, and they invoke the sultan's punitive measures against Majnun as proof of the seriousness of the poet's unacceptable conduct. According to her folks, Majnun is uninterested in anything as honorable as marriage. They adduce as evidence for their claim his instigation of the scandal concerning Layla and his repeated forced entry into their homes after the refusal of his marriage proposal, as well as his tendency to lampoon them in his poetry. The motif of trespass is best captured in the following passage from the romance of *Majnun Layla:*

> When Layla's father and his clan forbade Majnun from marrying her,
> he did not cease stealthily descending upon their homes, and trespassing
> upon their [property] [*yahjumu 'alayhi*]. They complained to the sultan

and he empowered them to shed his blood with impunity [*fa-ahdara dammahu lahum*]. They notified him of this, but this did not frighten him, and he declared: "Death is more peaceful for me, so let them slay me." When they learned of this and they realized that he still sought incaution on their part such that when they dispersed, he [could] gain entry into their homes, they moved away.[60]

Again what is at issue here is the trespass on their domestic spheres (in which Majnun engages surreptitiously), not to mention the impugning of Layla's chastity and their tribesmen's reputations through recited love poetry. Whereas these may not have violated pre-Islamic Bedouin norms and values of privacy, both the early Islamic seventh-century setting of the 'Udhri romance of *Majnun Layla* and its tenth-century retelling signaled something different.

In the 'Udhri romance of *Qays Lubna,* Qays the poet is barred from visiting Lubna once he divorces her. However, Qays, having been coerced into the divorce of his beloved wife by his parents, persists in seeing her. The following passage from the story foregrounds the trespass motif:

> [Lubna's] father had complained of Qays to Mu'awiya [ibn Abi Sufyan] and had informed him of his interference with her after . . . [the] divorce. Mu'awiya wrote to Marwan ibn al-Hakam to make his blood legal if he interfered with her. Then he [Mu'awiya] commanded her father to marry her to a man named Khalid b. Hillizah from the tribe of 'Abdallah b. Ghatafan. . . . Her father married her to him. . . . [Upon hearing of this], Qays' grief intensified and he began to sob and weep hot tears. Then he immediately set out on his mount until he reached her tribal quarter.[61]

This motif of trespass clearly involves an action-and-event-based plot. A patterned chain of events, including the initial love affair between the young Bedouins, the plot reversal instigated by the poet's indiscretions, the refusals (or breakdown) of marriage, the persistence of the poet-lover's subsequent clandestine visits and trespasses, and so forth, leads to the sultan's decree of waiving blood-vengeance rights on the lover's life. An explicitly legal angle depicts the beloved's kin seeking a government (provincial) decree that permits the lover to be murdered with impunity—that is, killed without the right to blood vengeance of his kin.[62]

The lover's transgressions or crimes consist of spatial trespass, and this form of trespass is accompanied, indeed instigated, by trespass in the verbal realms. Again and again the actions of the lover that are described (for example, declamation of scandalous verses about the beloved and other women of her tribe, public lampooning of her tribesmen, secret visitation of beloved even once she has married, stealthy entry into her tribal compound) suggest that invasiveness in both speech and action is what constitutes the lover's transgressions. Certainly these transgressions are framed in terms of unwanted access. In the romance of *Majnun Layla* we note, for example, the linkages between Majnun's forced entry into the homes of Layla's folks and his attack on their names and reputations in his poetry. Hence the motif of verbal indiscretion, that is, a motif of the revealed secret, is often interlocked with the motif of trespass or forced entry, which concerns privacy. The narrative syntax and imagery in the 'Udhri romances demonstrate the interlocking of these two motifs. Jamil, for instance, is faulted for publicizing invectives about his beloved's kin (*hijāʾ*) and intruding into the sanctity of their homes.

Such passages from the three 'Udhri romances demonstrate that the male lovers persist in desiring secret and private encounters with their beloveds. Even after the beloved is made another man's secret (that is, she is married to another man), the poet-lover does not refrain from visiting her. The marital bond between the beloved and her husband is repeatedly transgressed by the resumption of the lover's secret trysts with her. The resumption of the clandestine visits repeats the earlier dialectic of secrecy and revelation. Moreover, even after the woman's family is forced to induce the provincial authority to take legal action against him by depriving his kin of the right to blood vengeance (should he be slain), he is not completely deterred from visiting her. These conflicts between the lover's secret visitation and the marital bond are suggestive of tensions between the two models of marriage identified by W. Robertson Smith: the *ṣadīqa* model (which was increasingly becoming obsolete in early Islamic society) and a newly institutionalized form of matrimony in the Islamic Arabian ethos, described as "marriages of dominion," or *baʿal* marriages.[63] The latter increasingly sought to replace the vestiges of the far less fixed pre-Islamic form of conjugal relation.

In *Majnun Layla, Qays Lubna,* and *Jamil Buthayna* the women are not shown resisting the secret meetings, and at least one beloved, Layla, is shown inviting and arranging the trysts with her lover. This suggests that the beloved in question voluntarily engages in a consensual bond with her lover. She receives her lover of her own free will, even after marriage. At times she is shown turning down opportunities for trysts or postponing the meetings. In other words, the women or female beloveds choose to have trysts with their lovers. They choose to arrange, keep, and maintain the privacy and secrecy of these trysts. It is the fathers and husbands who seek to prevent the lovers' trysts. However, the presence of the motif of outlawing the lovers' rights to blood vengeance in both citations is, again, indicative of how the pre-Islamic *ṣadīqa* or *mutʿa* form of conjugal relations was being replaced the system of *baʿal* marriages. Apposite here is the mention that, in the *Majnun*

Layla romance, the word *baʿal* (the woman's "lord" or "owner," *baʿl, baʿal*) appears in some satirical verses uttered by Majnun when he hears that Layla's husband has cursed him. In these verses the exaggerated and excessive manner in which Majnun lays claim to being a *baʿal* of Layla only underscores that he is not her *baʿal* and that Ward is. He tries to usurp the position of Layla's husband by arrogating to himself the latter's conjugal title:

> If there is among you a lord [*baʿal*] of Layla, it's me
> By the Lord of the Throne, I have kissed her mouth
> eight times.[64]

The presence in the ʿUdhri romances of motifs of spatial trespass or forced entry illustrates how these love stories address changing norms regarding gender relations, marriage, courtship, and love as early Arab society made the transition from a pre-Islamic to a nascent Islamic ethos. In them a model of courtship and conjugality that perhaps allowed women and men greater choice and flexibility in their interactions with each other is juxtaposed against another model in which such interaction is fairly circumscribed. Again and again the romances foreground a tension or conflict in which what the lovers themselves desire, their own consensual desire to be together, is pitted against what their kinfolk and the prevailing social structures desire and mandate.

Conclusion

In their modes of indiscretion, of constantly revealing secrets, these ʿUdhri characters actually delineate what was increasingly deemed worthy of being kept secret as early Arab society made the transition from a pre-Islamic to a nascent Islamic ethos. Insofar as this is delineated, we obtain a glimpse into what aspects of the self were to be kept secret. First and foremost, discretion in speech was socially desirable. Discretion in speech was deemed highly desirable because increasingly speech came to be linked with gossip and slander—the opposites of privacy. The latter were regarded as an affront to emerging Islamic norms of, especially, female modesty and chastity. Clearly there are gender dimensions to this; this desirability of discretion in speech was an aspect of mainly the emerging Muslim male subjectivities. By contrast, the pre-Islamic models of masculinity allowed for, indeed celebrated, poetic and other indiscretions.

The most egregious male indiscretions that the ʿUdhri male poets engaged in were the following: speaking publicly about having been alone with women to whom they were not married; and secretly visiting the private homes and tribal compounds of these women—in effect, being secretly alone with them. This implies that what was to be kept secret was speech or talk involving women and intimacy with them. What was to be kept secret and private were meetings with unmarried women. What was to be kept secret and private were feelings that concerned areas of possible sexual misconduct. Conversely, the literature could be telling us that the reason speech or talk about this was unacceptable was because the act of being alone with a woman to whom one was not married was forbidden. Why? Because this act bore the potential for a range of intimacies that, according to Islamic norms, were disapproved of or illicit or on the borderline, such as possibly gazing at a woman, intimate speech with a woman, or acts ranging from touching to illicit fornication. Behaviors relating to the interaction between the two sexes were very much under watch. Tabooed, illicit sexuality is at the heart of these scenarios concerning the privacy of an unmarried couple.[65] This was under watch or scrutiny by various social agents: the tribes (that is, the symbolism of male guards, male kin, and servants) and the state. What is fascinating is that for transgressions of this kind of privacy in speech, the poets are punished socially: a poet-lover loses the woman he loves. However, for the transgression of privacy in space, the poets are punished by Islamic provincial authority. The passages regarding spatial trespasses corroborate that what was to be kept secret and private were homes and tribal compounds, especially where the women dwelled. Generally speaking, domestic space and the women inhabiting this space are rendered private. The passages also demonstrate that the state played a role in regulating privacy, because it enacted legal punitive measures for those who transgressed this privacy of the home.

'Udhri love literature's portrayal of changing norms regarding marriage and gender relations showcases issues of privacy. To reiterate, in this love literature the private becomes public through speaking, reciting, and (over)-hearing, through seeing and being seen. It becomes public through the circulation of risqué poetic language as well as talk and gossip, through spying and eavesdropping. It becomes public through clandestine physical access (trysts, secret visits) and even forms of trespass. The spatial trespass (of tribal compounds and homes) is coupled with verbal trespass (that is, indiscretions, scandal, and motifs of gossip) in the verse. The private also becomes public through the disclosures made by subordinates and servants. The strong presence of imagery of day and night as well as light and darkness is suggestive of how seeing or looking aided the private in becoming public. Daytime, when there is light, is very much linked with that which is public and visible, while nighttime is linked with privacy, with not being seen.

It is instructive to briefly compare the picture that emerges from early Arabic love literature with claims made by some scholars of medieval European literature. An examination of the meanings and functions of secrecy and privacy in early Arabic love literature refutes the claims, made by some scholars of European literature, that the emergence of phenomena such as subjectivity, interiority, and privacy can be dated to the twelfth century or thereafter. To digress briefly, in Duby's study of medieval European private life, one author claims that the focus is on "the emergence of the private sphere, the growing importance of the individual, and the new contours of domains henceforth regarded as secret or reserved."[66] By employing phrases such as "growing importance" and "emergence of," this author suggests that notions of the "private sphere" or even of "individual" came into existence only at a certain historical juncture. Such studies of European sources claim that individual subjectivity, interiority, the self's desire and/or need for privacy, and the existence of "domains . . . regarded as secret or reserved" are historical phenomena dating from during or after the twelfth century. Likewise, Spearing, in his study of medieval European narratives, declares that "the inner life begins to assume greater interest and importance in secular narratives from the twelfth century on."[67] He identifies what he terms the "private sphere" and stresses that this is conceived of not just as private space but also as inner life. My findings from an examination of early Arabic belles lettres and love literature do not support this dating. Certainly, the textual evidence from the 'Udhri romances, not to mention *Kitman* and early Arabic encyclopedias and dictionaries, demonstrates that secrecy (with its concomitant concerns with subjectivity and interiority) was a standard topic in thee Arabic sources from approximately the ninth century onward. Hence, Spearing's description of what he means by the "private sphere" (inner life) has striking similarities to descriptions of the act of revealing a secret found not just in *Kitman* by al-Jahiz but also in early Arabic love literature: "the thoughts and feelings, perhaps betrayed only fleetingly and ambiguously by glances or lowered eyes, blushing or turning pale, that are otherwise the most secret realm of all—'the chambir of my thought' as a late-medieval poet puts it."[68] As we have seen, early Arabic love literature both interrogates the prevailing psychosocial realities pertaining to the couple's secrecy and privacy and artfully represents interiority and secrecy in order to heighten the aesthetic experience of the narratives and poetry.

Conclusion

One spring I gave a lecture at the Oriental Club of Philadelphia entitled "A Semantics of Secrecy in the Qur'an," in which I expounded on how the scripture repeatedly describes God as the knower of what is hidden or concealed even though it often speaks of God as being the hidden one. I mentioned the central importance of the divine name of God as the All-Knowing (*al-'Alīm*) in the Qur'an and commented on the Qur'anic theme of God "knowing" the secrets of all human beings. After I finished, a member of the audience stood up and made comments that ended with the rather petulant protest "Since God can keep secrets, why can't I?" At the time I was both nonplussed and intrigued by the remark and had no idea how to respond to it. The protest has stayed with me over the years and provoked me to ponder further the links between secrecy and self in my material.

Could it be that early Arabo-Islamic ethical and literary discourses attempt to reassert a sense of secrecy and selfhood before an all-knowing God of the Qur'an? Could the Qur'anic promotion of the "transparency of self" (that is, God knows all your secrets) have generated an intense resistance to this very idea of the transparent self? Could the emphasis on secrets of the self found in classical ethical, literary, and didactic writings be considered, in part, a form of this intense resistance? Perhaps the internalization of this idea that one cannot have secrets from God generated the need to have secrets from other people. If there is the perception that one's relation with God is radically determined, then at least one can attempt to compensate for this by creating spheres of secrecy and privacy in interpersonal relations, that is, by keeping secrets from other human beings.

By no means am I suggesting that the emphasis on secrecy of the self found in some Arabo-Islamic ethical and literary writings is solely a function of this kind of dynamic. Social and legal norms as well as historical factors in Arabo-Islamic culture(s) are very much salient here. What I am suggesting is that, at the very least, the Qur'anic construction of the "religiously transparent self" is not irrelevant to the matter at hand. Indeed, even when it comes to early Islamic legal and ethical norms regarding public and private, the Qur'anic material is not irrelevant. Earlier I talked briefly about how the individual Muslim's ethical and legal duty of "commanding right and forbidding wrong" (*al-amr bi'l-ma'rūf wa'l-nahy 'an al-munkar*) also sheds light on the secrecy of the self, and this duty is not without its Qur'anic antecedents. Moreover, could not one suggest that to some extent the Qur'anic theme of the divine panoptic gaze comes to be internalized in this ethical individual responsibility of commanding right and forbidding wrong?

In this concluding chapter, I merely raise the possibility that numerous selections (dealing with secrecy) from early Arabo-Islamic ethical and literary discourses are suggestive of attempts to compensate for a perceived determining Qur'anic phenomenology of "self as transparent." How so? By persistently and consistently maintaining the need for creating spheres of secrecy and privacy in intrapersonal and interpersonal relations. What was vitally important was the acute need to feel that there were reserves within oneself that were secret and latent, and hence inaccessible to other human beings if not to God. I invoke once more the quotation from a well-known eleventh-century Arabic love treatise, *Tawq al-Hamama,* or *The Ring of the Dove,* by the Andalusian jurist and theologian Ibn Hazm. This quotation surfaces in a chapter entitled "The Vileness of Sinning," and importantly, Ibn Hazm lists those very Qur'anic verses discussed in chapter 1:

> Let no man say, "I was in privacy." Even if he be entirely alone, yet he
> is within the sight and hearing of "the Knower of all secrets" [5:108],
> "Who knoweth the perfidious eye, and what the breasts conceal" [60:20],
> "and knoweth the secret and that which is even more hidden" [20:6],
> "so that there shall not be three whispering together but He is the fourth
> of them, nor five but He is the sixth of them, nor fewer than that nor
> more but that He is with them wherever they may be" [68:8]. "He
> knoweth all that is in the breasts" [57:6], "and he knoweth alike the
> unseen and the visible" [6:73]; "and they conceal themselves from men,
> but they conceal not themselves from God, for He is with them" [4:107].
> Allah says, "And verily We have created man, and know all that his soul
> whispers within him, and We are nearer to him than his jugular vein;
> when two meet together, one sitting on the right and the other sitting
> on the left, neither uttereth a word, but beside him is a watcher
> watching" [50:15–17].[1]

Ibn Hazm seems almost to decry that there is no such thing as being "in privacy," declaring "[for even if one is] entirely alone, yet he is within the sight and hearing of the 'Knower of all secrets.'" However, that one cannot ever have secrets and / or privacy in relation to God certainly did not prevent him from emphasizing the need to have secrets from other human beings, especially in matters of love. His treatise contains several chapters on "secrecy and revelation in the matters of love" in which he insists on the merits of secrecy and discretion in interpersonal relations.

Just why is it that secrecy of the self in texts such as *The Ring of the Dove*—indeed in diverse Arabo-Islamic ethical, didactic, and literary works— is largely presented as something positive (that is, discretion in interpersonal bonds, interpersonal ethics of conduct, mystery and preciousness of love) whereas in the Qur'an this secrecy of the self (*kitmān*) is often associated with something negative (that is, deception)? One explanation is attributable to the conventions of the genre or discourse at hand and the intended audience(s). Put simply, the Qur'an is most concerned with the God-human relation, whereas the former discourses deal with interpersonal relations. In other words, Arabo-Islamic ethical and literary discourses address earthly contexts in which secrecy of the self is central to maintaining discretion, intensity, and power in interpersonal relations and modes of self-presentation, whereas the Qur'an presents the otherworldly context wherein nothing matters except individual moral transparency, accountability, and responsibility before God. Hence, on a cautionary note, the scripture more often than not connects the secrecy of the self with deception. Another explanation could be that the emphasis on the positive secrets of the self found in classical ethical, literary, and didactic writings is, in part, an aspect of the aforementioned resistance to the Qur'anic transparency of self. Perhaps the idea in the Qur'an that the secrets of the self are associated with deceptively hiding things from God or others generated the need to have good secrets of the self vis-à-vis others. In other words, the need for creating spheres of secrecy and privacy in interpersonal and intrapersonal realms (in the face of a perceived Qur'anic phenomenology of "self as transparent") often went hand in hand with conferring positive value to the hidden contents of these personal spheres—though ultimately the content of what one hid or concealed appeared not to matter as much as creating the inner reserves within oneself.

On a more contemporary note, one may ask how this book's examination of the secret in early Arabo-Islamic discourses could possibly shed light on what Farish Noor, a Malaysian political scientist and human rights activist, refers to as "the division between inside and outside, in-group and out-group" characterizing modern notions of identity and belonging among Muslims.[2] Writing in a post-9/11 context, Noor observes that "one of the defining features of the current Islamist resurgence worldwide is that it requires the presence of the trope of the negative Other, which manifests itself in a number of forms: secularism, the West, international Jewry/Zionism, capitalism, etc." He then describes these Islamist revolutionary movements as espousing a dialectic that puts them always "on the lookout for new enemies . . . as an opponent is required to give the revolution its identity." The word *identity* employed here is crucial—Noor intends to link his use of the word with notions of collective and/or individual identities among Muslims. This becomes clear from the next several observations he makes:

> Looking at the state of the world as a whole in the context of the aftermath of September 11, I feel that there is a desperate need for Muslims to re-learn the norms and rules of dialogue and communication. For despite the painfully and brutally obvious suffering that has been inflicted upon us, Muslims have not been able to communicate our pain and anxieties to the outside world (which at times may even be the neighbor next door), for the simple reason that we think of them as the *outside* world. The division between inside and outside, in-group and out-group, has been so forcibly enforced by this dialectical outlook which we have foisted upon ourselves that we have effectively exiled ourselves from the rest of humanity.[3]

A grave claim indeed "that we [Muslims] have . . . exiled ourselves from the rest of humanity"! How can one understand his assertion that this exile is due to what he describes as problematic communication strategies and insider-outsider dynamics? Are there resonances between what he describes as "the division between inside and outside, in-group and out-group" characterizing modern notions of identity and belonging among Muslims and some of this book's claims and arguments regarding premodern notions of self and identity?

My attempt to respond to these questions is speculative and cursory at best. One way to try to answer these questions is to focus briefly on the issue of boundaries. This book's study of the secret and secrecy can be thought of as an examination of all sorts of boundaries—the self's inner boundaries, boundaries between self and God, between consciousness and the unconscious; the body's inner/outer boundaries; boundaries between feeling and behavior, between self and other(s); as well as boundaries between self and society. Across the very different early Arabo-Islamic discourses (that is, the Qur'an, ethical writings, and love literature) examined in this book, the self is imagined in terms of the dialectic between keeping and revealing secrets. Furthermore, the boundary between the inner self and the outer body is crucial, especially to Qur'anic constructions of selfhood. Yet, what these Qur'anic constructions of the self impart to Arabo-Islamic ethical and literary discourses is an acute awareness of just how this boundary between the inner self and the outer body always gets subverted: given the self's embodied quality, its outer physical signs and signifiers inevitably and transparently attest to inner moral truths. Indeed, the construction of the human self and subjectivity throughout these diverse Arabo-Islamic discourses is characterized by the crossing, maintenance, blurring, fortification, and/or subversion of the body's boundaries. Needless to say, the symbolism of boundaries is pivotal. The anthropologist Mary Douglas, in her book *Purity and Danger,* offers a compelling analysis of the symbolism of boundary maintenance that helps us to bridge the gap between early Arabo-Islamic discourses and Farish Noor's comments. Douglas has observed that "when rituals express anxiety about the body's orifices, the sociological counterpart of this anxiety is a care to protect the political and cultural unity of a minority group."[4] She points out, "Just as it is true that everything symbolizes the body, so it is equally true (and all the more so for that reason) that the body symbolizes everything else. Out of this symbolism, which in fold upon fold of interior meaning leads back to the experience of the self with its body, the sociologist is justi- fied in trying to work in the other direction to draw out some layers of insight upon the self's experience in society."[5]

Here we return to Noor's observation regarding the "division between inside and outside, in-group and out-group" coloring modern notions of identity and belonging among Muslims. Such a division is expressive of an anxiety about inner/outer boundaries, self-other boundaries, and inside- outside borders that is found in other instances of identity and belonging, self and other relations in modern Arab/Islamic cultures. Consider the fol- lowing examples. The first is an excerpt from a twentieth-century auto- biographical work, *Return to Childhood: The Memoir of a Modern Moroccan Woman,* by Leila Abouzeid:

> Perhaps even more important a Muslim's private life is considered an *'awra* (an intimate part of the body), and *sitr* (concealing it) is imperative. As the Qur'an says, *Allah amara bissitr* (God ordered the concealing of that which is shameful and embarrassing). Hence the importance of *hijab* and *hajaba* or *yahjubu* from the root "to hide" words used for the veil that hides a woman's body and the screen that hides private quarters as in the Qur'anic verse that says *Kallimuhunnah min warai hijab* (talk to them from behind a screen), referring to the wives of the Prophet. The word for the ancient Arabo-Islamic walled city, *muhassanais* [is] the same as the term for chaste unmarried women, [and] it means literally "inaccessible." The concern about concealing is clear in Arabo-Islamic architecture, where inner courtyards and gardens are central, windows look inward rather than outward, and outside walls are blind.[6]

The second concerns a couple of contemporary jokes (difficult to translate from the Arabic) pertaining to secrecy that are current in Arab cultures and that have great resonances with two-liners found in the premodern texts examined:

Do you have "what it takes to keep a secret"?
As if in a well . . . [I am like a deep well.][7]

Another one goes something like this:

Do you have five bucks?
As if I didn't hear a thing. . . . [Nope!][8]

The third example concerns what was described by Saddam Hussein as the "mother of all wars" and is still being fought in Iraq. The issues of lying, secrecy, knowledge withheld, hiding, slander, invasion of privacy, and spying were at the forefront of the spiraling acrimonious verbal exchanges between Saddam Hussein and George W. Bush before the war began.[9] Recall, for instance, the controversy over Hussein's palaces. The Bush administration and the United Nations had insisted that his palaces needed to be thoroughly searched in case weapons of mass destruction were being concealed there. Hussein, on the other hand, had resisted this because he regarded the palace searches as nothing short of Western attempts to spy and collect intelligence within domains he considered private. What is striking is the recurrent charge that was leveled against the Arab leader: that of hiding, of concealing from the world community, of keeping secrets and not revealing them to inspectors and other officials.

Mary Douglas points out that notions of self and identity with an emphasis on and anxiety about inner/outer boundaries, self-body bounda- ries, and inside-outside borders have a sociological counterpart, namely, the "preservation of the unity of a minority group." Just how do Muslims, in the contemporary world, perceive themselves to be an "in-group," possibly a "minority in-group," vis-à-vis what they label as the "outside world"? It is remarkable that a similar impetus toward continually maintaining, fortify- ing, and policing the boundaries between an inner-outer binary informs the workings of the human self and subjectivity, as well as interpersonal relations in a selection of early Arabo-Islamic discourses, including the Qur'an. As I have argued, in these Arabo-Islamic sources, what is on the surface, external, outer, or visible as well as the realm of the public often carries negative connotations associated with deception, falsehood, corruption, or danger. Such negative connotations appear to inform the "division between inside and outside, in-group and out-group" that Noor discusses. Is such a division expressive of perceptions concerning collective self-preservation? Perhaps. There is no better evidence of this than the need of what actually is a tiny, fringe minority (Islamist groups) to find and/or create an external Other in order to define and bolster its own (fictive) unity and identity. As Noor points out, these Islamist groups are always "on the lookout for new enemies . . . as an opponent is required to give the revolution its identity." Douglas also identifies "four kinds of social pollution" relevant to the minority group's attempts to preserve its unity: "The first is danger pressing on external boundaries; the second, danger from transgressing the internal lines of the system; the third, danger in the margins of the lines. The fourth is danger from internal contradiction, when someof the basic postulates are denied by other basic postulates, so that at certain points the system seems to be at war with itself."[10]

All four, I would submit, are relevant to contemporary Islamist politics as well as to aspects of what Noor describes as "the fundamental notions of identity and belonging which have shaped and colored Muslim politics for so long." Noor demands, "The first thing that has to be attempted is a self-critique of ourselves and our own notions of identity and difference. For so long the Muslim world has been trapped in a dialectical impasse of its own making. The time has come for us to utilize the tools of contemporary social sciences and critical theory to interrogate some of the fundamental notions of identity and belonging which have shaped and colored Muslim politics for so long."[11] I, for one, find these suggestions very powerful. In addition, I see deep resonances between what Noor is calling for here and some of the imperatives behind the writing of this book. To paraphrase Noor, by utilizing the tools of contemporary social sciences and critical theory, I have sought to interrogate some of the fundamental notions of identity and belonging in the Qur'an and other early Arabo-Islamic discourses. I have done this by focusing on the concept of the secret in these discourses.

Notes

Introduction

1. Kristin Fathe, "Final Exam Response," Trinity University student paper, December 2004.

2. Frederick Mathewson Denny, *An Introduction to Islam,* 3rd ed. (New York: Macmillan, 2006), 144. See also Hanna E. Kassis, *A Concordance of the Qur'an* (Berkeley and Los Angeles: University of California Press, 1983), xvii: "It is not too bold to suggest that the Qur'an is to the Muslim what Jesus Christ, and not the Bible, is to the believing Christian." Moreover, Theodore Ludwig, *The Sacred Paths of the West* (Upper Saddle River, N.J.: Prentice Hall, 2001), asserts that "for Christians, the way to really know what God is like is through the revelation in Jesus Christ; here God's divine face is shown for all to see. Apart from Christ, God remains the almighty, righteous creator beyond human knowledge or contact; in Christ, the mystery has come to dwell among humans" (158).

3. Stefan Wild, "We Have Sent Down to Thee the Book with the Truth: Spatial and Temporal Implications of the Quranic Concepts of Nuzul, Tanzil, and Inzal," in *The Qur'an as Text,* ed. Stefan Wild (Leiden: Brill, 1996), 137. Wild also declares, "One can go even further and compare the Christian dogma that Christ was born of the virgin Mary with the Muslim concept of the *'ummīyya* of the prophet Muhammad. There was no human father for Jesus, and there was no written text taken down by man which might have influenced the prophet Muhammad."

4. Compare with discussion of images in Diana Eck, *Darsan: Seeing the Divine Image in India,* 3rd ed. (New York: Columbia University Press, 1998), 20–21.

5. The word *cipher* is related to the word *zero*, and both etymologically stem from the Arabic word *ṣifr* or *ṣafr*. By itself, a zero signifies "nought," but added after another numeral, it assigns value. One can imagine how the semantics of the word *cipher* (both as noun and as verb) came to acquire in general parlance the meanings related to secrecy and revelation. In the *Oxford English Dictionary* (*OED*), at least eight different meanings are given for it as a noun, and among them are "sign, number, figure, zero-point in thermometer, symbolic character," as well as "a secret or disguised manner of writing, whether by characters arbitrarily invented . . . or by an arbitrary use of letters or characters in other than their ordinary sense." *Webster's International* gives as one of its meanings "any method of transforming a message to conceal its meaning." One of its verbal meanings, according to the *OED,* is "to express, show forth, make manifest by any outward signs, portray, delineate."

OED on "cipher": The concept of "zero" is a legacy bequeathed to the Arabs by Indian civilization. *OED:* "Arab. *çifr* the arithmetical symbol 'zero' or 'nought' [written in Indian and Arabic numeration], a substantive use of the adj. *çifr* 'empty, void,' f. *çafara* to be empty. The Arabic was simply a translation of the Sanskrit name *śūnya,* literally 'empty.'"

6. The phrase "concept of the secret" is borrowed from the psychoanalyst Alfred Gross, who employed it in an article entitled "The Secret," trans. George Devereux, Gisela Ebert, and Joseph Noshpitz, *Bulletin of the Menninger Clinic* 2 (1951): 37–44. In it Gross differentiates the function of a secret from its content: "By contrast, the secret, once surrendered, is lost only insofar as its *content* is concerned. The *vessel* which contained it endures, ready to be filled with new content. We see then that in the study of the concept of the secret, one must differentiate between content and function; the hidden *content* of a secret is something different from the psychological state of *possessing* a secret" (38).

7. Contemporary popular culture in the United States has (arguably) embraced the idea of "telling secrets" to explore aspects of the self, identity, and relationships. Consider several examples. Whether it is the huge success of Frank Warren's postsecret.com or myriad television talk shows, such as *The Oprah Winfrey Show,* in which people willingly disclose all sorts of secrets and private details about their lives, contemporary popular culture has brought the "psychoanalytic couch" to the screen as well as to the virtual world. Warren, keenly recognizing the power of the secret as a burden, has remarked, "Above all . . . the release of a secret is like the release of a heavy weight." Exactly this view is found in my sources of nearly fifteen hundred years earlier and from a different culture. See http://www.cnn.com/2007/SHOWBIZ/books/01/30/postsecret.warren/index.html, "The Secrets People Reveal" (accessed January 2007).

8. Gerald J. Margolis, "The Psychology of Keeping Secrets," *International Review of Psycho-Analysis* 1 (1974): 291. Margolis points out that another reason psychoanalysis has special significance is that "the process of the patient laying his consciously held secrets and later his previously unconscious secrets at the feet of the judging and reacting analyst can be regarded as the central process of psychoanalytic therapy."

9. Modern Western theorists and scholars, including Georg Simmel, Sissela Bok, Alfred Gross, and Sigmund Freud, have influenced my examination of the idea or concept of the secret. Yet, throughout my research and writing of this book, the shuttling back and forth between the early Arabic and modern Western contexts has been a dialogic process, sometimes inspired and mandated by the exigencies of my primary texts and at other times instigated by insights and claims made by Western critics studying the subject of secrecy—insights and claims that resonate richly with the content of my own material.

10. Three edited collections on secrecy have been produced in history of religions scholarship during the last twenty years, and all three support my claim that both history of religions and Islamic studies scholarship have largely examined secrecy within the context of mysticism and/or traditions of the esoteric. See Kees W. Bolle, *Secrecy in Religions* (New York: Brill, 1987); H. G. Kippenberg and G. G. Stroumsa,

eds., *Secrecy and Concealment: Studies in the History of Mediterranean and Near Eastern Religions* (New York: Brill, 1995); and Elliot R. Wolfson, ed., *Rending the Veil: Concealment and Secrecy in the History of Religions* (New York: Seven Bridges Press, 1999). Among the topics addressed by these authors are secrecy in written and oral forms of early pagan teachings, secrecy's connections with early gnosticism, secrecy's links with the Gospels, secrecy's significance in Kabbalah traditions or in Islamic and Christian mystical writings, and secrecy's connections with Hindu tantric gnosis. However, the most recent of these collections, by Elliot Wolfson, appears to conflate the study of secrecy in the history of religions with the study of esotericism. Even the way that Wolfson assesses the contributions in his edited volume suggests that what he really is trying to glean from them are some common traits and features by which to define esotericism. I have benefited much from all three edited works, especially Wolfson's fine collection. More recently, excellent research has been done in the history of religions scholarship on secrecy by scholars such as Beryl Bellman, Michael Sells, Hugh Urban, and Paul Johnson. However, I believe there is an existing lacuna in history of religions scholarship regarding secrecy: this scholarship has not explored the links between secrecy and self, secrecy and identity, and secrecy and interpersonal bonds.

11. This latter I would couch within the framework of secrecy and the esoteric because esotericism is a hallmark of so much of Shi'ite theology and practices.

12. William Chittick, "The Paradox of the Veil in Sufism," in *Rending the Veil*, ed. Wolfson, 59–85; Annemarie Schimmel, "Secrecy in Sufism," in *Secrecy in Religions*, ed. Kees W. Bolle (New York: Brill, 1987), 81–98.

13. Etan Kohlberg, "Taqiyya in Shi'ite Theology and Religion," in *Secrecy and Concealment*, ed. Kippenberg and Stroumsa, 345–80. Consult Ann Williams Duncan's "Religion and Secrecy: A Bibliographic Essay," in the focus issue "Religion and Secrecy," *Journal of the American Academy of Religion* 74, no. 2 (2006): 469–82; and Maria Dakake, "Hiding in Plain Sight: The Practical and Doctrinal Significance of Secrecy in Shi'ite Islam," *Journal of the American Academy of Religion* 74, no. 2 (2006): 324–55.

14. Jean-Claude Vadet, *L'Esprit courtois en Orient dans les cinq premiers siècles de l'Hégire* (Paris: Maisonneuve et Larose, 1968). While history of religions largely has confined the consideration of secrecy within traditions and practices of the esoteric, medieval literary criticism (as represented in Vadet's work) has relegated the consideration of secrecy to the tradition of courtly love literature.

15. For this and other reasons, my book deals neither with Islamic mysticism nor with Shi'ism. Moreover the book does not deal with the topic of secrecy in hadith, wisdom literature ("mirror of princes" tradition), or Shari'a (Islamic law).

16. I am paraphrasing Gregory Gross here, who in his dissertation on secrecy in late medieval-European narrative observes that the texts he examines are "unified by the prominent way in which secrecy bears upon the representation of subjectivity in them (although with particular differences in each case)." See Gregory Walter Gross, "Secrecy and Confession in Late Medieval Narrative: Gender, Sexuality, and the Rhetorical Subject" (Ph.D. diss., Brown University, 1994), 1.

17. Issa Boullata, ed., *Literary Structures of Religious Meaning in the Qur'an* (Surrey: Curzon Press, 2000), x.

18. Excerpt from the following quote: "The importance of context (*maqām*) was recognized and formulated for the study of the text of the Qur'an by Muslim linguists whose work in this respect anticipated by many centuries modern linguistic thinking. Internal relationships were encapsulated in the dictum: *al-Qur'an yufassiru ba'ḍuhu ba'ḍan* (different parts of the Qur'an explain one another), which, given the structure of Qur'anic material, was argued to provide the most correct method of understanding the Qur'an." See M. A. S. Abdel Haleem, "Context and Internal Relationships: Keys to Quranic Exegesis; A Study of Sūrat al-Raḥmān (Qur'an Chapter 55)," in *Approaches to the Qur'an,* ed. G. R. Hawting and Abdul-Kader Shareef (London: Routledge, 1993), 71.

19. Mustansir Mir, "The Qur'an as Literature," *Religion and Literature* 20 (1988): 53.

20. Angelika Neuwirth, "Images and Metaphors in the Introductory Sections of the Makkan Suras," in *Approaches to the Qur'an,* ed. Hawting and Shareef, 33.

21. Abu 'Uthman 'Amr ibn Bahr al-Jahiz, *Kitab Kitman al-Sirr wa Hifz al-Lisan* in Majmu' Rasa'il al-Jahiz, ed. P. Kraus and M. T. al-Hajiri (Cairo: Lajnat al-Ta'lif wa-al-Tarjamat wa-al-Nashr, 1943), 37–60, translated by William Hutchins under the title "Keeping Secrets and Holding the Tongue," in *Nine Essays of al-Jahiz,* trans. William Hutchins (New York: P. Lang, 1989), 13–32.

22. Abu 'Uthman 'Amr b. Bahr b. Mahbub al-Kinani al-Basri is known as al-Jahiz. The French scholar Charles Pellat has undertaken the most comprehensive Western study of al-Jahiz. See his chapter entitled "Al-Jahiz" in *'Abbasid Belles-Lettres,* ed. Julia Ashtiany et al., Cambridge History of Arabic Literature (Cambridge: Cambridge University Press, 1990), 78–95. The author of *Kitman,* al-Jahiz was born in 776 C.E. in Basra. Al-Jahiz had no access to any kind of formal training beyond the attendance of Qur'anic schooling in that city. He frequented the mosque as well as study and debate circles, and he had the chance to hobnob with affluent and educated circles (with whom he read voraciously, especially translations of Greek and Persian Pahlavi texts). In eighth-century Basra there were lively daily discussions among intellectuals over matters such as "what school of theology was best and why?" and "could faith and reason be harmonized?" A rationalist school of theology called Mu'tazilism held sway in the Islamic world at this time. Al-Jahiz was known to have close contacts with some of the leading Mu'tazili figures of the city. Although the reigning 'Abbasid caliphs supported this school, it still encountered strong resistance in other parts of the Islamic world (see *Encyclopedia of the Quran,* s.v. "Mu'tazila"). As for his output, al-Jahiz's range of subjects was remarkable. Over two hundred authentic works are attributed to him, but only two dozen have survived intact. His major works are considered to be *Kitab al-Hayawan* (*Book of Animals*), *Kitab al-Bayan wa'l-tabyin* (*Book of Eloquence and Exposition*), and *Kitab al-Bukhala'* (*Book of Misers*)—all of these have been preserved intact. Among the most famous of al-Jahiz's works is his *Kitab al-Bayan wa'l-tabyin* (*Book of Eloquence and Exposition*). He also authored a book concened with the rhetorical structure of the Qur'an entitled *Kitab fi l-ihtijaj li-nazm al-Qur'an* (Book of Adducing of Proofs for the Composition of the Qur'an).

23. I am grateful to an anonymous reviewer with the University of South Carolina Press for pointing this out.

24. Unlike the "inorganization" attributed by Fedwa Malti-Douglas, *Structures of Avarice: The Bukhala' in Medieval Arabic Literature* (Leiden: Brill, 1985), 53, to one of al-Jahiz's major works, *Kitab al-Bukhala* (*Book of the Misers*)—a trait reflective of what may be described as his "confusingly digressive method of composition"— the treatise is a fairly coherent piece. Pellat, in "Al-Jahiz," 86–94, has also described the approach and style of al-Jahiz as being "digressive and untidy."

25. Several other works by al-Jahiz that address the subject of human secrecy and discretion are also considered in this book, among them *Kitab al-Bayan wa'l-tabyin* (*Book of Eloquence and Exposition*), ed. A. Muhammad Harun (Cairo: Matabat Lajnat al-Ta'lif wa al-Tarjama wa al-Nashr, 1948), vol. 1, specifically its chapters entitled "Bab al-Balagha" (On Eloquent Style) and "Bab al-Bayan" (On Eloquence), as well as *Risalat al-Ma 'ad wal-ma 'ash fi al-adab wa tadbir al-nas wa-mu 'amalatihim* (The Epistle of the Hereafter and *This Life on Decorum, Management of People and Interpersonal Relations*), in *Majmu' Rasa'il al-Jahiz*, ed. P. Kraus and M. T. al-Hajiri (Cairo: Lajnat al-Ta'lif wa-al-Tarjamat wa-al-Nashr, 1943), 1–36; and *Tafdil al-Nutq 'ala al-Samt* (*Virtues of Speech over Silence*), in *Majmu'at al-Rasa'il: Ithna 'asharah risalah*, edited by Muhammad al-Sasi al-Maghrribi (Cairo: Matba'at al-Taqaddam, 1906), 135.

26. Pellat, "Al Jahiz," 93.

27. The term *secrecy chapters* is a modification of one used by Malti-Douglas in *Structures of Avarice*.

28. These polythematic encyclopedias are characterized by an "intellectual methodology in which classification, categorization, and description were the ultimate tools for the acquisition and retention of knowledge," and hence they convey to us something of how knowledge was organized, presented, and even constructed (Kristen E. Brustad et al., *Interpreting the Self: Autobiography in the Arabic Literary Tradition,* ed. Dwight F. Reynolds [Berkeley and Los Angeles: University of California Press, 2001], 5).

29. Andre Miquel, *Deux histoires d'amour de Majnun à Tristan* (Paris: Editions Odile Jacob, 1996), has demonstrated the existence of commonalities between the 'Udhri romance of *Majnun Layla* and *Le Roman de Tristan*. Mahmoud Manzalaoui too, in "Tragic Ends of Lovers: Medieval Islam and the Latin West," *Comparative Criticism* 1 (1979): 40, 43, compares 'Udhri-style narrative accounts of "the sufferings and deaths of lovers" embedded in the medieval Arabic love treatises with Marie de France's *Lais* and the Tristan stories. Likewise, Andras Hamori, in "Love Poetry (*ghazal*)," in *'Abbasid Belles-Lettres*, ed. Ashtiany, makes the following brief comparison: "As with so much European love-poetry. . . the basic mode of 'Abbasid love poetry is paradox" (212).

30. *Kitab al-Aghani* (*The Book of Songs*), containing the tenth-century 'Udhri corpus, is the magnum opus of Abu al-Faraj al-Isfahani. He spent most of his life in Baghdad, where he seems to have received patronage from various sources but primarily from the Buyid court. He died in Baghdad in 967 c.e. Al-Isfahani, as one of the leading lights of the literary and artistic entourage patronized by the Buyid court, partook of an imperial courtly exercise in undertaking the enormous project of cataloging Arab culture and literature in his *Kitab al-Aghani*. Commissioned by an

unnamed patron to compose the work, al-Isfahani took fifty years to complete *Kitab al-Aghani.* The request of the patron arose from a need to rectify the situation concerning an existing *Kitab al-Aghani,* which had been discredited primarily among court and elite circles. The very project of rewriting the *Kitab al-Aghani* undertaken by al-Isfahani was, therefore, to resituate this work onto a court trajectory from whence the first *Kitab al-Aghani* had originated. See Abu al-Faraj al-Isfahani, *Kitab al-Aghani,* 24 vols. (Cairo: Al Haya al-Misriyya al-Amma li al-Kitab, 1992). Also see Hilary Kilpatrick, *Making the Great Book of Songs* (London: Routledge Curzon, 2003).

31. The Arabic titles of these romances are grammatical constructs of the names of the lovers; the name of the male lover is rendered a possessive construct of the name of the female beloved; for example, *Majnun Layla* really means "Majnun of Layla." In Persian and other Middle Eastern literary traditions, this is reversed such that the female beloved is made into a possessive construct of the male lover, *Layla Majnun.*

32. Not only has *Majnun Layla* crossed many cultural and linguistic boundaries in the Islamic world, but it has recently arrived in the West as well. Eric Clapton's composition of the song "Layla" is based on the medieval Persian version of the romance by Nizami. Since the mid-1800s this ancient romance often has been adapted to dramas in the Arab world, and a few have been staged or set to film, especially during the last century.

33. I borrow this concept (including the phrase) from F. V. Greifenhagen, "Garments of Disclosure and Deception: The Joseph Story in Islamic and Jewish Scripture and the Politics of Intertextuality" (master's thesis, Duke University, 1992), 13–14. Greifenhagen compares the Joseph stories in the Qur'an and the Bible, and in so doing, he discusses how "the Biblical and Qur'anic accounts thus inscribe differing ideologies of truth and deception. In the Qur'anic account, events unfold under the lucid light of both God's guidance of the events and of the exposition or telling of them. What is hidden is revealed (12:102)." He also points out that this is in contrast to, for example, the Bible, where deception paradoxically sometimes works in the service of truth and actually is a means of God's works. Joseph, of the "many-colored coat," is known in the Qur'an for his shirt rather than his coat. In chapter 12 (Sūrat Yūsuf), it is Joseph's shirt that ultimately tells the story of how his life is enmeshed in a tangled web of secrecy, deception, and love. Greifenhagen asserts that in this Qur'anic account, "Joseph's shirt functions to signify the disclosure of truth. . . . Garments do not deceive but disclose" (13–14). Given the context of accusations leveled against the prophet (of his being a fabricator and forger), Greifenhagen asserts that "a homology is created between the disclosing quality and reliability of Joseph's story, of God's plan and his prophet's messages."

34. *Encyclopedia of Islam,* s.v. "*nafs*": "in most cases, they [*nafs* and its plurals] mean the human self or person."

35. See Th. Emil Homerin's entry under *Encyclopedia of the Quran,* s.v. "soul." Also see al-Raghib al-Isfahani, *Muʿjam mufradat alfaz al-Qurʾan* (Beirut: Dar al-Kutub al-ʿIlmiyya, 1997), 557, under *Nafs;* and Hanna E. Kassis, under sec. 2, 824: "*nafs,* (pl. *anfus* and *nufus*)—soul, self, life, person, heart."

36. Kallistos Ware, " 'My Helper and My Enemy': The Body in Greek Christianity," in *Religion and the Body,* ed. Sarah Coakley (Cambridge: Cambridge University Press, 1997), 91.

37. Ibid. This is quite unlike the "Hellenic-Platonist approach, which—without being strictly dualist . . . makes a firm differentiation between soul and body."

38. Fazlur Rahman, *Major Themes of the Qur'an* (Minneapolis: Bibliotheca Islamica, 1994), 112.

39. This stress on *al-bāṭin* and the role of *al-bāṭin wa'l-ẓāhir* in the psychology of Sufism is especially evident in the thought and output of the early mystic al-Muhasibi (who would have been a contemporary of al-Jahiz). He discusses how the "actions of the members [or limbs] (*a'māl al-jawarih*), the outward conduct, are under the ultimate control of the heart, which may direct them towards evil or good" (Margaret Smith, *An Early Mystic of Baghdad* [New York: AMS Press, 1973], 87). But then he also draws attention to the "actions of the heart (*a'mal al-qulub*), including the motives and sources of the outward actions, the cognitive, emotional and volitional processes, the exercise of the virtues and vices, the reception of the psychological states (*aḥwāl*) and the attainment of the mystic stations (*maqamāt*)."

40. Chittick, 65–69: "The self is considered to be veiled in this life." Chittick analyzes the rich symbolism of the "veil" in Islamic mysticism.

41. *Encyclopedia of the Qur'an,* s.v. "secrets." Shigeru Kamada, the author of this entry, states that "many Sufis and mystic philosophers locate *sirr* at the deepest dimension in the human consciousness, where they realize enlightenment with a divine encounter" (572–73). Moreover, Kamada observes, "Because the words *sirr* and *khafī* (*akhfā*) in the Qur'an seem to refer to something secret or to hidden aspects of human consciousness, Sufis have incorporated them in their theories of the inner subtleties (*laṭāi'f*), a type of religious psychology that analyzes the structure of human inward consciousness."

Chapter 1: Self and Secrecy in the Qur'an

1. I borrow the phrase "ideology of truth and deception" from F. V. Greifenhagen's essay comparing the Joseph stories in the Qur'an and the Bible. See Greifenhagen, chap. 1, endnote 33.

2. The connections between *al-ghayb* and things eschatological (especially the resurrection day) are present throughout the Qur'an. Divine secrets are infinite, including, as just discussed, the timing of eschatological events and how human beings will be resurrected or "raised up from the dead." Yet another is the nature of the accounting process that will unfold on Judgment Day:

> Q 21:47 We shall set up scales of justice for the day
> of judgment, so that not a soul will be dealt with
> unjustly in the least. And if there be
> (No more than) the weight of a mustard seed,
> We will bring it (to account) . . .

3. Rahman, *Major Themes of the Qur'an,* 116.

4. Al-Raghib al-Isfahani, *Al-Mufradat fi gharib al-Qur'an* (Cairo: Maktabat al-Anjlu al-Misriyya, 1978), 1:108.

5. Consider the following verse from Abdullah Yusuf Ali, trans., *The Holy Qur'an* (Elmhurst, N.Y: Tahrike Tarsile Qur'an, Inc., 1987), 1244:

Q 39:23 God has sent down the best discourse in the form of a book . . . from it or as a consequence of it, the skins of those who fear their lord tremble. Then their skins and their hearts soften toward the remembrance of God. Such is the guidance of God, he guides whom he wants [to guide].

This verse is found in the last of the series of six chapters that, according to Abdullah Ali (1235) deal with the "mysteries of the spiritual world, as leading up to the Ma'ad, or the Hereafter." To shed some light on the reference to the "softening of the skins" in this verse, it is worth noting that in the verse preceding it, there is a phrase with opposing imagery: the phrase is *lil-qasiyat qulūbuhum min dhikr allah,* or "those whose hearts are hardened against the remembrance of God."

6. Mahmud ibn 'Umar al-Zamakhshari, *Al-Kashshaf 'an haqa'iq ghawamid al-tanzil* (Beirut: Dar al-Kitab al-'Arabi, 1947), 4:195.

7. Abu Ja'far Muhammad b. Jarir al-Tabari, *Mukhtasar tafsir al-Tabari* (Beirut: 'Alam al-Kutub, 1985), 2:417.

8. At least three passages in the Qur'an describe scenes in which human bodies rebel against and tell the secrets of their owners. The other two passages are from chapters 24 and 36 respectively:

24:23 Those who slander chaste women . . . are cursed in this life and the hereafter for them is a grievous penalty.
24:24 On the Day when their tongues, their hands, and their feet will bear witness against them as to their actions.
36:65 That day shall we set a seal on their mouths. But their hands will speak to us, and their feet will bear witness to what they had earned.

Here again one discerns the element of how "even one's limbs will testify to the accuracy of the judgment rendered"—in other words, the body acts as sacred testimonial against the self.

9. Muhammad ibn Ahmad al-Qurtubi, *Al-Jami' li-Ahkam al-Qur'an* (Beirut: Dar al-Kutub al-'Ilmiyya, 1996), 15:228.

10. Al-Raghib al-Isfahani, *Mu'jam,* 108. Al-Tabari also brings up the word *al-furuj* in his interpretation; see al-Tabari, *Jami al-bayan 'an ta'wil ay al-Qur'an* (Cairo: Mustafa al-Babi al-Halabi, 1954), 24:106.

11. See Mustansir Mir, *Dictionary of Qur'anic Terms and Concepts* (New York: Garland, 1987), 216–17. The word *shahāda* is also employed in the Qur'anic oppositions of the realm of the visible/seen (*'alam al-shahāda*) versus the realm of the unseen.

12. Mir, *Dictionary.*

13. This also characterizes the following verse:

75:13–14 On that day will the human being be informed of that which he has put forward and of that which he has left behind; in truth, the human being is a witness against himself [*'alā nafsihi basīra*].

14. Al-Tabari, *Jami al-bayan 'an ta'wil ay al-Qur'an,* 107.

15. Likewise in the chapter preceding this one we find:

40:16 The day when they will come forth, nothing concerning them will be hidden from God.

40:19 He knows the treachery of the eyes and what the breasts conceal.

16. Al-Tabari, *Jami al-bayan 'an ta'wil ay al-Qur'an,* 24:107–8.

17. See Abdul Hammid Siddiqui, trans., *Sahih Muslim,* book 038, no. 6682, *MSA-USC Hadith Database.* Muslim Students Association, University of Southern California, http://www.usc.edu/dept/MSA/fundamentals/hadithsunnah/muslim/004.smt.html

18. Neuwirth (6) has discussed how this "'eschatological scenery' passage . . . presents a picture that precisely presupposes a violent attack leading to the overturn of everything, since it portrays devastation, the dissipation of the groups . . . the emptying of the most concealed receptacles (v. 10: *mā fil-ṣudūr*)."

19. See al-Jahiz, *Kitab Kitman al-Sirr,* 47; and al-Jahiz, "Keeping Secrets and Holding the Tongue," 21.

20. Abu Muhammad Ibn Qutayba, *'Uyun al-Akhbar* (Cairo: Dar al-Kutub al-Misriyya, 1930), 1:39; Abi 'Umar Ahmad b. Muhammad Ibn 'Abd Rabbih al-Andalusi, *Kitab al-'Iqd al-Farid,* ed. Ahmad Amin, Ahmad al-Zayn, and Ibrahim al-Abyari (Cairo: Matba'at Lajnat al-Ta'lif wa al-Tarjama wa al-Nashr, 1940), 1:66.

21. A couple of contemporary jokes (difficult to translate from the Arabic) that pertain to secrecy echo these sayings:

> Do you have "what it takes to keep a secret"?
> As if in a well . . . [I am like a deep well.]
> Do you have five bucks?
> Nope, as if I didn't hear a thing. . . .

22. Within the context of Old Testament studies, Balentine examines the theological implications of God's hiddenness in prophetic literature as well as Psalms: "Whereas the prophets stress the 'specific sense' of God's hiddenness in reaction to a guilty people, the psalmists complain of a hiddenness which to them seem inexplicable" (Samuel E. Balentine, *The Hidden God: The Hiding of the Face of God in the Old Testament* [New York: Oxford University Press, 1983], 166).

23. Andrew Rippin, in an article exploring the Qur'anic phrase "desiring the face of God," has put it thus: "God is declared present for the human who seeks him. The human presence is one that is demanded." See Andrew Rippin, "Desiring the Face of God: The Qur'anic Symbolism of Personal Responsibility," in *Literary Structures of Religious Meaning in the Qur'an,* ed. Boullata, 123. Rippin argues that the theme of "personal responsibility" in the Qur'an, while often analyzed in "terms of free will versus predestination," is "embedded in a variety of [Qur'anic] symbolic expressions" (ibid., 117). The expression "desiring the face of God," he maintains, is really about "submitting one's face [which] provides a sense of being open, just as God's face suggests his being open to humans. But the emphasis falls on personal responsibility and this is conveyed, at least in part, through the symbol of the face" (ibid., 122). Likewise, I argue (and here I paraphrase Rippin), that the Qur'anic symbolism of human secrecy and revelation concerns being open, sincere, and transparent before God, just as his communication and revelation (in the form of the divine Qur'an) suggests his disclosure to humans. Yet, the ultimate emphasis is on

individual (or collective) accountability, and this is partly conveyed through the symbolism of human concealment and secrecy (ibid.).

24. Apposite here is the mention that in an ancient ode by the celebrated, pre-Islamic pagan poet Zuhayr b. Abi Salma there is a verse that has a striking resemblance to the Qur'anic refrain "Do not conceal from God what is in your heart that it may be hidden; whatever is concealed, God knows all about it." See A. J. Arberry, *The Seven Odes* (London: Allen & Unwin, 1957), 115–16. While this verse did not necessarily contradict the poet's pagan values (there did exist a high god known as "Allah" in Mecca of pagan Arabia), it could also be that he was influenced by elements of the Qur'anic refrain. Zuhayr was a pagan poet, and it is possible that he was a Mukhaḍram—the Arabic term for those that lived during the transition from pre- to early Islamic times. In other words, if he lived through the years of Muhammad's early call to Islam, he therefore would have been exposed, to some degree, to the early revelations of the Qur'an.

25. Qur'anic-studies scholars often characterize the scripture's chapters/revelations as being of two types: those that correspond to the Meccan phase of Muhammad's prophethood (610 to 622 C.E.) and those that correspond to the Madinan phase of his calling as Prophet and leader of the nascent community of Muslims (622 to 632 C.E.). The Hijra, or emigration of the Prophet from Mecca (due to Muhammad's experiences of opposition from, and persecution by, the Meccans), to Madina took place in 622 C.E.

26. Consult Q 3:118, 3:154, 3:179, 4:63, 5:52, 6:13, 6:28, 6:59, 6:103, 8:43, 9:78, 10:61, 11:31, 11:123, 12:77, 16:77, 29:10, 29:52, 31:16–17, 33:51–52, 34:3, 72:25–26, and 96:14.

27. The verse numbering is based on Abdullah Yusuf Ali's translation *The Holy Qur'an.* I have closely consulted his and other translations, including A. J. Arberry, trans., *The Koran Interpreted* (New York: Simon & Schuster, 1996); and M. A. S. Abdel Haleem, *The Qur'an* (Oxford: Oxford University Press, 2004). The translations in this book draw upon all three of these sources (mainly that by A. Yusuf Ali) but with modifications by me to ensure accuracy and readability.

28. Margolis, "Psychology of Keeping Secrets," 291: "Secret keeping is a psychological process of considerable importance if only for its ubiquity."

29. Georg Simmel, "The Secret and Secret Society," in *The Sociology of Georg Simmel,* ed. Kurt H. Wolff (Glencoe, Ill.: Free Press, 1950), 334, declares, "Out of the counterplay of these two interests, in concealing and revealing, spring nuances and fates of human interaction that permeate it in its entirety . . . every human relation is characterized, among other things, by the amount of secrecy that is in and around it." Bolle (1) has observed that "not only is there no religion without secrecy, but there is no human existence without it." Also see Wolfson, 2.

30. According to the *Princeton Encyclopedia of Poetry and Poetics* (Alex Preminger, *Princeton Encyclopedia of Poetry and Poetics,* enl. ed. [Princeton, N.J.: Princeton University Press, 1965], 686–87), the term *refrain* consists of "a line, lines or part of a line, repeated at intervals . . . it may be as short as a single word or as long as a stanza. In stanzaic verse . . . it may appear at the beginning or in the middle [rather than the end of a stanza]. It may be used in such a way that its meaning varies or

develops from one recurrence to the next . . . or it may be used each time with a slight variation of wording appropriate to its immediate context." While the term is usually applied to poetry including stanzaic or free verse, I believe its application to the Qur'an is defensible given the poetic and rhythmic qualities associated with Qur'anic language.

31. Sissela Bok, *Secrets: On the Ethics of Concealment and Revelation* (New York: Pantheon, 1983), 7.

32. Al-Tabari, *Jami al-bayan 'an ta'wil ay al-Qur'an,* 1:366–67. Other relevant Qur'anic verses implicating the Madinan Jews and/or the Meccan pagans are:

> 36:76 Let not their sayings [of the unbelievers] then sadden you. Indeed we know what they keep secret and what they reveal.
> 47:26 This because they said to those who hate what God has revealed, "We will obey you in part of [this matter]." And God knows their secrets.
> 96:13–14 Do you see if/when he gives lies and turns away? Does he not know that God sees?

33. John Burton, *The Sources of Islamic Law: Islamic Theories of Abrogation* (Edinburgh: Edinburgh University Press, 1990), 192.

34. Ibid. Burton further remarks: "Nothing in these passages, nor in their Kur'ā-nic contexts remotely suggests that Muhammad, in the course of his own polemic with his Jewish compatriots, ever accused them of tampering with the written texts of the scriptures. Only one passage [2:75 cited above] uses the term: the Word of God, a form of words which in another Kur'ānic context refers, not to the Tora, but to the Word of God as mediated through the administrative instructions and regulations promulgated by Muhammad himself" (Burton, *Sources of Islamic Law,* 193).

35. In the Gospels a different sort of disparity between public and private is associated with certain Jewish groups—Jesus is shown decrying how their public piety is motivated by their desire for honor and admiration. In addition to Matthew 6 and 23, we find this issue mentioned in Luke 12. I provide examples from both Gospels:

> Matthew 23:12 (sayings against hypocrisy directed mainly to scribes and Pharisees) They do all their deeds to be seen by others, for they make their phylacteries broad and their fringes long.
> Luke 12:1–3 Meanwhile when the crowd gathered by the thousands, so that they trampled on one another, he began to first speak to his disciples, "Beware of the yeast of the Pharisees, that is, their hypocrisy. Nothing is covered up that will not be uncovered, and nothing secret that will not become known.
> Therefore whatever you have said in the dark will be heard in the light, and what you have whispered behind closed doors will be proclaimed from the housetops."

36. Abu Ja'far Muhammad b. Jarir al-Tabari, *Jami al-bayan 'an ta'wil al-Qur'an,* vol. 11 (Cairo: Dar al-Ma'arif, 1961); al-Zamakhshari, 1:209. See also Richard Bell, *A Commentary on the Qur'an,* ed. C. E. Bosworth and M. E. J. Richardson, 2 vols. (Manchester: Manchester University Press, 1991).

37. Mir, *Dictionary of Qur'anic Terms,* 55.

38. Burton, *Sources of Islamic Law,* 193. Burton remarks: "The assertion is frequent in the Kur'ān, being represented by the functions of the root *k t m* whose use in Kur'ānic verses averring the truth of Muhammad's claims is a Kur'ānic cliché: 'Who is more heinous in guilt than he who would conceal a testimony in his keeping from God?'"

39. Rahman, *Major Themes of the Qur'an,* 162.

40. Mahmoud Ayoub, "Muhammad the Prophet (circa 570–632)," in *Dictionary of Literary Biography,* vol. 311, *Arabic Literary Culture, 500–925,* ed. Michael Cooperson and Shawkaw M. Toorawa (Detroit: Thomson Gale, 2005), 268–87.

41. For an understanding of the history and cultural context of the relationship between Muhammad and the Jews of Madina, consult Barakat Ahmad, *Muhammad and the Jews: A Re-examination* (New Delhi: Vikas, 1979). Ahmad points to the presence of the word *khiyāna* (treachery) in 8:58 as referring to the breaking of covenant (made with Muhammad) by certain Jewish tribes in Madina. He asserts regarding 8:57–58 that "according to the commentators both these verses refer to the B. Qurayzah and not to the B. Qaynuqa" (61). Also consult David Marshall, *God, Muhammad and the Unbelievers: A Qur'anic Study* (Surrey: Curzon Press, 1999). Interestingly enough it seems that Muhammad himself partook in "the literary technique . . . known as *lahn,* that is, mistaking or misrepresenting the truth without lying" (see Ayoub, 280).

42. Rahman, *Major Themes of the Qur'an,* 37–38. Richard Bell (360) also alludes to the Madinan Jews as being the referent in verses 58:7–14.

43. Actually 58:7 launches an important sequence of verses (8–13) revolving around this concept of the *najwā*. The first series of verses (verses 7–10) addresses the secrecy of those engaging in deceptions and conspiracies. Verse 8 depicts those who secretly consult and meet for purposes or motives of deception. Secret consultations that are convened for hostile aims and/or for conspiring against the Prophet are not sanctioned.

44. Rahman, *Major Themes of the Qur'an,* 37–38.

45. Check 4:1, 5:117, 11:93 (96), 33:52, and 50:18 (17). In 5:117, in which Jesus is shown speaking to God: "And I was a witness over them as long as I remained among them, but since/as of when you caused me to die, you have been the watcher/spy [*al-raqīb*] over them and you are the witness over all things." Also see Kassis, s.v. "*raqīb.*"

46. According to the lexica, the word *najwā* in this verse means "secret talk between two or more persons" or "telling secrets to another person or holding secret consultations or conferences." It is derived from the root *n-j-w*, which has several verb forms (I, III, IV, VI) that possess a range of related meanings such as "to whisper (a secret to)," "to disclose, to lay bare," and "to whisper back and forth." Cf. al-Raghib al-Isfahani, *Mu'jam,* 538, and *Al-Mufradat,* 2:739.

47. Not surprisingly then, in Q 43:80 the verb "to hear," or *sama'*, instead of "to know," or *'alama,* is used in describing God's omniscience regarding these secret conferences: "Do they think that we hear not their secrets and their secret consultations? [We do] and our messengers are by them, recording."

48. M. Muhsin Khan, trans., *Sahih Bukhari,* vol. 1, book 8, no. 405, *MSA-USC Hadith Database,* Muslim Students Association, University of Southern California,

http://www.usc.edu/dept/MSA/fundamentals/hadithsunnah/bukhari/ (accessed January 2007).

49. Ibid., vol. 8, book 73, no. 96.

50. I am thankful to an anonymous press reader for pointing this out to me. According to this reader, *munājāt* gets applied to Moses' speaking with God, as well as Muhammad's "intimate colloquy" with God on the night of his ascension as recorded in some late hadith.

51. Mir, *Dictionary of Qur'anic Terms,* 141–42, s.v. "*najwā.*"

52. The Kuwaiti-born scholar Khaled Abou El Fadl has observed that "it would be disingenuous to deny that the Qur'an and other Islamic sources offer possibilities of intolerant interpretation." See Abou El Fadl et al., *The Place of Tolerance in Islam,* ed. Joshua Cohen and Ian Lague (Boston: Beacon Press, 2002), 23. It is certainly possible to see how these verses regarding the deceptions of the Madinan Jews could lend themselves to "intolerant interpretations."

53. David Marshall, *God, Muhammad and the Unbelievers: A Qur'anic Study* (Surrey: Curzon Press, 1999), 25.

54. See Simmel, 330: "In this situation emerges that the purposive hiding and masking, that aggressive defensive, so to speak, against the third person, which alone is usually designated as secret."

55. Kippenberg and Stroumsa, xiv.

56. Eye symbolism is an aspect of verse 40:19 from the refrain, especially the symbolism of the dichotomy or juxtaposition of breast versus the eye. Though both the eyes and the breast are shown hiding in this verse, by contrast in Arabic belles lettres the eye or eyes are generally associated with "revelation" or "disclosure": "He knows the treachery of the eyes and what the breasts conceal" (Q 40:19). The reference to deception or treachery has a general import even though the context for 40:19 is eschatological. As Abdullah Yusuf Ali points out, the phrase "treachery of the eyes" (*khā'inata al-'ayn*) may refer to the following: "1) how the eyes deceive in so far [*sic*] as what may be seen does not actually happen; 2) [how the] deceiver's eyes deceive others; 3) that the beholder sees things he ought not to (for example, *zinā'* [fornication] of the eyes)" (Abdullah Yusuf Ali, *Holy Qur'an,* 1267).

57. Given that the Arabic word for "heart," or *qalb,* as the lexica attest, also means "soul, mind, and intellect," I argue that it too functions as a metaphor for the inner, latent aspects of the self (al-Raghib al-Isfahani, *Mu'jam,* 458). Toshihiko Izutsu, *God and Man in the Koran: Semantics of the Koranic Weltanschauung* (Tokyo: Keio Institute of Cultural and Linguistic Studies, 1964), points out that *qalb,* as used in the Qur'an, should be understood as an inward psychological and mental capacity.

58. Consult Q 2:235, 5:52, 5:117, 11:31, and 33:37.

59. In the Christian East too, "the heart is in this way the hidden core of the self, the *temenos* or inner shrine. It is the secret place of meeting between body and soul, between soul and spirit, between the unconscious and the conscious, between the created and the uncreated" (Ware, 101).

60. *Encyclopedia of Islam,* new ed., s.v. "*kalb,*" by L. Gardet.

61. English translations of the Qur'an cannot convey the important nuances in and differences between the various kinds of concealment and revelation. A. Yusuf

Ali and other well-known English-language translators use the same English verb "to reveal" for what in the Arabic original are different verbs. Indeed, the identity of the agent of revelation can determine the content of the secret and the language employed to describe its revelation. Actually there exist two clusters of Arabic words for "to reveal" in the Qur'an: those describing God's revelations and those describing disclosures and revelations on the part of all nondivine agents. For instance, the oft-used word *wahy* (inspiration, revelation) and its verbal derivations are mostly employed throughout the scriptural text to describe God's revelations. By contrast the verb *badā* and its derivations, meaning "to appear, to be manifest," are applied only to human beings and other nondivine agents. I would strongly agree with a statement made in an excellent student paper that "the character [or content] of the secret to be revealed . . . determines the agent of revelation and the Arabic word used to describe the revelation in the Qur'an. Contrary to Simmel's claim, the content of the secret is not only important in Qur'anic revelation, it is defining" (Emily Manetta, Swarthmore student paper: "The Sacred and the Shameful: An Analysis of Secrecy and Revelation in Quranic Text," May 1999).

62. Two other verbs conveying the semantics of "disclosure, revelation" are *badā*, meaning "to appear, to be manifest"; and *jahara*, "to proclaim, publish, be loud in speech." See Kassis, sec. 2, *'alana*, 256; *jahara*, 590–91.

63. Al-Raghib al-Isfahani, *Mu'jam*, 256–57. Also see al-Raghib al-Isfahani, *Al-Mufradat*, 2:334; Edward William Lane, *Arabic-English Lexicon* (Cambridge: Islamic Texts Society, 1984), 1:1337–40; Abu al-Fadl Jamal al-Din Ibn Mukarram Ibn Manzur al-Ifriqi al-Misri, *Lisan al-'Arab*, 15 vols. (Beirut: Dar Sadir/Dar Beirut, 1956); and the *Encyclopedia of the Qur'an*, s.v. "secrets." Other oft-used Qur'anic verbs employed for conveying the semantics of human secrecy and concealment are *khafiya* and *katama*.

64. The form I verb, *sarra*, and, especially, the form IV verb, *asarra*, have these two opposing significations respectively: he kept it secret and he revealed it. The most oft-used verb in the refrain appears to be the IV form *asarra*, although other verbs with meanings that are just shades different from *asarra* are also employed.

65. Simmel, 331.

66. Ibid.

67. Ibid., 335.

68. Wolfson, 3.

69. This form implies the "concept of the secret," as discussed earlier. Wolfson (2) identifies secrecy and revelation as being essential to the very constitution of human subjectivity: "The centrality of the secret in the phenomenology of religious experience should come as no surprise given the importance of secrecy in the human condition. Of the various traits that distinguish humans from other sentient beings, dissimulation is certainly one of the most obvious examples. Indeed, to dissimulate is basic to the human way of being: we are who we are primarily because we are not who we profess to be. The masks by which our lives are constructed are multiple, and it is precisely through the obscurity of these masks that we are rendered transparent. In this regard, the sphere of religion is not distinct. On the contrary, the repeated emphasis on the category of the mystery in the religious domain is an

extension of the more general emphasis on concealment that is so essential to our disclosure in the realm of intersubjectivity."

70. Of course, the very distinctions in the Qur'an between the hidden and the open, the concealed and the revealed are, as Izutsu, in his study of the Qur'an (83), has declared, "meaningful only in reference to the basic epistemological capacity of the human mind." The hadith corpus indicates that such inextricability of the secret and revealed was also an aspect of worship and prayer: "Abu Huraira reported [that] The Messenger of Allah . . . used to say while prostrating himself: 'O Lord, forgive me all my sins, small and great, first and last, open and secret.' " See Siddiqui, book 004, number 0980.

71. This is demonstrated through the many hundreds of entries under its verbal root, listed in Kassis, sec. 1, "The Divine Name," 17–20; sec. 2, "The Remaining Vocabulary of the Qur'an," 239–55.

72. Derivations from the verbal root *kh-b-r*, "to discern, be aware," are often found in conjunction with or in place of the aforementioned verbal derivation of "to know." See Kassis, sec. 1, "The Divine Name," 52–53; sec. 2, "The Remaining Vocabulary of the Qur'an," 678–79.

73. The "Ninety-Nine Divine Names or Attributes of God" are known in Arabic as *al-asmā' al-ḥusnā*, the "Beautiful Names of God." Consult Q 17:110: "Say: Call on God or on the Merciful—whatever names you call him, his are the most beautiful names."

74. Rahman, *Major Themes of the Qur'an*, 37–38.

75. *Encyclopedia of the Qur'an*, s.v. "faith."

76. See Siddiqui, book 001, no. 0228, *MSA-USC Hadith Database* (adjustments made for the sake of readability):

> It is reported on the authority of Abu Huraira that when it was revealed to the Messenger of Allah . . . "To Allah belongs whatever is in the heavens and whatever is in the earth and whether you disclose that which is in your mind or conceal it, Allah will call you to account according to it. Then He forgives whom He pleases and chastises whom He Pleases; and Allah is over everything Potent" (2:284), the Companions of the Messenger . . . felt it hard and severe and they came to the Messenger . . . and sat down on their knees and said: "[O] Messenger, we were assigned some duties which were within our power to perform, such as prayer, fasting, struggling . . . charity. Then this (the above-mentioned) verse was revealed unto you and it is beyond our power to live up to it."

An almost identical hadith follows this one (see *Sahih Muslim*, book 001, number 0229, *MSA-USC Hadith Database*):

> It is narrated on the authority of Ibn 'Abbas: When this verse was revealed: "Whether you disclose that which is in your mind or conceal it, Allah will call you to account according to it" (2:284), there entered in their minds something (of that fear) such as had never entered their hearts (before). The Apostle (may peace be upon him) observed: Say: We have heard and obeyed and submitted ourselves. He (the reporter) said: Allah instilled faith in their hearts and He revealed this verse: "Allah burdens not a soul beyond its capacity. It gets every good that it earns and it suffers every ill that it earns. Our Lord, call us not to

account if we forget or make a mistake. He the (Lord) said: I indeed did it. Our Lord! do not lay on us a burden as Thou didst lay on those before us. He (our Lord) said: I indeed did it. And pardon us, have mercy on us. Thou art our Protector" (2:286). He said: I indeed did it.

77. Ibid., See Sahih Muslim, book 001, no. 0228, *MSA-USC Hadith Database*.

78. Muhsin Khan, trans., *Sahih Bukhari,* volume 6, book 60, nos. 68–69, *MSA-USC Hadith Database.* Muslim Students Association- University of Southern California. http://www.usc.edu/dept/MSA/fundamentals/hadithsunnah/bukhari/060.sbt.html (accessed January 2007). In this *Sahih Bukhari* collection, we find two brief hadith that state this verse (2:284) was abrogated:

> Narrated Ibn 'Umar: This verse—"Whether you show what is in your minds or conceal it . . ." (2:284) was abrogated.
>
> Narrated Marwan Al-Asghar: A man from the companions of Allah's Apostle who I think, was Ibn 'Umar said The Verse:—"Whether you show what is in your minds or conceal it . . ." was abrogated by the Verse following it.

79. John Burton, foreword to *The Sources of Islamic Law: Islamic Theories of Abrogation* (Edinburgh: Edinburgh University Press, 1990), x, quoting the Muslim scholar al-Suyuti (from his work *Itqan*). Among the most noted of Western authorities on the subject on abrogation or *naskh,* Burton has pointed out that "Western scholars have hitherto shown an incomprehensible indifference to Muslim discussions on *naskh*" (ix). To paraphrase David Powers, another noted authority on the subject, most Islamic scholars have defined it as comprising any of the following (or a combination thereof): "removal, change and/or cancellation followed by replacement." David Powers, "The Exegetical Genre nasikh al-Qur'an wa mansukhuhu," in *Approaches to the History of the Interpretation of the Qur'an,* ed. Andrew Rippin (Oxford: Clarendon Press, 1988) 124–25.

80. A. F. L. Beeston et al., eds., "Early Arabic Prose," in *Arabic Literature to the End of the Umayyad Period,* ed. Beeston et al., Cambridge History of Arabic Literature (Cambridge: Cambridge University Press, 1983), 121.

81. M. Muhsin Khan, trans., *Sahih Bukhari,* vol. 3, book 48, no. 809.

82. Pamela Eisenbaum, private correspondence, Crosscurrents: The Association for Religion and Intellectual Life, Union Theological Seminary, New York City, July 2004.

83. Michael Cook, *Forbidding Wrong in Islam* (Cambridge: Cambridge University Press, 2003), 62.

84. Ibid., 57. Here I am paraphrasing Cook, who uses the term "immunity of hidden wrongs." Cook analyzes early textual evidence concerning the Islamic duty of "commanding right and forbidding wrong."

85. Ibid.

86. Ibid.

87. ibid., 61–63.

88. "We may not spy on people nor may we enter a home on the off-chance of discovering some wrongdoing in it" (ibid., 58).

89. Ibid., 61–63.

90. M. Muhsin Khan, trans., *Sahih Bukhari,* vol. 3, book 48, no. 809.

91. Denise Spellberg, *Politics, Gender and the Islamic Past: The Legacy of 'A'isha Bint Abi Bakr* (New York: Columbia University Press, 1994), 61.

92. Ibid., 63.

93. Ibid., 71–72. The relevant events surrounding the controversy had come to the public's knowledge, and though what resulted from this were false accusations, deceptive appearances, they still loomed large. 'A'isha, in her moments of despair, is shown turning to a Qur'anic incident wherein appearances were deceptive: "Then I tried to recall the name of Jacob, but I could not remember it. I said, 'I will say what the father of Joseph said: "[My course is to show] comely patience. The help of Allah needs be sought [to defend] me against what you describe"'" (71); "She refuses to accept the communal rumours that suggest her guilt, just as Jacob, the father of Joseph, in the Qur'anic verse 12:18 she cites, refuses to believe the false evidence of his son's bloodied shirt" (71).

94. Spellberg, 71.

95. Ibid., 79. It is interesting to note comparisons that resonate across cultures with the Indian Sage Valmiki's epic *Ramayana*. Sita, abducted by the demon king Ravana from her husband Ram, is also subject to criticism and doubt for having lived (despite the fact that she was held captive) in the house of someone other than her husband for over a year. When compelled to prove her innocence, she beseeches Agni, the god of fire, who vouches for her chastity.

96. See Ibn Hazm, *Tawq al-Hamama*, ed. al-Tahir Ahmad Makki (Cairo: Dar al-Ma'arif, 1975), 119; and Ibn Hazm, *The Ring of the Dove: A Treatise on the Art and Practice of Arab Love,* trans. A. J. Arberry (London: Luzac, 1953), 250. For the sake of readability and consistency, the format of the Qur'anic verse citations has been altered from that found in Arberry's translation.

97. Briefly stepping outside of the Abrahamic monotheistic framework, Eck (8–9) analyzes how it is that the ocular and the visual predominate in the worshiper-deity relationship in Hinduism. In the Hindu ritual of *darshan,* "seeing" is conceived of and practiced in a wholly immanent sense. Eck furthermore draws our attention to how in the Hindu Indian milieu, the god's gaze involves a perceived tactile and affective dimension: "When Hindus stand on tiptoe and crane their necks to see . . . the image of Lord Krsna, they wish not only to 'see,' but to be seen. The gaze of the huge eyes of the image meets that of the worshiper, and that exchange of vision lies at the heart of Hindu worship. . . . In the Indian context, seeing is [also] a kind of touching. The art historian Stella Kramrisch writes . . . 'Seeing, according to Indian notions, is a going forth of the sight towards the object. . . . Touch is the ultimate connection by which the visible yields to being grasped.'"

98. A. Rizzuto, paper delivered at Margaret Mahler Symposium hosted by the Margaret S. Mahler Psychiatric Research Foundation, Philadelphia, May 2000.

99. Ibid.

100. See the text of the Hadith of Gabriel in Sachiko Murata and William C. Chittick, *Vision of Islam* (St. Paul, Minn.: Paragon House, 1994), xxv.

101. Ibid., xxvii–xxviii.

102. This hadith is described by Murata and Chittick (xxvii) as presenting the religion in a nutshell. Acknowledging its pedagogical value (even in the classical

sources), they use the hadith as a focal point for the organization of their entire text (xxv).

103. Murata and Chittick, 276.

104. Ana-Maria Rizzuto, *The Birth of the Living God: A Psychoanalytic Study* (Chicago: University of Chicago Press, 1979), 198–99.

105. Murata and Chittick, 276.

106. The theology of the Qur'an presents rather conflicting claims on this tension. See *Encyclopedia of the Qur'an,* s.v. "Hidden and the Hidden."

107. Denny aptly describes Hadith Qudsī as a "divine saying" that Islamic tradition deems to be "a revelation from God but couched in Muhammad's own words" (159).

108. A. J. Arberry, *An Introduction to the History of Sufism* (London: Longman, 1943), 28.

Chapter 2: Sharing and Withholding Secrets

1. Bolle, 5.

2. Again the verse numbering is based on Abdullah Yusuf Ali's *Holy Qur'an.* I have closely consulted his and other translations, including Arberry, *Koran Interpreted;* and Abdel Haleem, *Qur'an.* The translations in this book draw on all three of these sources (mainly that by A. Yusuf Ali) but with modifications by me to ensure accuracy and readability.

3. In her *Encyclopedia of the Qur'an* entry, J. Smith remarks that "Faith is not so much believing in something or adhering to some kind of acceptance of the unseen" (167). Actually, in the way that the *ghayb* or the unseen is conceived of in the Qur'an, eschatological elements are very much a part of this "unseen," and Smith notes that "Faith in God is both trust in God's mercy . . . and fear of the reality of the day of judgment." See *Encyclopedia of The Quran,* s.v. "Faith."

4. Jacques Derrida, *The Gift of Death,* trans. David Wills (Chicago: University of Chicago Press, 1995), 108.

5. Izutsu, 83.

6. Ibid., 82–83.

7. Shi'ite Qur'anic commentators especially were interested in teasing out what was included in the domain of the unseen or the hidden, and much was discussed concerning Q 31:34, "which lists five items the knowledge of which is reserved for God alone: knowledge of the hour (of the last judgment); knowledge of the future of rainfall . . . knowledge of the gender of the infant in the mother's womb . . . knowledge of people's fate . . . and knowledge of an individual's place of death." See *Encyclopedia of the Qur'an,* s.v. "Hidden and the Hidden." The idea of "a glorious Qur'an in a guarded tablet," an idea that touches on the divine prehistory of the Qur'anic text, is also deemed an element of the unseen and hidden.

8. Izutsu, 83.

9. Ibid., 85. Izutsu observes that "there seems to be no trace in pre-Islamic heathenism of the word's having been used in a religious sense."

10. Ibid., 84.

11. Al-Razi defined the *ghayb* to include those "things concealed from senses." "Furthermore . . . Razi says that things can be divided into those that can be discovered by means of an indication from God and those that cannot be so discovered. Relying on this dichotomy, claims al-Razi, one can remove the contradiction apparent in the verses of the Qur'an: those claiming God's exclusive access to the world of 'the hidden' refer to the areas that cannot be discovered by means of an indication from God, whereas those speaking of God sharing his knowledge of 'the hidden' with some of his creatures refer to things that can be discovered in this fashion" (*Encyclopedia of the Qur'an*, s.v. "Hidden and the Hidden").

12. Al-Raghib al-Isfahani, *Mu'jam*, 411–12. Also see al-Raghib al-Isfahani, *Al-Mufradat*, 2:552.

13. Edward W. Lane, 2:2313. Also see al-Raghib al-Isfahani, *Mu'jam*, 411–12; and al-Raghib al-Isfahani, *Al-Mufradat*, 2:552.

14. *Encyclopedia of the Qur'an*, s.v. "Hidden and the Hidden."

15. Charles Pellat, *The Life and Works of Jahiz* (Berkeley and Los Angeles: University of California Press, 1969), 204.

16. The quotation reads: "a reply to . . . 'Why [believe in] God at all?' takes the form of a 'belief in and awareness of the unseen' (2:3, 5:94, 21:49, 35:18, 36:11, 50:33, 57:25 67:12); this 'unseen' has been, to a greater or lesser extent, made 'seen' through Revelation for some people such as the Prophet (examples: 81:24; 68:47; 52:41; 53:35; 12:102), although it cannot be fully known to anyone except God (examples: 72:26; 64:18; 59:22; 49:18; 39:46; 35:38; 32:6; 27:65; 23:92; 18:26; 16:77; 13:9; 12:81; 11:31; 7:188, etc.)" (Rahman, *Major Themes of the Qur'an*, 2).

17. *Encyclopedia of the Qur'an*, s.v. "Hidden and the Hidden."

18. This is what God says to the angels after Adam tells the "names" of things created.

19. Izutsu, 182.

20. Even the *jinn* are depicted as recognizing that their ignorance of the *al-ghayb* could have grave consequences. In 34:14 the *jinn* who are working for the prophet Sulayman are unaware of his death until the very last moment.

21. Bolle, 5.

22. Izutsu, 84.

23. Al-Raghib al-Isfahani, *Mu'jam*, 167.

24. Abdullah Yusuf Ali, *Holy Qur'an*, 1158.

25. Grammatically the case could be made for both types of referents. Arabic-English translations of the Qur'an only heighten this ambiguity. In Edward W. Lane's *Arabic-English Lexicon* we find that there is a derivation of the root of *ghayb* (the IV form verb *aghabat*) that means "she had her husband or one of her family absent from her" (the verb implies a necessarily female agent or *fa'il*). Although the use of the preposition *li* is not immediately clear in the following verse, the phrase *lil-ghayb* in it reflects this same sense:

> 4:34 Men are protectors/maintainers of women by virtue of God favoring some over others, and by virtue of what they spend of their wealth. So righteous women are obedient and guardful in the absence [of mates] by virtue of what God guards . . . [*hafizat lil-ghayb bi-mā hafiza allah*].

26. Often the object of the verb *khashiya* is the word *rabb*, or Lord (for example, 35:18 *yakhshūna rabbahum bil-ghayb*) or other words signifying God. It is also the case that the phrase *bil-ghayb* functions as its object. Certain Arabic expressions exist in which *bil-ghayb* functions as an object of a verb; for example, there is a saying, *rajama bil-ghayb*, that means "He spoke of that which is unknown [to him]." This supports the aforementioned prevailing translations and not the alternative one I propose. But the question arises: could the phrase *bil-ghayb* be grammatically used as a descriptive state that refers back to the human agents of the verb *khashiya*, the ones engaging in the "fearing with awe or veneration"? The descriptive state I am referring to here is grammatically known as "circumstantial accusative," and in Arabic grammar the term for it is *ḥāl*. It is possible that the verb *khashiya* is one of the *'afāl al-qulūb*, which can take two objects (a direct or indirect object). These, according to the grammarian W. Wright, "signify an act that takes place in the mind or *'afāl al-yaqīn wal-shakk aw al-rujḥān* or verbs of certainty and doubt or preponderance (of probability), such as . . . *wajada, ẓanna, ḥasiba*" (W. Wright, *A Grammar of the Arabic Language* [Cambridge: Cambridge University Press, 1988], pt. 2:48).

27. Derrida, 57.

28. Bolle, 5.

29. Al-Tabari, *Jami al-bayan 'an ta'wil ay al-Qur'an*, 24:153; al-Qurtubi, *Al-Jami' li-Ahkam al-Qur'an* (1996), 15:9.

30. Regarding this verse, Ali remarks, "those who in their innermost hearts and in their most secret doings were actuated by God-fearing love, the fear that is akin to love" (Abdullah Yusuf Ali, *Holy Qur'an*, 1416).

31. Ibid., 833.

32. *Encyclopedia of the Qur'an*, s.v. "Faith."

33. There are also verses that enjoin this in one's interaction with the Prophet, for example:

> 49:2 O you who believe! raise not your voices above the voice of the prophet
> nor speak loudly to him as you speak loudly to one another lest your works
> become in vain and you perceive not.

34. Modern commentators occasionally straddle both interpretations. The Pakistani commentator Syed Anwer Ali states: "The words '. . . fear their Lord unseen . . .' in the verse [35:18] imply that this fear must be sincere and from within the depth of their hearts, because while accepting the Message of warning or admonition, they also accept the Faith that the Authority before whom they are submitting is All-Seeing although He Himself is Invisible." See Syed Anwer Ali, *Qur'an: The Fundamental Law of Human Life* (Karachi, Pakistan: Hamdard Foundation Press, 1987), 11:459.

35. *Encyclopedia of the Qur'an*, s.v. "Almsgiving."

36. Ibid.

37. Ibid.

38. Ibid.

39. Examples of verses in which secrecy's links with "good deeds" are discerned are the following:

Q 4:149 Whether you manifest a good deed or hide it or pardon an evil, God effaces and is all-powerful.

Q 4:148 God loves not the publicizing of bad speech, except [on behalf of] one who has been wronged. God is all-knowing and all-hearing.

40. Tarif Khalidi, *The Muslim Jesus: Sayings and Stories in Islamic Literature* (Cambridge, Mass.: Harvard University Press, 2001), 53.

41. M. Muhsin Khan, trans., *Sahih Bukhari,* vol. 8, book 76, no. 506, *MSA-USC Hadith Database,* Muslim Students Association, University of Southern California, http://www.usc.edu/dept/MSA/fundamentals/hadithsunnah/bukhari/076.sbt.html (accessed January 2007).

42. Among the "occasions of revelation," or *asbāb al-nuzūl,* associated with this verse is the following: Ali (b. Abi Talib) had only four dirhams. He gave away one of the dirhams at night, one at day, one secretly and one publicly. The Prophet said to him, "What has made you do this?" He said, "I did it so that I would be worthy of God who has made a promise to me." The Prophet said to him, "Now that is yours." So God revealed the verse (Q 2:274), "Those who give their possessions at night and at day, secretly and in public, they will have their reward with their lord." [Wāḥidī, *Asbāb* , 86]. See *Encyclopedia of the Qur'an,* s.v. "Occasions of Revelation."

43. Kassis, sec. 2, *'alana,* 256; *jahara,* 590–91.

44. Th. Emil Homerin, "Altruism in Islam," in *Altruism in World Religions,* ed. Jacob Neusner (Washington, D.C.: Georgetown University Press, 2005), 15.

45. Ibid., 16. Furthermore, "like *zakat, ṣadaqa,* or voluntary alms, should be given in secret if possible so as to avoid spiritual pride and to save the recipient from embarrassment" (ibid., 18).

46. Abu Ja'far Muhammad b. Jarir al-Tabari, *Jami' al-bayan fi tafsir al-Qur'an* (Beirut, 1992), 93.

47. Earlier we saw how the term *najwā* embraces the meanings of "private and/or secret converse" that is of a sacred, religious nature "between God and his believer," especially on Judgment Day.

48. *Encyclopedia of the Qur'an,* s.v. "Anatomy." Qamar-ul Huda remarks that "as an expression of unbelief, the Qur'an frequently uses the metaphor of the 'sealed heart.'"

49. Consult the lexical dictionaries, including the Qur'anic lexicon by al-Raghib al-Isfahani, *Mu'jam,* under the relevant Arabic terms.

50. Al-Raghib al-Isfahani, *Mu'jam,* 458.

51. See *khatm* in al-Raghib al-Isfahani, *Mu'jam,* 160. Here I am not so concerned with the question of free will versus God's determinism as raised by this phrase.

52. Al-Tabari, *Jami' al-bayan 'an ta'wil ay al-Qur'an,* intro. and notes by J. Cooper (Oxford: Oxford University Press, 1987), 1:110–11.

53. Ibid.

54. Rahman, *Major Themes of the Qur'an,* 20.

55. The mention of the stained heart is found in 83:14: "Nay, but on their hearts is the stain of which they do or earn."

56. Al-Tabari, *Jami' al-bayan,* introduction by J. Cooper, 1:110.

57. Helmut Gatje, *The Qur'an and Its Exegesis: Selected Texts with Classical and Modern Muslim Interpretations,* trans. and ed. Alford T. Welch (Berkeley and Los Angeles: University of California Press, 1976), 221.

58. Elaine Scarry, *The Body in Pain: The Making and Unmaking of the World* (New York: Oxford University Press, 1985), 203.

59. Ibid., 204.

60. Ibid., 202.

61. Ware, 91.

62. Ibid. This is quite unlike the "Hellenic-Platonist approach, which—without being strictly dualist . . . makes a firm differentiation between soul and body."

63. Indeed, one could argue that "the character [or content] of the secret to be revealed . . . determines the agent of revelation and the Arabic word used to describe the revelation in the Qur'an. Contrary to Simmel's claim, the content of the secret is not only important in Qur'anic revelation, it is defining" (Emily Manetta, Swarthmore student paper: "The Sacred and the Shameful: An Analysis of Secrecy and Revelation in Quranic Text," May 1999).

Chapter 3: Self as Cipher in *Kitab Kitmān al-Sirr*

1. I have closely consulted the Arabic text of the treatise throughout this book. However, all the translations of excerpts from al-Jahiz's *Kitman* are (with occasional and minor modifications on my part for greater accuracy) from *Nine Essays of al-Jahiz,* trans. Hutchins. See al-Jahiz, *Kitab Kitman al-Sirr,* 54; and al-Jahiz, "Keeping Secrets and Holding the Tongue," trans. Hutchins, 27.

2. Sissela Bok's work (*Secrets,* 11) demonstrates a perceptive assertion that "at the heart of secrecy lies discrimination of some form, since its essence is sifting, setting apart, drawing lines," which resonates powerfully with this conceptualization of *kitmān al-sirr.*

3. Admittedly, al-Jahiz rather infrequently relies on the Qur'an in fashioning his ideas regarding secrecy (references to Qur'anic verses are made six times throughout the sixty-page treatise, *Kitman*), but as we shall see, the very first citation of a Qur'anic verse (89:5) in his work is an important element in his conceptualization of concealing the secret (*kitmān al-sirr*).

4. The most comprehensive Western studies of al-Jahiz remain those by the French scholar Charles Pellat. See his "Al-Jahiz," 78–95. More recent comprehensive studies of al-Jahiz are those authored by James E. Montgomery, including "Al-Jahiz's *Kitab al-Bayan wa-l-Tabyin,*" in *Writing and Representation in Medieval Islam: Muslim Horizons,* ed. Julia Bray (New York: Routledge, 2006); and "Al-Jahiz," in *Dictionary of Literary Biography,* vol. 311, *Arabic Literary Culture, 500–925,* ed. Cooperson and Toorawa, 231–42.

5. Pellat, in "Al-Jahiz," 94, remarks that he was dubbed "the teacher of reason and polite learning," or *mu'allim al-'aql wa l-adab,* by some early writers. For al-Jahiz, "*adab* was indeed a process of building up a new culture in which reflection, doubt, observation and even experiment were involved." One would think that the strain of his *adab* trajectory that dealt with, in Pellat's words "the study of manners and morals, analyzing character and emotion and building up pictures of entire

social groups characterized by some particular moral or psychological feature," generated a wide readership.

6. It is somewhat difficult to assess how his Muʿtazilite affiliation and background informed his ideas regarding secrecy in *Kitman*. It is sufficient to note that the Muʿtazilite views of the "created Qurʾan" and the fact that the Qurʾan contained metaphorical language (the Muʿtazilites maintained that scriptural phrases such as "the throne of God" or "the face of God" were not to be literally interpreted) would have exerted an influence on his ideas; certainly the latter view suggests that he would have readily accepted the tropological qualities of language.

7. Wen-Chin Ouyang, *Literary Criticism in Medieval Arabic-Islamic Culture* (Edinburgh: Edinburgh University Press, 1997), 102–3.

8. The third major work of al-Jahiz is *Kitab al-Bukhala*ʾ, or *Book of Misers*. His three major works have been preserved intact.

9. Ouyang, 103.

10. Jamal El-Attar, "Al-Jahiz's View of Arabic in Relation to the Qurʾan," in *Democracy in the Middle East: Proceedings of the Annual Conference of the British Society of Middle Eastern Studies, 8–10 July 1992, University of St. Andrews, Scotland* (Exeter: BRISMES, 1992), 26.

11. El-Attar quoting (and translating) al-Jahiz in ibid., 26.

12. Ouyang, 103.

13. Montgomery, "Al-Jahiz," 238.

14. See al-Jahiz, *Kitab Kitman al-Sirr,* 59; and al-Jahiz, "Keeping Secrets and Holding the Tongue," trans. Hutchins, 31.

15. Al-Jahiz, *Kitab Kitman al-Sirr,* 39; al-Jahiz, "Keeping Secrets and Holding the Tongue," trans. Hutchins, 15.

16. Ibid.

17. See al-Jahiz, *Tafdil al-Nutq ʿala al-Samt,* in *Majmuʿat al-Rasaʾil: Ithna ʿasharah risalah,* edited by Muhammad al-Sasi al-Maghribi (Cairo: Matbaʿat al-Taqaddam, 1906), 136. In *Tafdil al-Nutq* he lauds the efficacy of the spoken word, remarking that only through the tongue can "you express your needs and declare your aims," and moreover, "you can describe silence with words, while you cannot do the converse." Furthermore, he notes that "were silence more preferable . . . the superiority . . . [of] human beings over other [creatures] would not be recognized."

18. Brustad, Reynolds, and their coauthors have pointed out that this particular verse and its emphasis on a "godly way to use speech" were explicitly invoked by some medieval Arab autobiographers as motivations for writing the genre. It could be that this Qurʾanic injunction was invoked to legitimate not just the desire to speak through a particular genre but also the need or desire to speak publicly or make a claim known. See Brustad et al., 61–62.

19. Montgomery, "Al-Jahiz," 238.

20. Ibid.

21. Pellat, "Al-Jahiz," 80. Al-Jahiz earned a living through his writing, and some of his early writings were "designed to legitimate the ʿAbbasid caliphate or to justify important government measures."

22. To some extent then, this treatise on secrecy and discretion likely elicited the same audience as his possibly apocryphal *Kitab al-Hajib* (Book of the Chamberlain)

and his now lost work *Kitab Akhlaq al-Wuzara* (Book on the Morals of Viziers), a manual of conduct for viziers.

23. See Geert Jan van Gelder, "Compleat Men, Women and Books: On Medieval Arabic Encyclopaedism," in *Pre Modern Encyclopaedic Texts,* ed. Peter Binkley (New York: Brill, 1997), 254. These encyclopedic anthologies were also a part of a general trajectory of humanistic belletristic writings which—in their emphasis on *urbanitas,* literary style, ethics, and language—appealed to various strata of the court elites including the caliph and nobles and their entourage.

24. The first and last works are separated by more than four centuries. The author of the first work, *'Uyun,* was Ibn Qutayba, who was a contemporary of al-Jahiz.

25. However, since the chapters partake in a different genre—i.e., the encyclopedia as opposed to the treatise or monograph that al-Jahiz authored—the presentation of these ideas and elements is unique. In other words, rather than employing discursive prose, these chapters rely on, as van Gelder describes, "countless quotations in prose and poetry, including maxims, proverbs, anecdotes, jokes, homilies," to convey and frame the central ideas and elements concerning secrecy present in *Kitman.* See van Gelder, 254.

26. Paraphrased from Akhtar's discussion on "distance." See Salman Akhtar, *Inner Torment* (Northvale, N.J.: Jason Aronson, 1999), 241.

27. Ibn Manzur al-Ifriqi al-Misri, s.v. "*katama.*"

28. In the Qur'anic refrain, the word's negative value is certainly evinced by 3:167 (in which the act of concealing involves hypocrisy and what is concealed is "unbelief" [*kufr*]) and implied by 21:110. Examples of this abound generally in the Qur'an: 2:228, in which the use of the verb refers to divorced women concealing pregnancy (something unlawful), as well as 4:81 and 5:51, in which its use signifies deceptions on the part of the pagan Meccans or the Madinan Jews. Consult 2:228, 3:71, 4:37, 4:42, 4:81, 4:108, 4:114, and 5:61. Burton's observation supports this: "The assertion is frequent in the Kur'ān, being represented by the functions of the root *k t m* whose use in Kur'ānic verses averring the truth of Muhammad's claims is a Kur'ānic cliché: 'Who is more heinous in guilt than he who would conceal a testimony in his keeping from God?'" (Burton, *Sources of Islamic Law,* 193). However, in a few instances, such as the following, the word is used in a Qur'anic context in which the act of concealing is positive, and not surprisingly, it is faith, or *imān,* that is concealed: "and a believing man from the people of Pharoah who concealed his faith . . ." (40:28).

29. *Wal-ḥadīth kulluhu illāmā lā bāla bihi ḏhikr al-nās wa-laghw* [trifle, slip of language, useless word] *wa-khaṭal* [coarse talk] *wa-hujr* [delirium, unseemly language] *wa-hudhā* [raving and ranting] *wa-ghība* [backbiting, slander] *wa-hamz* [backbiting, faultfinding] *wa-lamz* [reproach] *wa qāla ba'aḍ al-ḥukamā' li-ibnihi: yā bunayya innamā al-insān ḥadīth fa-in istaṭa'ta an takūna ḥadīth ḥasan, fa-'uf'al. wa kullu sirr fil-arḍ innama huwa khabar 'an insān wa-ṭayy 'an insān. . . .* Hutchins has translated *Wal-ḥadith kulluhu illāmā lā bāla bihi ḏhikr al-nās* as "All conversation, except what is pointless, is talk about people . . ." (see al-Jahiz, "Keeping Secrets and Holding the Tongue," trans. Hutchins, 25). It could be argued that there is a corruption of the original text here and that more consistent with the import of al-Jahiz's

views is the translation "All talk (*ḥadīth*), except what is to the point, is talk about people (*dhikr al-nās*). . . ."

30. Again I have closely consulted the Arabic text of the treatise throughout this article. However, all the translations of excerpts from al-Jahiz's *Kitman* are (with occasional and minor modifications on my part for greater accuracy) from *Nine Essays of al-Jahiz,* translated by William Hutchins. See al-Jahiz, *Kitab Kitman al-Sirr,* 52; and al-Jahiz, "Keeping Secrets and Holding the Tongue," trans. Hutchins, 25.

31. "By reporting secrets, biography assumes an air of veracity . . . [and therefore] . . . commands interest, and exudes authority because it offers (or purports to offer) insights into 'character and disposition' that were missing from annalistic history" (Michael Cooperson, *Classical Arabic Biography: The Heirs of the Prophets in the Age of al-Ma'mun* [Cambridge: Cambridge University Press, 2000], 23).

32. Ibn 'Abd Rabbih al-Andalusi, 1:65; Ahmad ibn 'Abd al-Wahhab al-Nuwayri, *Nihayat al-Arab fi Funun al-Adab* (Cairo: Dar al-Kutub al-Misriya, 1923), 6:84. Also see the seven volumes of Ibn 'Abd Rabbih al-Andalusi's work and the nineteen volumes of al-Nuwayri's work.

33. Al-Jahiz, *Kitab Kitman al-Sirr,* 40.

34. Ibid., 38; al-Jahiz, "Keeping Secrets and Holding the Tongue," trans. Hutchins, 14.

35. Al-Jahiz, *Kitab Kitman al-Sirr,* 60; al-Jahiz, "Keeping Secrets and Holding the Tongue," trans. Hutchins, 31.

36. Al-Jahiz, *Kitab Kitman al-Sirr,* 39; al-Jahiz, "Keeping Secrets and Holding the Tongue," trans. Hutchins, 15.

37. Ibid.

38. Al-Jahiz, *Kitab Kitman al-Sirr,* 54; al-Jahiz, "Keeping Secrets and Holding the Tongue," trans. Hutchins, 27.

39. Edward W. Lane, 1:761–62.

40. Specifically, this work's chapters entitled "Bab al-Balagha" and "Bab al-Bayān" contain material that suggests complementarities with his ideas regarding concealment of the secret (*kitmān al-sirr*).

41. See al-Jahiz, *Kitab al-Bayan,* 1:77. "The intellect is the scout of the soul, knowledge is the scout of the intellect and eloquence [*al-bayān*] is the interpreter of knowledge"; "The life of chivalry is truth, the life of the spirit is chastity, the life of forbearance is knowledge and the life of knowledge is eloquence [*al-bayān*]"; "A logician said: The goal of a human being is an eloquently, expressive life; The self is a pillar of the body, knowledge is a pillar of the self and eloquence [*al-bayān*] is a pillar of knowledge." Repeatedly, *al-bayān* links with knowledge are rendered prominent. Here, knowledge (*'ilm*) carries class connotations: to be knowledgeable is to be at once a member of an elite or refined class and to be spiritually enlightened. These sayings foreground the interconnections of morality, ethics, and spirituality in the conception of *al-bayān* as the eloquent use of the spoken word. *Al-bayān,* or one's eloquence, is a marker of this class and enlightenment: to be inarticulate is to be inelegant and unchivalrous. (These translations from the Arabic original are my own.)

42. Al-Jahiz, *Kitab Kitman al-Sirr,* 40; al-Jahiz, "Keeping Secrets and Holding the Tongue," trans. Hutchins, 15.

43. Modern Western theories (especially those that are psychoanalytically oriented) shed light on this connection between secrets and bodily organs. The principal theorist who conveys this is Alfred Gross, who, after describing the secret as "a concealed and an abstract possession," observes: "The secret is also more closely identified with its owner than other possessions; it perishes with him and thus is analogous to such corporal 'possessions' of man as his head, his heart or his hands" (37).

44. Al-Jahiz, *Kitab Kitman al-Sirr,* 39; al-Jahiz, "Keeping Secrets and Holding the Tongue," trans. Hutchins, 14.

45. Al-Jahiz, *Kitab Kitman al-Sirr,* 43–44.

46. Ibid., 39.

47. In contrast the modern theorist and founder of psychoanalysis, Sigmund Freud, conceptualized a difference between the two forms of secrets thus: "In his essay, 'The Unconscious' though he did not specifically mention secrets by name, Freud was trying to produce a topographical and descriptive model for what is hidden from consciousness and for the dynamics which kept some mental processes from entering awareness. These were no longer 'secrets' in the narrow clinical sense. The dynamically repressed was the result of the complex mental processes far beyond the conscious act of keeping secrets." What Freud views as "'secrets' in the narrow clinical sense" is akin to consciously kept secrets. He implies that unconscious secrecy concerns that which is "dynamically repressed" or that which, according to him, is "hidden from consciousness." See James W. Barron et al., "Sigmund Freud: The Secrets of Nature and the Nature of Secrets," *International Review of Psycho-Analysis* 18, no. 2 (1991): 156.

48. Freud's theory of the unconscious initially had a mechanistic cast to it, a cast similar to the kind of "hydraulics of secrecy" (in which bodily imagery is important) evident in al-Jahiz's writings.

49. Consult Lois Giffen and Joseph N. Bell on the term *hawa* in general and especially as understood by al-Jahiz. Giffen points out that al-Jahiz was not as strict and conservative as other authors (for example, Ibn al-Jauzi or Ibn al-Qayyim) in his ideas regarding passion or *al-hawa*. A quotation of al-Jahiz conveyed by Giffen sheds some light on his views of the relationship between *'ishq* (passionate love) and *al-hawa*: "*Hubb* is at the root of *hawa*, and *'ishq* branches off from *hawa*. *'Ishq* is that which causes a man to wander aimlessly about in a state of rapture or to die heartsick on his bed; and the starting point of all this is the bringing about of injury to his *murū'a* [pagan sense of manly honor] and his being filled with a feeling of submissiveness towards those who surround his beloved" (Lois Anita Giffen, *Theory of Profane Love among the Arabs: The Development of the Genre* [New York: New York University Press, 1971], 118). See also Joseph Norment Bell, *Love Theory in Later Hanbalite Islam* (Albany: State University of New York Press, 1979).

50. Al-Jahiz, *Kitab Kitman al-Sirr,* 38.

51. Ibid.

52. Al-Jahiz, *Kitab Kitman al-Sirr,* 38; al-Jahiz, "Keeping Secrets and Holding the Tongue," trans. Hutchins, 14.

53. Primarily for the sake of readability, I have used a translation other than that provided by A. Yusuf Ali. His translation is: "Is there (not) in these an adjuration (or evidence) for those who understand?" (*Holy Qur'an,* 1732).

54. Edward W. Lane, 2:2115.

55. Al-Jahiz, *Kitab Kitman al-Sirr,* 39; al-Jahiz, "Keeping Secrets and Holding the Tongue," trans. Hutchins, 14.

56. Ibid.

57. Al-Jahiz, *Kitab Kitman al-Sirr,* 41; al-Jahiz, "Keeping Secrets and Holding the Tongue," trans. Hutchins, 16.

58. Modern theories of secrecy—psychosocial and psychoanalytic—also identify and discuss this tension. For example, Alfred Gross observes: "The secret tempts its owner both to surrender its content and to retain it. Or to put it in psychoanalytic terms, the secret pushes its owner into the familiar ambivalence and conflict between expulsion and retention" (38). Gross describes this "struggle between retention and the surrender of a possession" as a psychological state that "all varieties and forms of resistance" have in common (39). A very important psychological insight to be derived from these claims is the idea of a somatic component to the unconscious, to the id. In this vein, the Iranian psychoanalyst and scholar of Sufism Muhammad Shafii has observed: "The fascinating part of Sufi psychology is that the unconscious in Sufism is not a psychological abstract, but has concrete reality. It originates from the gut, viscera, and the heart. It has a physiological basis. Vegetative and autonomic functions of the nervous system are a part of the unconscious. The concept of the unconscious in psychoanalysis has been plagued by the limitations of the topographical theory. Psychoanalytic theory has not paid enough attention to the role of visceral, autonomic, and vegetative aspects of the central nervous system as a building block for the development of unconscious fantasies, perceptions, and thought processes" (Mohammad Shafii, *Freedom from the Self: Sufism, Meditation, and Psychotherapy* [New York: Human Science Press, 1985], 35).

59. Moreover, the word *wa'y* embraces the meanings of "consciousness," and the same word prefixed with the negative Arabic article *lā* means "the unconscious." The Arabic expression *wa'ā 'alā nafsihi* means "to dawn on someone, to become clear to someone." See Hans Wehr, *A Dictionary of Modern Written Arabic,* ed. J. Milton Cowan (London: Macdonald & Evans, 1980), 1082.

60. Alfred Gross, after having established an analogy between the secret and a body organ, goes on to argue that the most fundamental trait of the secret that differentiates it from an organ is that "it is capable of regenerating itself. However faithful a lost arm may be to its master, it will not grow back again." An individual must always keep his organs: "they stubbornly demand to remain always with their master. . . . It is otherwise with the secret whose owner may keep it when and as long as he sees it fit or may dispose of it when chooses. He can give it away, he can sell it, and he can exchange it" (38).

61. Al-Jahiz, *Kitab Kitman al-Sirr,* 17.

62. It seems that this motif of disclosing secrets to holes in the ground is found in Greek antiquity too (in the Midas story) and in the Sanskrit corpus of didactic narratives as well.

63. Ibn Qutayba, *'Uyun al-Akhbar,* 1:41.

64. Ibid., 1:38.

65. Ibn 'Abd Rabbih al-Andalusi, 1:65; al-Nuwayri, 6:80.

66. The maxim and its minicommentary rely on bodily imagery also to convey the danger of disclosing one's secret—telling one's secrets may lead to one's bloodshed. This is somewhat similar to the idea found in al-Jahiz's *Kitman* that a wrong or harmful word can cause bloodshed.

67. Ibrahim Ibn Muhammad al-Bayhaqi, *Kitab al-Mahasin wal-Masawi* (Beirut: Dar Beirut, 1960), 374–75.

68. In the following verses from the Qur'an, God instructs Adam and then tests the angels:

2:31 And he taught Adam the names of all things; then he placed them before the angels, and said: "Tell me the names of these if you are right."

2:32 They said: "Glory to you: of knowledge we have none, except what you have taught us; indeed you are all-knowing and perfect in wisdom."

2:33 He said: "O Adam! tell them their names." When he had told them, God said: "Did I not tell you that I know the unseen [*ghayb*] of the heavens and earth, and I know what you show and what you conceal?"

69. See Pellat, *Life and Works of Jahiz,* 214.

70. Al-Jahiz, *Kitab Kitman al-Sirr,* 44; al-Jahiz, "Keeping Secrets and Holding the Tongue," trans. Hutchins, 19.

71. See Sigmund Freud, "Fragment of an Analysis of a Case of Hysteria" (1905), in *The Standard Edition of the Complete Psychological Works of Sigmund Freud,* ed. James Strachey (London: Hogarth Press and the Institute of Psycho-Analysis, 1953), 7:77–78. Freud asserts that the unconscious secrets of a patient can be made conscious, or brought to consciousness, through the intuition and understanding of bodily signs and symptoms.

72. Al-Jahiz, "Keeping Secrets and Holding the Tongue," 19.

73. Al-Jahiz, *Kitab Kitman al-Sirr,* 45; al-Jahiz, "Keeping Secrets and Holding the Tongue," trans. Hutchins, 19.

74. See al-Jahiz, *Kitab Kitman al-Sirr,* 14; and al-Jahiz, "Keeping Secrets and Holding the Tongue," trans. Hutchins, 39.

75. See al-Jahiz, *Kitab Kitman al-Sirr,* 52; and al-Jahiz, "Keeping Secrets and Holding the Tongue," trans. Hutchins, 29.

76. Al-Jahiz, *Kitab Kitman al-Sirr,* 41; al-Jahiz, "Keeping Secrets and Holding the Tongue," trans. Hutchins, 16. Freud, many centuries later, identified a similar phenomenon when he posited contrariness in the very structure of repression in the unconscious. He claimed that "the repressed has a pressure in the direction of consciousness" and furthermore that "the unconscious . . . has a natural 'upward drive' and desires nothing better than to press forward across its settled frontiers into the ego and so to consciousness." See Sigmund Freud, "An Outline of Psycho-Analysis" (1940), in *The Standard Edition of the Complete Psychological Works of Sigmund Freud* (1964), ed. Strachey, 23:36.

77. See al-Jahiz, *Kitab Kitman al-Sirr,* 39; and al-Jahiz, "Keeping Secrets and Holding the Tongue," trans. Hutchins, 14.

78. Bok, 76.

79. Henri F. Ellenberger, "The Pathogenic Secret and Its Therapeutics," *Journal of the History of Behavioral Sciences* 2 (1966): 40.

80. When in 1882 J. Breuer discussed with Freud his treatment of Anna O. and related "that Anna O. was relieved of her symptoms by being induced 'to express in words the affective phantasy by which she was at the moment dominated,'" Freud was deeply impressed (Barron et al., 152).

81. Frank Kermode talks about a similar process in the literary sphere when he notes how all parables require interpretive action. He calls it the need for completion, similar to that in the interpretation of dreams, "for the dream-text, when understood, disappears, is consumed by its interpretation, and ceases to have affective force." See Frank Kermode, *The Genesis of Secrecy: On the Interpretation of Narrative* (Cambridge, Mass.: Harvard University Press, 1979), 24. The mention of "affective phantasy" in the exchange between Freud and Breuer (see note 81) and the presence of a similar reference by Kermode ("affective force") are critical here and further shed light on why, according to al-Jahiz, "an effective cure for the 'constricted breast' can only stem from self-disclosure that is relational and interpersonal." Only when the secret is communicated to another can, in the words of Michael Hoyt, this affective force be discharged: "Making the secret public, at least to the therapist-confessor, allows for the discharge of its associated affect, thus freeing energies for future growth" (Michael F. Hoyt, "Secrets in Psychotherapy: Theoretical and Practical Considerations," *International Review of Psycho-Analysis* 5 [1978]: 238). Such a discharge is accompanied by a sense of release or unburdening of the breast that is experienced as very desirable by the secret-holder.

82. Al-Jahiz, *Kitab Kitman al-Sirr,* 44; al-Jahiz, "Keeping Secrets and Holding the Tongue," trans. Hutchins, 18.

83. See al-Jahiz, *Kitab Kitman al-Sirr,* 43; and al-Jahiz, "Keeping Secrets and Holding the Tongue," trans. Hutchins, 17–18.

84. See Ibn Qutayba, 1:39; Ibn 'Abd Rabbih al-Andalusi, 1:65; and al-Nuwayri, 6:82.

85. Ibn Qutayba, 1:39.

86. Ibn 'Abd Rabbih al-Andalusi, 1:66; al-Nuwayri, 6:82.

87. Al-Nuwayri, 6:85.

88. Al-Jahiz, *Kitab Kitman al-Sirr,* 47–48.

89. Ibn Hazm, *The Ring of the Dove,* 99.

90. Simmel, 346.

91. Ibid., 330: "The sociological characteristic of all these combinations is that the secret of a given individual is acknowledged by another; that what is intentionally or unintentionally hidden is intentionally or unintentionally respected. The intention of hiding, however, takes on a much greater intensity when it clashes with the intention of revealing. In this situation emerges that purposive hiding and masking, that aggressive defensive, so to speak, against the third person, which alone is designated as secret."

92. Al-Jahiz, *Kitab Kitman al-Sirr,* 46.

93. See ibid., 47; and al-Jahiz, "Keeping Secrets and Holding the Tongue," trans. Hutchins, 21.

94. Al-Jahiz, *Kitab Kitman al-Sirr,* 45.

95. Ibid.

96. Pellat, "Al-Jahiz," 202–3.

97. Carl Fulton Sulzberger, "Why It Is Hard to Keep Secrets," *Psychoanalysis* 2, no. 2 (1953): 39. Simmel (326) talks about the idea of "differentiation of friend-ships": that each friend is, in a sense, reserved for a particular role and, furthermore, that these friends may not know about each other's existence nor know what others of them know. Each friendship is compartmentalized, and Simmel explains: "These differentiated friendships that connect us with one individual in terms of affection, with another in terms of common intellectual aspects, with a third in terms of religious impulses and with a fourth in terms of common experiences—all these friendships present a very peculiar synthesis in regard to the question of discretion, of reciprocal revelation and concealment. They require that the friends do not look into those mutual spheres of interest and feeling which . . . are not included in the relation and which if touched upon would make them feel painfully the limits of their mutual understanding."

Chapter 4: The Rhetoric of the Secret

1. Unless otherwise indicated, nearly all translations from the 'Udhri romances, including (specially) *Majnun Layla,* are mine. Regarding *Tawq al-Hamama* (treatise authored by Ibn Hazm), throughout I consult the Arabic text, but the translations of excerpts of the text are from *The Ring of the Dove,* translated by A. J. Arberry, with occasional and minor modifications by me to ensure readability and accuracy. In a few instances I cite only excerpts from Arberry's translations of the text or from the original Arabic text. Refer to Ibn Hazm, *The Ring of the Dove.*

2. "Object relations": the word *object* here denotes the primary love objects of infancy. "When Freud summarized his understanding of love with the epigram 'all finding is refinding' he was again echoing platonic doctrine. However, what was to Plato the refinding of the prenatal bliss of the soul became to Freud the refinding the early love object of infancy in adult love (Freud 1905b:202)." See M. S. Berg-mann, *The Anatomy of Love* (New York: Columbia University Press, 1987), 146.

3. See Simmel.

4. Hamori, 213–14.

5. Ibn Manzur al-Ifriqi al-Misri, s.v. *sirr;* Edward W. Lane, 1:1337–40; al-Raghib al-Isfahani, *Mu'jam,* 256–57. Also see al-Raghib al-Isfahani, *Al-Mufradat,* 334.

6. Ibn Manzur al-Ifriqi al-Misri, s.v. *sirr.*

7. See, for example, 24:30–31, 4:51, and 21:91.

8. Giffen, 64. Also see Michael W. Dols, *Majnun: The Madman in Medieval Islamic Society,* ed. Diana E. Immisch (Oxford: Clarendon Press, 1992), 315.

9. Ibn Hazm, *The Ring of the Dove,* 33.

10. Abu Bakr Muhammad Ibn Dawud al-Zahiri, *Kitab al-Zahra,* ed. Ibrahim al-Samura'i (Amman: Maktab al-Minar, 1985), 1:table of contents.

11. Ibid., 117. Another well-known variant reads: "He who loves passionately, hides his love, remains chaste, will be forgiven by God, Who will admit him to the Garden."

12. Ibn Hazm, *Tawq al-Hamama,* 12; Ibn Hazm, *The Ring of the Dove,* 25.

13. Ibid.

14. Ibn Hazm, *Tawq al-Hamama,* 60.

15. Ruqayya Y. Khan, "Qays ibn al-Mulawwah (circa 680–710)," in *Dictionary of Literary Biography*, vol. 311, *Arabic Literary Culture, 500–925*, ed. Cooperson and Toorawa, 288–91.

16. Abu al-Faraj al-Isfahani, "Majnun Layla," in *Kitab al-Aghani* (Cairo: Al-Hay'a al-Misriyya al-'Amma li al-Kitab, 1992), 2:11.

17. Qays ibn al-Mulawwah's biographical accounts in both Ibn Qutayba's *Book of Poetry and Poets* and Abu al-Faraj al-Isfahani's *Book of Songs* suggest that at the time that Nawfal b. Musahiq, the governor of Medina in 702 C.E., attempted to help him in his disputes with the tribe and kin of his beloved, Layla bint al-Harish, he was a mere youth.

18. Abu al-Faraj al-Isfahani, "Majnun Layla," 15.

19. Ibid., 43.

20. As pointed out by Catherine Bates, the link between rhetoric and courtship is very strong in medieval European literature as well. Bates states: " 'Courting' lent itself to the art of love-making because wooing a member of the opposite sex came to be regarded as a highly complex, tactical, and strategic rhetorical procedure." See Catherine Bates, *The Rhetoric of Courtship in Elizabethan Language and Literature* (Cambridge: Cambridge University Press, 1992), 11.

21. Speech itself was gendered male. The Arabic word for "phallus" or "penis" is *dhakar*, derived from the word *dhakara*, which has among its meanings "to speak, tell, mention, and narrate."

22. See "al-Muraqqish al-Akbar," in Mufaddal ibn Muhammad al-Dabbi, *The Mufaddaliyat: An Anthology of Ancient Arabian Odes*, trans. and ed. Sir Charles James Lyall (Oxford: Clarendon Press, 1921), 2:170–71.

23. Concealment and revelation were well-recognized rhetorical tropes in early Arabic literature. Early Qur'anic studies assigned immense importance to the examination of tropes (*majāz*) in the Arabic language. Ibn Qutayba's *Ta'wil Mushkil al-Qur'an*, a work analyzing rhetorical structures of the Qur'an, presents a list of the subcategories of tropes, or *majāzāt*, and it includes the mention of concealment and revelation: "*ikhfā' wa-iẓhār* (concealing and revealing)." See Abu Muhammad Ibn Qutayba, *Ta'wil Mushkil al-Qur'an*, commentary by Al-Sayyid Ahmad Saqr (Cairo: Dar Ihya'i al-Kitab al-'Arabi, n.d.), 11.

24. Abu al-Faraj al-Isfahani, "Jamil Buthayna," in *Kitab al-Aghani* (Cairo: Al-Hay'a al-Misriyya al-'Amma li al-Kitab, 1992), 8:125.

25. Ibn Hazm, *The Ring of the Dove*, 86; Ibn Hazm, *Tawq al-Hamama*, 67.

26. Jamil b. 'Abd Allah al-'Udhri, *Sharh Diwan Jamil*, commentary by Ibrahim Jazini (Beirut: Dar al-Katib al 'Arabi, 1968), 22–23.

27. Ibn Hazm, *The Ring of the Dove*, 78.

28. Ibid.

29. Ibid.

30. Simmel, 346–47.

31. Ibn Hazm, *The Ring of the Dove*, 84.

32. Abu al-Faraj al-Isfahani, "Majnun Layla," 4.

33. R. Howard Bloch, *Medieval Misogyny and the Invention of Western Romantic Love* (Chicago: University of Chicago Press, 1991), 123.

34. Ibid.

35. Ibid.

36. Ibid.

37. Ibid., 122.

38. J. C. Burgel, "Love, Lust, and Longing: Eroticism in Early Islam as Reflected in Literary Sources," in *Society and the Sexes in Medieval Islam,* ed. Afaf Lutfi Al-Sayyid- Marsot (Malibu, Calif.: Undena Press, 1979), 84.

39. "Qays' public expressions about Layla usurped the traditional Arab right of the families, represented by the father, to announce a marriage. Qays' public display of love, his tashbīb—the rhapsodizing about a beloved woman and one's relationship to her—violated recognized Arab custom. It brought shame and dishonor to Layla and her family" (Dols, 332).

40. Abu al-Faraj al-Isfahani, "Jamil Buthayna," 98–99.

41. "The inamorata is often said to belong to an enemy tribe, and thus she serves the double role of a person sought after, but also proudly rejected when her demands grow excessive" (Beeston et al., 44); "[Qays al-Ruqayyat] . . . used his great gift for writing love poetry to satirize the Umayyads by writing love songs on their women. As has been mentioned before, this idea was based on a tradition of love satire resorted to in pre-Islamic times" (ibid., 419).

42. Vadet has maintained that the conventions of *tashbīb,* as an aspect of the Bedouin conception of *l'amour-folie,* acquired certain negative associations with satire in the later context of Hijazi poetry of the Umayyad period. During the Umayyad period, "la folie, sans espoir et sans remede . . . parce qu'infligee par une puissance superieure, licence de propos qui depasse la mesure et risque d'entrainer un conflit" (Vadet, 103). At this juncture, "l'amant plaisantim feigne d'etre victime du isq," and *tashbib* becomes "presque synonyme de satire, hagw," and thereby, a threat to the honor of the tribe (ibid.). "Nous craignons qu'il [le poete] ne dirige ses satires contre nous ou qu'il ne compose sur nos femmes des poemes d'amour tasbib, disent des Bedouins alarmes par la passion" (ibid., 103–4).

43. Abu al-Faraj al-Isfahani, "Majnun Layla," 75.

44. Alfred Gross, 37.

45. Ibid.

46. Ibid.

47. Ibid., 41.

48. Al-Jahiz, *Kitab Kitman al-Sir,* 39.

49. Ibn Hazm, *Tawq al-Hamama,* 60; Ibn Hazm, *The Ring of the Dove,* 76.

50. Here, Arberry has translated this as "expression of his eyes" when in Arabic the only word present is *eye* (*'ayn*). Yet, I concur with this translation because once this word is coupled with *ḥarakāt,* it does suggest eye movements/expressions.

51. The Arabic translation is *Ammā al-maḥabba fa-khilqa wa-innama yamlik al-insān ḥarakāt jawārihihi al-muktasiba.* See Ibn Hazm, *Tawq al-Hamama,* 76.

52. Ibn Hazm, *Tawq al-Hamama,* 60.

53. The preponderance of this kind of imagery concerning the turbulence of the natural elements to express the upheaval of bodily humors attests to the presence of Gaelic influences in medieval Arabic love theory. The etymological links between "secretions" and "secrets" are also interesting in this regard. "Alfred Gross went so far as to ask 'whether there is not in our subconscious a complete identity between

the secret on the one hand, and bodily excretions (respectively the organs of secretion) on the other'" (Bok, 32).

54. Ibn Hazm, *Tawq al-Hamama*, 69.

55. Abu al-Faraj al-Isfahani, "Majnun Layla," 13–14.

56. Simmel, 308.

57. Abu al-Faraj al-Isfahani, "Majnun Layla," 14.

58. Ibid., 16.

59. Ibid., 14.

60. Ibid., 16.

61. Manzalaoui has pointed out that in a later collection of stories, *Alf Layla wa Layla*, "the mutuality of the simultaneous faint is the sentimental romance's surrogate for sexual intercourse." See Mahmoud Manzalaoui, "Swooning Lovers: A Theme in Arab and European Romance," *Comparative Criticism* 8 (1986): 75.

62. Ibn Qutayba, 1:39; Ibn 'Abd Rabbih al-Andalusi, 1:65; al-Nuwayri, 6:82.

63. Modification of Arthur Wormhoudt's translation of Ibn Zaydun, *The Diwan of Ibn Zaidun* (Oskaloosa, Iowa: William Penn College, 1973), 100.

64. See Hans Hinrich Biesterfeldt and Dimitri Gutas, "The Malady of Love," *Journal of the American Oriental Society* 104, no. 1 (1984): 21–55.

65. Here, the idea of the body wasting away could be equated with an emotional state of being hungry or empty—an interesting equation, given how some psychologists have described loving as an impoverishment for the ego. Bergmann, for instance, has shown how object libido depletes ego libido in the process of loving. Moreover, insofar as the secret is defined as a valuable, internal property and possession, and hence, a valuable addendum to and augmenting quality for the self, it is not surprising that the secret's revelations draw upon metaphors associated with impoverishment and depletion.

66. Ibn Hazm, *Tawq al-Hamama*, 95.

67. A. J. Arberry, *Arabic Poetry: A Primer for Students,* ed. Arthur John (Cambridge: Cambridge University Press, 1965), 19.

68. Abu al-Faraj al-Isfahani, "Majnun Layla," 19.

69. Ibid., 67.

70. Abu al-Faraj al-Isfahani, "Jamil Buthayna," 125.

71. Ibn Hazm, *The Ring of the Dove*, 42: "Weeping is a well-known sign of Love; except that men differ very greatly from one another in this particular. Some are ready weepers; their tear-ducts are always overflowing and their eyes respond immediately to their emotion, the tears rolling down at a moment's notice. Others are dry-eyed and barren of tears."

72. Ibid., 71.

73. Ibid.

74. Ibid.

75. Ibid., 72.

76. Ibid.

77. Ibid., 186.

78. Sigmund Freud, "The Dream Work" (1900), in *The Standard Edition of the Complete Psychological Works of Sigmund Freud* (1953), ed. Strachey, 5:359.

79. Abu al-Faraj al-Isfahani, "Kuthayyir 'Azza," in *Kitab al-Aghani* (Cairo: Al-Hay'a al-Misriyya al-'Amma li al-Kitab, 1992), 9:29.

80. See Joseph N. Bell, 36: "The primary cause of passionate love is *nazar*. For love, as is evident from Ibn al-Jawzi's definition, occurs when the soul meets an object which conforms to its nature. Obviously, it is the faculty of vision which is most often responsible for bringing about this meeting. It is persistent gazing, he adds, and not a lone glance, which results in love." In Ibn al-Jawzi's view (*mahabba*) love and affection (*wadd*), together with an inclination toward the beautiful and suitable, are not to be blamed, since they are natural in mankind. "But *'ishq*, which exceeds the limit of mere inclination and [normal] love and by possessing the reason causes its victim to act unwisely, is blameworthy and ought to be avoided by the prudent" (ibid., 37).

81. In these two passages the word *samn* also could be interpreted to signify both chaste (secret) speech and chaste femininity. The word *samīn*, morphologically related to *samun*, means "fat, chaste, abundant." *Kalām samin* means "chaste speech" as well as "chaste, eloquent or excellent language." Arab literary critics of the Middle Ages, such as Ibn Qutayba, often described language using corporeal words such as "fat" and "lean." In *Ta'wil*, Ibn Qutayba contrasts the terms *samin* and *ghaththa* with reference to language: the former means "plump or good language," whereas the latter means "lean language" and "bad speech." See Ibn Qutayba, *Ta'wil Mushkil al-Qur'an*, 11. Language that is characterized as *samin* is speech that is rich in allegorical and metaphorical meanings. Such language is also described as "chaste" precisely because it is full of concealed allegorical meanings, and chastity, we must remember, is intimately connected with secrecy in the medieval Arabic discourse on love. Some of Suzanne Stetkevych's work suggests that the symbolism of a blood versus milk dichotomy is important in early Arabic literature. See Suzanne Pinckney Stetkevych, *The Mute Immortals Speak: Pre-Islamic Poetry and the Poetics of Ritual* (Ithaca, N.Y.: Cornell University Press, 1993), 208–10.

82. Abu al-Faraj al-Isfahani, "Majnun Layla," 32.

83. Ibid., 31–32.

84. The classical Urdu poet Sauda has a verse that is relevant to this anecdote: *Adam ka jisam jab ke anasir say mil bana, kuch agh bach rahi thi so ashiq ka dil bana* (When the body of Adam was created from the elements, some fire was leftover; thus the heart of the lover was made). See Muhammad 'Abd al-Rahman Barker, Shah Abdus Salam, and M. Akbaruddin Siddiqi, *Classical Urdu Poetry*, vol. 3 (New York: Spoken Language Services, 1977), 1:111:68.

85. A. C. Spearing, *The Medieval Poet as Voyeur: Looking and Listening in Medieval Love Narratives* (Cambridge: Cambridge University Press, 1993), 22.

86. Ibid.

87. Michel Foucault, *An Introduction*, vol. 1 of *The History of Sexuality*, trans. Robert Hurley (New York: Vintage, 1980), 37.

Chapter 5: Toward a Literary Archaeology of the Private and the Secret

1. The term *Hanbalites* refers to the adherents of one of the four schools of Islamic law (Hanbali, Hanafi, Maliki, and Shafi'i). See Cook, *Forbidding Wrong*, 59.

2. Cook, *Forbidding Wrong*, 59–61.

3. Ruqayya Khan, "Qays ibn al-Mulawwah," 288–91.

4. Susan Crane, *Gender and Romance in Chaucer's Canterbury Tales* (Princeton, N.J.: Princeton University Press, 1994), 94–95.

5. See W. R. Smith, *Kinship and Marriage in Early Arabia,* ed. Stanley Cook (London: Adam and Charles Black, 1903). He lays out the argument in chapters 3–6.

6. W. R. Smith, 87. According to Gertrude Stern, *zinā'* may have been applied by the prophet to "very loose matrimonial bonds and the consequent abuses thereof, rather than to adultery in the strict sense of the word." Stern observes that, for example, the *ṣadīqa* system, as labeled by Smith, "has been referred to as 'the general conception of unchastity' while W. R. Smith defined it as 'a kind of Nair polyandry in which the number of husbands was not defined.'" See Gertrude Stern, *Marriage in Early Islam* (London: Royal Asiatic Society, 1939), 18:73.

7. W. R. Smith, 92–94.

8. Ibid., 92.

9. Ibid.

10. Ibid., 87–88.

11. Hamori, 205.

12. Ibid.

13. In his dissertation Gregory Gross discusses William G. Dodd's interpretation of medieval love poetry. Gross points out that, "in the criticism on medieval literature, secrecy has received the most attention as an ingredient in the code of courtly love" (10). This first paradigm views courtly love poetry "to be accepted as an accurate reflection of actual social practices, rather than as a highly stylized body of fiction"; hence Gross argues that some critics of medieval love poetry such as Dodd have regarded secrecy as "nothing more than one of the straightforward obligations of the courtly lover" (Gross, 12). Spearing echoes this when, in his study of secrecy and privacy in medieval European love narratives, he declares, "Much of it [the evidence about secular social life] comes from romances themselves, which, with all their distortion and idealization, are sometimes all the social history we possess" (Spearing, 14–15).

14. Peter Dronke is another critic who has followed this second paradigm. Dronke, in the words of Gregory Gross, maintains that the "numerous injunctions for secrecy between lover and beloved found in medieval love-lyrics have more to do with the artful representation of the emotional experience of love itself than with the practical concerns of adulterous lovers" (Gregory W. Gross, 12). Dronke observes that "not because love is always illicit! . . . The secrecy of amour courtois springs rather from the universal notion of love as a mystery not to be profaned by the outside world, not to be shared by any but lover and beloved" (Peter Dronke, *Medieval Latin and the Rise of European Love-Lyric,* 2nd ed. [London: Oxford University Press, 1968], 1:48). Gregory Gross also cites another critic, namely John Stevens, who explains the ubiquity of secrecy in romantic love literature thus: "We do not have to accept the 'code's' rational explanation—the preservation of the Lady's good name—as fully sufficient; it clearly is not. Obligation of secrecy . . . corresponds to a deep psychological need . . . to isolate and intensify" (Gregory Gross, 13).

15. Danielle Regnier-Bohler remarks, "Fiction can be used as evidence in a literary archaeology of the private." See Regnier-Bohler, "Imagining the Self," in *Revelations of the Medieval World: A History of Private Life,* ed. George Duby (Cambridge, Mass.: Belknap Press of Harvard University Press, 1988), 2:315.

16. Unless otherwise indicated in this chapter, nearly all translations from the 'Udhri romances, including especially *Majnun Layla,* are mine.

17. Bok, 10–11.

18. Ibid.

19. Ibid., 11.

20. Talal Asad, "Boundaries and Rights in Islamic Law," in *Islam: The Public and Private Spheres,* ed. Arien Mack, *Social Research* 70, no. 2 (2003): 684. Likewise, Roy Mottahdeh and Kristen Stilt have argued that "relational standing is perhaps the most important key to understanding public and private in Islamic legal thinking. The differentiation of space reflects the relational status of different members of society" (Mottahedeh and Stilt, "Public and Private as Viewed through the Work of the *Muhtasib,*" in *Islam: The Public and Private Spheres,* ed. Arien Mack, *Social Research* 70, no. 2 [2003]: 745).

21. Cook, *Forbidding Wrong,* 62.

22. Ibid., 57. Michael Cook analyzes early textual evidence concerning the Islamic duty of "commanding right and forbidding wrong."

23. Spearing, 19.

24. Ibid.

25. Bok, 90.

26. Ibid.

27. Ibid., 91

28. Ibid., 94–95.

29. Sir Charles James Lyall, trans., verses 1–6, in al-Dabbi, 2:329.

30. Spearing, 22.

31. Michael Sells, *Early Islamic Mysticism: Sufi, Qur'an, Miraj, Poetic and Theological Writings* (New York: Paulist Press, 1996), 65–66. Also see al-Dabbi, *The Mufaddaliyat,* trans. Lyall, 2:334–35, for the Arabic text translated into English.

32. Spearing, 22.

33. Verses 24–27, in al-Dabbi, trans. Lyall, 2:162. This pre-Islamic poet is al-Aswad son of Ya'fur (boon companion of King of Hirah al-Nu'man).

34. Michael Sells, trans., *Desert Tracings: Six Classic Arabian Odes by Alqama, Shanfara, Labid, Antara, Al-Asha, and Dhu Al-Rumma* (Middletown, Conn.: Wesleyan University Press, 1989), 60.

35. A well-known incident associated with the life of the Prophet Muhammad (captured in the hadith collections and the earliest biography of the Prophet) that involves issues of gossip, slander, and the public/private dichotomy is conveyed through the hadith al-Ifk, or "the account of the lie" involving his young wife 'A'isha. This incident offers yet another glimpse into how speech networks, especially in the form of gossip networks and rumor mills, loomed large in early Arab culture and society. Spellberg (62) suggests that this incident is "not about private conduct or matters of conscience, but about public definitions of social control, behavior, and gender." My research indicates that issues regarding secrecy and

privacy, especially as they pertain to gender, sexuality, and marital relations in this milieu, are very salient to this incident.

36. Abu al-Faraj al-Isfahani, "Qays Lubna," in *Kitab al-Aghani* (Cairo: Al-Hay'a al-Misriyya al-'Amma li al-Kitab, 1992), 9:208–9. Unless otherwise indicated, nearly all the translations from the 'Udhri romances are mine.

37. Abu al-Faraj al-Isfahani, "Majnun Layla," 2:47.

38. Ibid., 43.

39. Ibid., 14.

40. Ibid., 94.

41. Ibid.

42. Abu al-Faraj al-Isfahani, "Kuthayyir 'Azza," 9:33.

43. Joseph N. Bell, 28.

44. Bok, 94–95.

45. Abu al-Faraj al-Isfahani, "Jamil Buthayna," 8:106–7.

46. Regnier-Bohler, 332.

47. Abu al-Faraj al-Isfahani, "Majnun Layla," 2:36.

48. Burgel, 94.

49. Abu al-Faraj al-Isfahani, "Jamil Buthayna," 8:122–23.

50. Abu al-Faraj al-Isfahani, "Majnun Layla," 2:72.

51. See Joseph Schacht, *An Introduction to Islamic Law* (Oxford: Clarendon Press, 1964), 7, 184–87

52. Suzanne Stetkevych, 251–52.

53. Sulzberger, 41.

54. Ibn Qutayba, 1:41.

55. Stern, 73.

56. Abu al-Faraj al-Isfahani, "Jamil Buthayna," 8:108.

57. Ibid., 8:122–23.

58. The term *al-sultān* deserves some comment. According to Schacht, "the word *sultān* . . . came to be used as a title only from the 4th/10th century onward." See Schacht, *An Introduction to Islamic Law,* 206.

59. Abu al-Faraj al-Isfahani, "Jamil Buthayna," 8:123–24.

60. Abu al-Faraj al-Isfahani, "Majnun Layla," 2:26.

61. Abu al-Faraj al-Isfahani, "Qays Lubna," 9:197–98.

62. Interesting semantic and symbolic connections between the leaking of secrets and the spilling of blood are found in the verbal texture of these textual exempla from the 'Udhri romances. For example, in the romance of *Jamil Buthayna,* the phrase that is employed to describe the sultan's measures after the beloved's kin petition him is *fa-abāhahum dammahu,* or literally "he declares lawful to them his [that is, Jamil's] blood" (8:122–23). This is telling because the word *abāha* is also a verb often used in the early Arabic love lexicon for "to reveal a secret." Recall that semantic and symbolic connections between the leaking of secrets and the spilling of blood are also inscribed in early Arabic polythematic encyclopedic sources.

63. W. R. Smith, 92–94.

64. Abu al-Faraj al-Isfahani, "Majnun Layla," 2:75.

65. But it is not just the sexual dimensions of the couple that are deemed threatening and illicit; the very existence of the couple (especially unmarried) threatens

the hierarchies of other social relations. Hence there is a profound tension between the couple and a larger web of social relations. This web of relations includes horizontally structured bonds such as friendships or pacts between same-sex parties, kin ties between same-sex members (for example, female cousins), and spousal links in a polygamous marriage (for example, cowives), as well as vertically structured bonds such as relations between a superior and his subordinate (for example, master-servant or mistress-maid relations). Privacy and secrecy in their verbal and spatial dimensions are rendered crucial to the couple's bond (marital or nonmarital), and it is precisely through this definition of the couple as private and secret that the secrecy of the couple is ineluctably challenged and sometimes preserved by this web of social relations. Several literary motifs construct a kind of dichotomy between, especially, the unmarried couple and the larger social group. The couple is set in opposition to the web of social relations through the presence of motifs of gossip (for example, imagery of tale bearers, guards, and tattle-tale servants). Often these couples represent improper or illicit kinds of bonds.

66. Regnier-Bohler, 313.

67. Spearing, 21.

68. Ibid.

Conclusion

1. See Ibn Hazm, *Tawq al-Hamama,* 119; and Ibn Hazm, *The Ring of the Dove,* 250.

2. Farish A. Noor, "What Is the Victory of Islam? Towards a Different Understanding of the *Ummah* and Political Success in the Contemporary World," in *Progressive Muslims: On Justice, Gender and Pluralism,* ed. Omid Safi (Oxford: Oneworld, 2003), 325.

3. Ibid.

4. Mary Douglas, *Purity and Danger: An Analysis of Concepts of Pollution and Taboo* (London: Routledge & Kegan Paul, 1966), 148.

5. Ibid., 146.

6. Leila Abouzeid, *Return to Childhood: The Memoir of a Modern Moroccan Woman,* trans. Heather Logan Taylor (Austin: University of Texas Press, 1998), preface.

7. Nasir al-Attahi, Syrian graduate student, personal conversations with the author, 2002, University of California, Santa Barbara.

8. Ibid.

9. *New York Times,* January 24, 2003: "The Bush Administration's case against Iraq can be summed up in one sentence: Iraq has not led United Nations inspectors to the weapons Washington insists Baghdad is hiding . . . Iraq's government would have to abandon its authoritarian and secretive ways and become an open partner in disarmament, one that would make its weapons [and] scientists available, provide military archives of its weapons development efforts and open its hidden weapons vaults."

10. Douglas, 147.

11. Noor, 326.

Bibliography

'Abd al-Baqi, Muhammad Fu'ad. *Al-Mu'jam al-mufahras li-alfaz al-Qur'an al-Karim.* Beirut: Dar al-Andalus, 1945.

Abdel Haleem, M. A. S. "Context and Internal Relationships: Keys to Quranic Exegesis; A Study of Sūrat al-Raḥmān (Qur'an Chapter 55)." In *Approaches to the Qur'an,* edited by G. R. Hawting and Abdul-Kader A. Shareef. London: Routledge, 1993.

———, trans. *The Qur'an.* Oxford: Oxford University Press, 2004.

Abou El Fadl, Khaled, et al. *The Place of Tolerance in Islam.* Edited by Joshua Cohen and Ian Lague. Boston: Beacon Press, 2002.

Abouzeid, Leila. *Return to Childhood: The Memoir of a Modern Moroccan Woman.* Translated by Heather Logan Taylor. Austin: University of Texas Press, 1998.

Abu-Lughod, Lila. *Veiled Sentiments: Honor and Poetry in a Bedouin Society.* Berkeley and Los Angeles: University of California Press, 1986.

Ahmad, Barakat. *Muhammad and the Jews: A Re-examination.* New Delhi: Vikas, 1979.

Akhtar, Salman. *Inner Torment.* Northvale, N.J.: Jason Aronson, 1999.

Ali, Abdullah Yusuf, trans. *The Holy Qur'an.* Elmhurst, N.Y.: Tahrike Tarsile Qur'an, 1987.

Ali, Syed Anwer. *Qur'an: The Fundamental Law of Human Life.* 11 vols. Karachi, Pakistan: Hamdard Foundation Press, 1982.

Arberry, A. J. *Arabic Poetry: A Primer for Students.* Edited by Arthur John. Cambridge: Cambridge University Press, 1965.

———. *An Introduction to the History of Sufism.* London: Longman, 1943.

———. *The Seven Odes.* London: Allen & Unwin, 1957.

———, trans. *The Koran Interpreted.* New York: Simon & Schuster, 1996.

Arjomand, Said Amir. *The Shadow of God and the Hidden Imam: Religion, Political Order, and Societal Change in Shi'ite Iran from the Beginning to 1890.* Chicago: University of Chicago Press, 1984.

Asad, Talal. "Boundaries and Rights in Islamic Law." In *Islam: The Public and Private Spheres,* edited by Arien Mack, *Social Research* 70, no. 2 (2003): 683–86.

Ayoub, Mahmoud M. "Muhammad the Prophet (circa 570–632)." In *Dictionary of Literary Biography,* vol. 311, *Arabic Literary Culture, 500–925,* edited by Michael Cooperson and Shawkaw M. Toorawa. Detroit: Thomson Gale, 2005.

Balentine, Samuel E. *The Hidden God: The Hiding of the Face of God in the Old Testament.* New York: Oxford University Press, 1983.

Barker, Muhammad 'Abd al-Rahman, Shah Abdus Salam, and M. Akbaruddin Siddiqi. *Classical Urdu Poetry.* Vol. 3. Ithaca, N.Y.: Spoken Language Services, 1977.

Barron, James W., Ralph Beaumont, Gary N. Goldsmith, Michael J. Good, Robert L. Pyles, Ana-Maria Rizzuto, and Henry F. Smith."Sigmund Freud: The Secrets of Nature and the Nature of Secrets." *International Review of Psycho-Analysis* 18, no. 2 (1991): 143–63.

Barthelemy, Dominique, and Philippe Contamine. "The Use of Private Space." In *Revelations of the Medieval World: A History of Private Life,* edited by George Duby, vol. 2. Cambridge, Mass.: Belknap Press of Harvard University Press, 1988.

Bates, Catherine. *The Rhetoric of Courtship in Elizabethan Language and Literature.* Cambridge: Cambridge University Press, 1992.

al-Bayhaqi, Ibrahim Ibn Muhammad. *Kitab al-Mahasin wal-Masawi.* Beirut: Dar Beirut, 1960.

Beeston, A. F. L., T. M. Johnstone, R. B. Serjeant, and G. R. Smith, eds. *Arabic Literature to the End of the Umayyad Period.* Cambridge History of Arabic Literature. Cambridge: Cambridge University Press, 1983.

Bell, Joseph Norment. *Love Theory in Later Hanbalite Islam.* Albany: State University of New York Press, 1979.

Bell, Richard. *A Commentary on the Qu'ran.* Edited by C. E. Bosworth and M. E. J. Richardson. 2 vols. Manchester: Manchester University Press, 1991.

Bergmann, M. S. *The Anatomy of Love.* New York: Columbia University Press, 1987.

Biesterfeldt, Hans Hinrich, and Dimitri Gutas. "The Malady of Love." *Journal of the American Oriental Society* 104, no. 1 (1984): 21–55.

Bledsoe, Caroline H. "Arabic Literacy and Secrecy among the Mende of Sierra Leone." *Man* 21 (1986): 202–26.

Bloch, R. Howard. *Medieval Misogyny and the Invention of Western Romantic Love.* Chicago: University of Chicago Press, 1991.

Bok, Sissela. *Secrets: On the Ethics of Concealment and Revelation.* New York: Pantheon, 1983.

Bolle, Kees W., ed. *Secrecy in Religions.* New York: Brill, 1987.

Boullata, Issa, ed. *Literary Structures of Religious Meaning in the Qur'an.* Surrey: Curzon Press, 2000.

Brustad, Kristen E., et al. *Interpreting the Self: Autobiography in the Arabic Literary Tradition.* Edited by Dwight F. Reynolds. Berkeley and Los Angeles: University of California Press, 2001.

Burgel, J. C. "Love, Lust, and Longing: Eroticism in Early Islam as Reflected in Literary Sources." In *Society and the Sexes in Medieval Islam,* edited by Afaf Lutfi Al-Sayyid-Marsot. Malibu: Undena Press, 1979.

Burton, John. *The Collection of the Qur'an.* Cambridge: Cambridge University Press, 1977.

———. *The Sources of Islamic Law: Islamic Theories of Abrogation.* Edinburgh: Edinburgh University Press, 1990.

Chittick, William C. "The Paradox of the Veil in Sufism." In *Rending the Veil: Concealment and Secrecy in the History of Religions,* edited by Elliot R. Wolfson. New York: Seven Bridges Press, 1999.

Cline, Ruth H. "Heart and Eyes." *Romance Philology* 25 (1972): 263–97.

Cook, Michael. *Commanding Right and Forbidding Wrong in Islamic Thought.* Cambridge: Cambridge University Press, 2000.

———. *Forbidding Wrong in Islam.* Cambridge: Cambridge University Press, 2003.

Cooperson, Michael. *Classical Arabic Biography: The Heirs of the Prophets in the Age of al-Ma'mun.* Cambridge: Cambridge University Press, 2000.

Crane, Susan. *Gender and Romance in Chaucer's Canterbury Tales.* Princeton, N.J.: Princeton University Press, 1994.

al-Dabbi, Mufaddal ibn Muhammad. *The Mufaddaliyat: An Anthology of Ancient Arabian Odes.* 2 vols. Edited and translated by Sir Charles James Lyall. Oxford: Clarendon Press, 1918, 1921.

Dakake, Maria. "Hiding in Plain Sight: The Practical and Doctrinal Significance of Secrecy in Shi'ite Islam." *Journal of the American Academy of Religion* 74, no. 2 (2006): 324–55.

Denny, Frederick Mathewson. *An Introduction to Islam.* 3rd ed. New York: Macmillan, 2006.

Derrida, Jacques. *The Gift of Death.* Translated by David Wills. Chicago: University of Chicago Press, 1995.

Dols, Michael W. *Majnun: The Madman in Medieval Islamic Society.* Edited by Diana E. Immisch. Oxford: Clarendon Press, 1992.

Douglas, Mary. *Purity and Danger: An Analysis of Concepts of Pollution and Taboo.* London: Routledge & Kegan Paul, 1966.

Dronke, Peter. *Medieval Latin and the Rise of European Love-Lyric.* 2 vols. 2nd ed. London: Oxford University Press, 1968.

Duncan, Ann Williams. "Religion and Secrecy: A Bibliographic Essay." *Journal of the American Academy of Religion* 74, no. 2 (2006): 469–82.

Eck, Diana L. *Darsan: Seeing the Divine Image in India.* 3rd ed. New York: Columbia University Press, 1998.

El-Attar, Jamal. "Al-Jahiz's View of Arabic in Relation to the Qur'an." In *Democracy in the Middle East: Proceedings of the Annual Conference of the British Society of Middle Eastern Studies, 8–10 July 1992, University of St. Andrews, Scotland,* 20–33. Exeter: BRISMES, 1992.

Ellenberger, Henri F. "The Pathogenic Secret and Its Therapeutics." *Journal of the History of Behavioral Sciences* 2 (1966): 29–42.

Foucault, Michel. *An Introduction.* Vol. 1 of *The History of Sexuality.* Translated by Robert Hurley. New York: Vintage, 1980.

Freud, Sigmund. "The Dream Work" (1900). In *The Standard Edition of the Complete Psychological Works of Sigmund Freud,* edited by James Strachey, vol. 5. London: Hogarth Press and the Institute of Psycho-Analysis, 1953.

———. "Five Lectures on Psycho-Analysis" (1910). In *The Standard Edition of the Complete Psychological Works of Sigmund Freud,* edited by James Strachey, vol. 11. London: Hogarth Press and the Institute of Psycho-Analysis, 1957.

———. "Fragment of an Analysis of a Case of Hysteria" (1905). In *The Standard Edition of the Complete Psychological Works of Sigmund Freud,* edited by James Strachey, vol. 7. London: Hogarth Press and the Institute of Psycho-Analysis, 1953.

———. "The Future Prospects of Psycho-Analytic Therapy" (1910). In *The Standard Edition of the Complete Psychological Works of Sigmund Freud,* edited by James Strachey, vol. 11. London: Hogarth Press and the Institute of Psycho-Analysis, 1957.

———. "An Outline of Psycho-Analysis" (1940). In *The Standard Edition of the Complete Psychological Works of Sigmund Freud,* edited by James Strachey, vol. 23. London: Hogarth Press and the Institute of Psycho-Analysis, 1964.

———. "Psycho-Analysis and the Establishment of the Facts in Legal Proceedings" (1906). In *The Standard Edition of the Complete Psychological Works of Sigmund Freud,* edited by James Strachey, vol. 9. London: Hogarth Press and the Institute of Psycho-Analysis, 1959.

———. *The Standard Edition of the Complete Psychological Works of Sigmund Freud.* 24 Vols. Edited and translated by James Strachey. London: Hogarth Press and the Institute of Psycho-Analysis, 1999.

———. "Three Essays on Sexuality" (1905). In *The Standard Edition of the Complete Psychological Works of Sigmund Freud,* edited by James Strachey, vol. 7. London: Hogarth Press and the Institute of Psycho-Analysis, 1953.

Gatje, Helmut. *The Qur'an and Its Exegesis: Selected Texts with Classical and Modern Muslim Interpretations.* Translated and edited by Alford T. Welch. Berkeley and Los Angeles: University of California Press, 1976.

Gelder, Geert Jan van. "Compleat Men, Women and Books: On Medieval Arabic Encyclopaedism." In *Pre Modern Encyclopaedic Texts,* edited by Peter Binkley. New York: Brill, 1997.

Giffen, Lois Anita. *Theory of Profane Love among the Arabs: The Development of the Genre.* New York: New York University Press, 1971.

Goffman, Erving. *The Presentation of the Self in Everyday Life.* Garden City, N.Y.: Doubleday, 1959.

Graham, William A. *Divine Word and Prophetic Word in Early Islam: A Reconsideration of the Sources, with Special Reference to the Divine Saying or Hadith Qudsi.* The Hague: Mouton, 1977.

Greifenhagen, F. V. "Garments of Disclosure and Deception: The Joseph Story in Islamic and Jewish Scripture and the Politics of Intertextuality." Master's thesis, Duke University, 1992.

Gross, Alfred. "The Secret." Translated by George Devereux, Gisela Ebert, and Joseph Noshpitz. *Bulletin of the Menninger Clinic* 2 (1951): 37–44.

Gross, Gregory Walter. "Secrecy and Confession in Late Medieval Narrative: Gender, Sexuality, and the Rhetorical Subject." Ph.D. diss., Brown University, 1994.

Hamori, A. "Love Poetry (*ghazal*)." In *'Abbasid Belles-Lettres,* edited by Julia Ashtiany and A. F. L. Beeston. Cambridge History of Arabic Literature. Cambridge: Cambridge University Press, 1990.

Hawting, G. R., and Abdul-Kader Shareef, eds. *Approaches to the Qur'an.* London: Routledge, 1993.

Homans, Peter. "Once Again, Psychoanalysis, East and West: A Psychoanalytic Essay on Religion, Mourning, and Healing." *History of Religions* 24 (1984): 133–54.

Homerin, Th. Emil. "Altruism in Islam." In *Altruism in World Religions,* edited by Jacob Neusner. Washington, D.C.: Georgetown University Press, 2005.

Hoyt, Michael F. "Secrets in Psychotherapy: Theoretical and Practical Considerations." *International Review of Psycho-Analysis* 5 (1978): 231–41.

Ibn 'Abd Rabbih al-Andalusi, Abi 'Umar Ahmad b. Muhammad. *Kitab al-'Iqd al-Farid.* Edited by Ahmad Amin, Ahmad al-Zayn, and Ibrahim al-Abyari. 7 vols. Cairo: Matba'at Lajnat al-Ta'lif wa al-Tarjama wa al-Nashr, 1940.

Ibn Dawud al-Zahiri, Abu Bakr Muhammad. *Kitab al-Zahra.* Edited by Ibrahim al-Samura'i. Vol. 1. Amman: Maktab al-Minar, 1985.

Ibn Hazm. *The Ring of the Dove: A Treatise on the Art and Practice of Arab Love.* Translated by A. J. Arberry. London: Luzac, 1953.

———. *Tawq al-Hamama.* Edited by al-Tahir Ahmad Makki. Cairo: Dar al-Ma'arif, 1975.

Ibn Hisham, Abd al-Malik. *The Life of Muhammad: A Translation of Ibn Ishaq's Sirat Rasul Allah.* Edited by A. Guillaume. Karachi: Oxford University Press, 1967.

Ibn Manzur al-Ifriqi al-Misri, Abu al-Fadl Jamal al-Din Ibn Mukarram. *Lisan al-'Arab.* 15 vols. Beirut: Dar Sadir / Dar Beirut, 1956.

Ibn Qutayba, Abu Muhammad. *Al-Shi'r wa al-Shu'ara.* 2 vols. Edited by Ahmad Muhammad Shakir. Cairo: Dar al-Ma'arif bi Misr, 1966.

———. *Ta'wil Mushkil al-Qur'an.* Commentary by Al-Sayyid Ahmad Saqr. Cairo: Dar Ihya'i al-Kitab al-'Arabi, n.d.

———. *'Uyun al-Akhbar.* 4 vols. Cairo: Dar al-Kutub al-Misriyya, 1930.

Ibn Zaydun. *The Diwan of Ibn Zaidun.* Translated by Arthur Wormhoudt. Oskaloosa, Iowa: William Penn College, 1973.

al-Isfahani, Abu l-Faraj. "Jamil Buthayna." In Abu al-Faraj al-Isfahani, *Kitab al-Aghani,* vol. 8, 91–154. Cairo: Al-Hay'a al-Misriyya al-'Amma li al-Kitab, 1992.

———. *Kitab al-Aghani.* 24 vols. Cairo: Al-Hay'a al-Misriyya al-'Amma li al-Kitab, 1992.

———. "Kuthayyir 'Azza." In *Kitab al-Aghani,* vol. 9, 3–48. Cairo: Al-Hay'a al-Misriyya al-'Amma li al-Kitab, 1992.

———. "Majnun Layla." In *Kitab al-Aghani,* vol. 2, 1–97. Cairo: Al-Hay'a al-Misriyya al-'Amma li al-Kitab, 1992.

———. "Qays Lubna." In *Kitab al-Aghani,* vol. 9, 180–249. Cairo: Al-Hay'a al-Misriyya al-'Amma li al-Kitab, 1992.

al-Isfahani, al-Raghib. *Al-Mufradat fi gharib al-Qur'an.* 2 vols. Cairo: Maktabat al-Anjlu al-Misriyya, 1978.

———. *Mu'jam mufradat alfaz al-Qur'an.* Beirut: Dar al-Kutub al-'Ilmiyya, 1997.

Izutsu, Toshihiko. *God and Man in the Koran: Semantics of the Koranic Weltanschauung.* Tokyo: Keio Institute of Cultural and Linguistic Studies, 1964.

Jacobs, Janet Liebman, and Donald Capps, eds. *Religion, Society, and Psychoanalysis: Readings in Contemporary Theory*. Boulder: Westview Press, 1997.

al-Jahiz, Abu 'Uthman 'Amr ibn Bahr. "Keeping Secrets and Holding the Tongue." In *Nine Essays of al-Jahiz*, translated by William Hutchins, 13–32. New York: Lang, 1989.

———. *Kitab al-Bayan wa'l-tabyin*. Edited by A. Muhammad Harun. Vol. 1. Cairo: Matabat Lajnat al-Ta'lif wa al-Tarjama wa al-Nashr, 1948.

———. *Kitab Kitman al-Sirr wa Hifz al-Lisan*. In *Majmu' Rasa'il al-Jahiz*, edited by P. Kraus and M. T. al-Hajiri, 37–60. Cairo: Lajnat al-Ta'lif wa-al-Tarjamat wa-al-Nashr, 1943.

———. *Risalat al-Ma'ad wal-ma'ash fi al-adab wa tadbir al-nas wa-mu 'amalatihim*. In *Majmu' Rasa'il al-Jahiz*, edited by P. Kraus and M. T. al-Hajiri, 1–36. Cairo: Lajnat al-Ta'lif wa-al-Tarjamat wa-al-Nashr, 1943.

———. *Tafdil al-Nutq 'ala al-Samt*. In *Majmu'at al-Rasa'il: Ithna 'asharah risalah*, edited by Muhammad al-Sasi al-Maghribi, 135–40. Cairo: Matba'at al-Taqaddam, 1906.

Jeffery, Arthur. *The Qur'an as Scripture*. New York: Books for Libraries, 1980.

Johansen, Baber. "Apostasy as Objective and Depersonalized Fact: Two Recent Egyptian Court Judgments." In *Islam: The Public and Private Spheres*, edited by Arien Mack, *Social Research* 70, no. 2 (2003): 687–710.

Johnson, Paul Christopher. *Secrets, Gossip and Gods: The Transformation of Brazilian Candomble*. New York: Oxford University Press, 2002.

Kamada, Shigeru. "A Study of the Term *Sirr* (Secret) in Sufi Lata'if Theories." *Orient: The Reports of the Society for Near Eastern Studies in Japan* 19 (1983): 7–28.

Kassis, Hanna E. *A Concordance of the Qur'an*. Berkeley and Los Angeles: University of California Press, 1983.

Kelber, Werner H. "Narrative and Disclosure: Mechanisms of Concealing, Revealing, and Reveiling." *Semeia* 43 (1988): 1–20.

Kermode, Frank. *The Genesis of Secrecy: On the Interpretation of Narrative*. Cambridge, Mass.: Harvard University Press, 1979.

Kernberg, Otto F. *Love Relations: Normality and Pathology*. New Haven, Conn.: Yale University Press, 1995.

Khairallah, As'ad. *Love, Madness, and Poetry: An Interpretation of the Magnun Legend*. Beirut: Orient-Institut der Deutschen Morgenl andischen Gesellschaft, 1980.

Khalidi, Tarif. *The Muslim Jesus: Sayings and Stories in Islamic Literature*. Cambridge, Mass.: Harvard University Press, 2001.

Khan, M. Muhsin, trans. *Sahih Bukhari. MSA-USC Hadith Database*. Muslim Students Association, University of Southern California. http://www.usc.edu/dept/MSA/fundamentals/hadithsunnah/bukhari/ (accessed January 2007).

Khan, Ruqayya Y. "On the Significance of Secrecy in the Medieval Arabic Romances." *Journal of Arabic Literature* 31 (2000): 238–53.

———. "Qays ibn al-Mulawwah (circa 680–710)." In *Dictionary of Literary Biography*, vol. 311, *Arabic Literary Culture, 500–925*, edited by Michael Cooperson and Shawkat M. Toorawa. Detroit: Thomson Gale, 2005.

Kierkegaard, Soren. "Fear and Trembling." In *Kierkegaard's Writings*, edited and translated by Howard V. Hong and Edna Hong, vol. 6. Princeton, N.J.: Princeton University Press, 1983.

Kilpatrick, Hilary. *Making the Great Book of Songs: Compilation and the Author's Craft in Abu l-Faraj al-Isbahani's Kitab al-Aghani.* London: Routledge Curzon, 2003.

Kippenberg, H. G., and G. G Stroumsa, eds. *Secrecy and Concealment: Studies in the History of Mediterranean and Near Eastern Religions.* New York: Brill, 1995.

Kohlberg, Etan. "Taqiyya in Shi'ite Theology and Religion." In *Secrecy and Conceal-ment: Studies in the History of Mediterranean and Near Eastern Religions,* edited by H. G. Kippenberg and G. G. Stroumsa. New York: Brill, 1995.

Lane, Edward William. *Arabic-English Lexicon.* 2 vols. Cambridge: Islamic Texts Society Trust, 1984.

Lane, Julie D., and Daniel M. Wegner. "The Cognitive Consequences of Secrecy." *Journal of Personality and Social Psychology* 69 (1995): 237–53.

Loomis, Roger Sherman, and Laura Hibbard Loomis, eds. *Medieval Romances.* New York: Random House, 1957.

Ludwig, Theodore. *The Sacred Paths of the West.* Upper Saddle River, N.J.: Prentice Hall, 2001.

Madigan, Daniel A. *The Qur'an's Self-Image: Writing and Authority in Islam's Scrip-ture.* Princeton, N.J.: Princeton University Press, 2001.

Majnun Layla. *Diwan Majnun Layla.* Edited by 'Abd al-Sattar Ahmad Farraj. Cairo: Maktabat Misr, 1973.

Malti-Douglas, Fedwa. *Structures of Avarice: The Bukhala' in Medieval Arabic Litera-ture.* Leiden: Brill, 1985.

Manzalaoui, Mahmoud. "Swooning Lovers: A Theme in Arab and European Romance." *Comparative Criticism* 8 (1986): 71–90.

———. "Tragic Ends of Lovers: Medieval Islam and the Latin West." *Comparative Criticism* 1 (1979): 37–52.

Margolis, Gerald J. "The Psychology of Keeping Secrets." *International Review of Psycho-Analysis* 1 (1974): 291–96.

———. "Secrecy and Identity." *International Review of Psycho-Analysis* 47 (1966): 517–22.

Marshall, David. *God, Muhammad and the Unbelievers: A Qur'anic Study.* Surrey: Curzon Press, 1999.

McAuliffe, Jane Dammen, ed. *Encyclopedia of the Quran.* 6 vols. Leiden: Brill, 2001–6.

Middleton, John. "Secrecy in Lugbara Religion." *History of Religions* 12(1973): 299–316.

Miquel, Andre. *Deux histoires d'amour: de Majnûn à Tristan.* Paris: Editions Odile Jacob, 1996.

Mir, Mustansir. *Dictionary of Qur'anic Terms and Concepts.* New York: Garland, 1987.

———. "The Qur'an as Literature." *Religion and Literature* 20 (1988): 49–64.

Montgomery, James E. "Al-Jahiz." In *Dictionary of Literary Biography,* vol. 311, *Arabic Literary Culture, 500–925,* edited by Michael Cooperson and Shawkaw M. Toorawa. Detroit: Thomson Gale, 2005.

————. "Al-Jahiz's *Kitab al-Bayan wa-l-Tabyin*." In *Writing and Representation in Medieval Islam: Muslim Horizons,* edited by Julia Bray. New York: Routledge, 2006.

Mottahedeh, Roy, and Kristen Stilt. "Public and Private as Viewed through the Work of the *Muhtasib*." In *Islam: The Public and Private Spheres,* edited by Arien Mack, *Social Research* 70, no. 2 (2003): 735–48.

Murata, Sachiko, and William C. Chittick. *Vision of Islam.* St. Paul, Minn.: Paragon House, 1994.

Neuwirth, Angelika. "Images and Metaphors in the Introductory Sections of the Makkan Suras." In *Approaches to the Qur'an,* edited by G. R. Hawting and Abdul-Kader Shareef. London: Routledge, 1993.

Noor, Farish A. "What Is the Victory of Islam? Towards a Different Understanding of the *Ummah* and Political Success in the Contemporary World." In *Progressive Muslims: On Justice, Gender and Pluralism,* edited by Omid Safi, 320–33. Oxford: Oneworld, 2003.

al-Nuwayri, Ahmad ibn 'Abd al-Wahhab. *Nihayat al-Arab fi Funun al-Adab.* 19 vols. Cairo: Dar al-Kutub al-Misriyya, 1923.

Ouyang, Wen-Chin. *Literary Criticism in Medieval Arabic-Islamic Culture.* Edinburgh: Edinburgh University Press, 1997.

Pellat, C. "Al-Jahiz." In *'Abbasid Belles-Lettres,* edited by Julia Ashtiany et al. Cambridge History of Arabic Literature. Cambridge: Cambridge University Press, 1990.

————. *The Life and Works of Jahiz.* Berkeley and Los Angeles: University of California Press, 1969.

Powers, David S. "The Exegetical Genre nasi<u>kh</u> al-Qur'an wa mansū<u>kh</u>uhu." In *Approaches to the History of the Interpretation of the Qur'an,* edited by Andrew Rippin. Oxford: Clarendon Press, 1988.

Preminger, Alex, ed. *Princeton Encyclopedia of Poetry and Poetics.* Enl. ed. Princeton, N.J.: Princeton University Press, 1965.

Qays Lubna. *Diwan Qays Lubna.* Edited by Amil Badi' Ya'qub. Beirut: Dar al-Kitab al-'Arabi, 1993.

Qudamah b. Ja'afar, Abi al-Faraj. *Naqd al-Shi'r.* Edited by S. A. Bonnebaker. Leiden: Brill, 1956.

al-Qurtubi, Muhammad ibn Ahmad. *Al-Jami' li-Ahkam al-Qur'an.* Cairo: Dar al-Kutub al-Misriyya, 1944.

————. *Al-Jami' li-Ahkam al-Qur'an.* 21 vols. Beirut: Dar al-Kutub al-'Ilmiyya, 1996.

Rahman, Fazlur. *Major Themes of the Qur'an.* Minneapolis: Bibliotheca Islamica, 1994.

————, ed. *Avicenna's Psychology: An English Translation of Kitab al-najat, Book II, Chapter VI, with Historico-Philosophical Notes and Textual Improvements on the Cairo Edition.* Westport, Conn.: Hyperion Press, 1981.

Ramaswamy, Sumathi. *Passions of the Tongue: Language Devotion in Tamil India, 1891–1970.* Berkeley and Los Angeles: University of California Press, 1997.

Regnier-Bohler, Danielle. "Imagining the Self." In *Revelations of the Medieval World: A History of Private Life,* edited by George Duby, vol. 2. Cambridge, Mass.: Belknap Press of Harvard University Press, 1988.

Rippin, Andrew. "Desiring the Face of God: The Qur'anic Symbolism of Personal Responsibility." In *Literary Structures of Religious Meaning in the Qur'an,* edited by Issa Boullata. Surrey: Curzon Press, 2000

———. *The Qur'an and Its Interpretative Tradition.* Aldershot: Ashgate, 2001.

Rippin, Andrew, ed. *Approaches to the History of the Interpretation of the Qur'an.* Oxford: Clarendon Press, 1988.

Rizzuto, Ana-Maria. *The Birth of the Living God: A Psychoanalytic Study.* Chicago: University of Chicago Press, 1979.

Scarry, Elaine. *The Body in Pain: The Making and Unmaking of the World.* New York: Oxford University Press, 1985.

Schacht, Joseph. *An Introduction to Islamic Law.* Oxford: Clarendon Press, 1964.

Schimmel, Annemarie. "'I Take off the Dress of the Body': Eros in Sufi Literature and Life." In *Religion and the Body,* edited by Sarah Coakley. Cambridge: Cambridge University Press, 1997.

———. "Secrecy in Sufism." In *Secrecy in Religions,* edited by Kees Bolle. New York: Brill, 1987.

Sells, Michael. *Approaching the Qur'an: The Early Revelations.* Ashland, Oreg.: White Cloud Press, 1999.

———. *Early Islamic Mysticism: Sufi, Qur'an, Miraj, Poetic and Theological Writings.* New York: Paulist Press, 1996.

———. *Mystical Languages of Unsaying.* Chicago: University of Chicago Press, 1994.

———, trans. *Desert Tracings: Six Classic Arabian Odes by Alqama, Shanfara, Labid, Antara, Al-Asha, and Dhu Al-Rumma.* Middletown, Conn.: Wesleyan University Press, 1989.

Shafii, Mohammad. *Freedom from the Self: Sufism, Meditation, and Psychotherapy.* New York: Human Science Press, 1985.

Siddiqui, Abdul Hammid, trans. *Sahih Muslim. MSA-USC Hadith Database.* Muslim Students Association, University of Southern California. http://www.usc.edu/dept/MSA/fundamentals/hadithsunnah/muslim/ (accessed January 2007).

Simmel, Georg. "The Secret and Secret Society." In *The Sociology of Georg Simmel,* edited by Kurt H. Wolff. Glencoe, Ill.: Free Press, 1950.

Smith, H. F., J. W. Barron, R. Beaumont, G. N. Goldsmith, M. I. Good, R. L. Pyles, and A. Rizzuto. "Sigmund Freud: The Secrets of Nature and the Nature of Secrets." *International Review of Psycho-Analysis* 18 (1991): 143–63.

Smith, Jane Idleman, and Yvonne Y. Haddad. *The Islamic Understanding of Death and Resurrection.* Albany: State University of New York Press, 1981.

Smith, Margaret. *An Early Mystic of Baghdad: A Study of the Life and Teaching of Harith B. Asad al-Muhasibi,* A.D. 781–A.D. 857. New York: AMS Press, 1973.

Smith, W. R. *Kinship and Marriage in Early Arabia.* Edited by Stanley Cook. London: Adam & Charles Black, 1903.

Spacks, Patricia Meyer. *Privacy: Concealing the Eighteenth-Century Self.* Chicago: University of Chicago Press, 2003.

Spearing, A. C. *The Medieval Poet as Voyeur: Looking and Listening in Medieval Love Narratives.* Cambridge: Cambridge University Press, 1993.

Spellberg, Denise. *Politics, Gender and the Islamic Past: The Legacy of 'A'isha Bint Abi Bakr.* New York: Columbia University Press, 1994.

Stetkevych, Jaroslav. *The Zephyrs of Najd: The Poetics of Nostalgia in the Classical Arabic Nasib.* Chicago: University of Chicago Press, 1993.

Stetkevych, Suzanne Pinckney. *The Mute Immortals Speak: Pre-Islamic Poetry and the Poetics of Ritual.* Ithaca, N.Y.: Cornell University Press, 1993.

Stern, Gertrude. *Marriage in Early Islam.* Vol. 18. London: Royal Asiatic Society, 1939.

Stevens, John. *Medieval Romance: Themes and Approaches.* New York: Norton, 1973.

Stewart, Devin. "Taqiyya as Performance: The Travels of Baha' al-Din al-'Amili in the Ottoman Empire (991–93/1583–85)." *Princeton Papers in Near Eastern Studies* 4: 1–70. Reprinted in Stewart, Baber Johansen, and Amy Singer, *Law and Society in Islam*, 1–70. Princeton, N.J.: Marcus Weiner, 1996.

Sulzberger, Carl Fulton. "Why It Is Hard to Keep Secrets." *Psychoanalysis* 2, no. 2 (1953): 37–43.

al-Tabari, Abu Ja'far Muhammad b. Jarir. *Jami' al-bayan 'an ta'wil al-Qur'an.* 16 vols. Edited by Mahmud Muhammad Shakir. Cairo: Dar al-Ma'arif, 1961.

———. *Jami' al-bayan 'an ta'wil ay al-Qur'an.* 30 vols. Cairo: Mustafa al-Babi al-Halabi, 1954–68.

———. *Jami' al-bayan 'an ta'wil ay al-Qur'an.* Vol. 1. Introduction and notes by J. Cooper. Oxford: Oxford University Press, 1987.

———. *Jami' al-bayan fi tafsir al-Qur'an.* 12 vols. Beirut: Dar al-Kutub al-'Ilmiyya, 1992.

———. *Majma' al-Bayan fi tafsir al-Qur'an.* Vol. 4. Damascus: Matba'at al-'Irfan, 1983.

———. *Mukhtasar tafsir al-Tabari.* 2 vols. Beirut: 'Alam al-Kutub, 1985.

At-Tarjumana, A'isha Abdarahman and Ya'qub Johnson, trans. *Malik's Muwatta. MSA-USC Hadith Database.* Muslim Students Association—University of Southern California. http://www.usc.edu/dept/MSA/fundamentals/hadithsunnah/muwatta/ (accessed January 2007).

Terrien, Samuel L. *The Elusive Presence: Toward a New Biblical Theology.* Vol. 26 of *Religious Perspectives,* edited by Ruth Nanda Anshen. San Francisco: Harper & Row, 1978.

al-'Udhri, Jamil b. 'Abd Allah. *Sharh Diwan Jamil.* Commentary by Ibrahim Jazini. Beirut: Dar al-Katib al 'Arabi, 1968.

'Umar ibn Abi Rabi'a. *Diwan.* Kitab al-Turath, 2. Cairo: al-Hay'a al-Misriyya al-'Amma li al-Kitab, 1978.

Urban, Hugh B. "The Torment of Secrecy: Ethical and Epistemological Problems in the Study of Esoteric Traditions." *History of Religions* 37 (1998): 209–48.

Vadet, Jean-Claude. *L'Esprit courtois en Orient dans les cinq premiers siècles de l'Hégire.* Paris: Maisonneuve et Larose, 1968.

Vawter, Bruce. *Job and Jonah: Questioning the Hidden God.* New York: Paulist Press, 1983.

Waines, David. *An Introduction to Islam.* Cambridge: Cambridge University Press, 1995.

Ware, Kallistos. "'My Helper and My Enemy': The Body in Greek Christianity." In *Religion and the Body,* edited by Sarah Coakley. Cambridge: Cambridge University Press, 1997.

Wehr, Hans. *A Dictionary of Modern Written Arabic.* Edited by J. Milton Cowan. London: Macdonald & Evans, 1980.

Wild, Stefan, ed. *The Qur'an as Text.* Leiden: Brill, 1996.

———. "We Have Sent Down to Thee the Book with the Truth: Spatial and Temporal Implications of the Qur'anic Concepts of Nuẓūl, Tanẓīl, and 'Inẓāl." In *The Qur'an as Text,* edited by Stefan Wild. Leiden: Brill, 1996.

Wolfson, Elliot R., ed. *Rending the Veil: Concealment and Secrecy in the History of Religions.* New York: Seven Bridges Press, 1999.

Wright, W. *A Grammar of the Arabic Language.* Cambridge: Cambridge University Press, 1988.

Young, M. J. L., J. D. Latham, and R. B Serjeant, eds. *Religion, Learning and Science in the 'Abbasid Period.* Cambridge History of Arabic Literature. Cambridge: Cambridge University Press, 1990.

al-Zamakhshari, Mahmud ibn 'Umar. *Al-Kashshaf 'an haqa'iq ghawamid al-tanzil.* 4 vols. Beirut: Dar al-Kitab al-'Arabi, 1947.

Index

medieval European literature, 102,
124–25
Medieval Poet as Voyeur, The, 99
Mir, Mustansir, 5, 15, 22, 21
Montgomery, James, 54, 55
Moses, 14, 22
Mufaddaliyat, The, 103
Muhammad, 21–22, 27, 29–30, 32, 37,
45, 54, 65, 110, 168–69n35
Mu'jam mufradat alfaz al-Qur'an, 14
Murata and Chittick, 32
Muraqqish the Elder, al-, 78

Naqd al-Shi'r, 82
New Testament, 12, 44–45
nafs, 8–9, 24, 27, 33, 38, 59–60, 64, 68.
najwā. See Qur'an
Neuwirth, Angelika, 5
nighttime, 94–95, 113–18, 124
Nihayat al-Arab fi Funun al-Adab, 6, 55,
57, 63, 67–68
Noah, 37
Noor, Farish, 128, 130, 131, 132
Nuwayri, al-, 55

Ouyang, Wen-chin, 53, 54

Pellat, Charles, 6, 53
Politics, Gender and the Islamic Past, 29
pre-Islamic ode, 82, 102–5, 118
pre-Islamic "public self," 8–9, 28–29, 31.
See also secrecy; *nafs;* Qur'an
privacy, 31, 66, 97, 99–102, 105–25. *See
also* secrecy
Prophet. *See* Muhammad
Proverbs, 12
Psalms, 12
psychoanalysis, 3, 66, 72, 84
Purity and Danger, 130

qalb, 24, 48–49, 65. See also *sadr*
Qays ibn Dharih, 108–9, 121
Qays Lubna, 105–7, 121–22
Qudama ibn Ja'far, 82
Qur'an: and *bil-ghayb,* 39–43; and divine
ghayb, 34–39; and eschatology, 13–
17, 42; *al-furūj,* 14; *julūd,* 14; *al-
munāfiqūn,* 20; *najwā,* 22, 24; refrain

on secrecy, 17–19, 141–42n23, 142–
43n30; *sadr* (or *sudūr*), 19, 22, 23, 24;
Sūrat al-'Ādiyāt, 16; Sūrat al-Baqara,
35; Sūrat al-Mā'ida, 37; Sūrat al-
Mā'ūn, 46; Sūrat al-Mujādila, 21–23;
Sūrat al-Nūr, 14; Sūrat al-Zilzāl, 16;
Sūrat Hā-Mīm, 13–16; and Sūrat Yā
Sīn, 14; and transparency of self, 17,
23, 26–33; and women, 74, 110. *See
also* secrecy
Qurtubi, al-, 14, 42

Rahman, Fazlur, 9, 13, 21–22, 26, 36, 49
raqīb, 22, 52
Razi, Fakhr al-Din, al-, 36
Regnier-Bohler, Danielle, 100, 113
*Return to Childhood: The Memoir of a
Modern Moroccan Woman,* 130
Risalat al-Ma'ad wal-ma'ash, 70
Rizzuto, Ana-Marie, 32–33

sadaqa, 44.
sadīqa, 98–100. *See also* marriage among
early Arabs
sadr (or *sudūr*) 19, 22, 23, 24, 61–67. *See
also* secrecy
Sahih Muslim, 15
salat, 22, 43
Scarry, Elaine, 50
Schacht, Joseph, 117
Schimmel, Annemarie, 3
self. *See* secrecy; *nafs;* Qur'an; pre-Islamic
"public self"
secrecy: and alterity in the Qur'an, 20–23;
and charity in the Qur'an, 43–47; and
gossip in early Arabic love literature,
102–5, 105–7; and human speech,
54–59, 63–71, 103, 107; and interpersonal secrets, 67–70; and *kitmān
al-sirr,* 52, 56, 59–62, 67, 70–71; and
pithy sayings, 16–17, 57, 63, 65–66,
68, 88; and Qur'anic faith-belief system, 47–50; and religiously transparent self, 8–11, 13, 17, 23–33, 50–51,
70–71, 126–28; and revelation, 79–
81, 85, 91–95; and sexuality, 72–75,
78, 82–83, 88, 90–96, 117–18, 124,

About the Author

RUQAYYA YASMINE KHAN is an associate professor of Islamic studies at Trinity University in San Antonio, Texas. Her research interests include Arabic literary studies, Qur'anic studies, the psychology of religion, progressive Islamic theologies, and the intersections between religion and childhood.